Pra
Renée Robertson an(

MW01068603

In reading *The Coaching Solution*, I could feel how Renée's authenticity as a person and as a professional coach is invested in these pages. Her book offers a very solid toolbox for successfully establishing coaching in any organization. And on a personal —and professional—note, Renée offers true value-add to our clients' change projects by leveraging her business experience and knowledge.

DR. ALEXANDER DOUJAK, Managing Partner, Doujak Corporate Development

Coaching is one of the new—and misused—buzzwords across organizations today. So, what is coaching and how and why should you implement it across your organization?

Renée Robertson provides cogent answers to these questions, and does so based on her own real-world experience of implementing an award-winning coaching program in a large organization that was in crisis. That company was MCI as it emerged from the WorldCom scandal—and bankruptcy—and sought to re-establish itself as an elite and trusted player in telecommunications again. The stakes—retaining our best employees in spite of the scandal.

Renée's book captures her experience at MCI and broadens across a larger organization at Verizon. It is a "must read" for anyone even considering a coaching program.

STEPHEN P. YOUNG, retired Senior Vice President, MCI and Verizon
Visiting Instructor, Georgia State University
Founding Director, Sales Executive RoundTable

In the mosaic of life we are all just a composite of our exposure. We owe gratitude for the impact that others have had on us, specifically those that coach us on how we can improve ourselves and in turn improve the lives of those around us. In *The Coaching Solution*, Renée shares her personal experience through a multitude of corporate positions and very challenging situations, highlighting the role of coaching in the improvement of individual performance and corporate transformation. All of us can relate to, and benefit from, her story.

CHARLES A. HELLINGS, Executive Vice President,
Strategic Business Development, ePath Learning, Inc.

I believe there is a leader to some degree in everyone, but very few of us embrace change. Change affects all; therefore, all must be included if a company is to successfully transform. Renée does a phenomenal job of listening to the organization and recognizing the hurdles of change across a company's culture, its personnel, and the markets it serves to effectively drive the right path for its evolutionary change.

KEVIN BANDY, Senior Vice President, Enterprise Transformation, salesforce.com

In *The Coaching Solution*, Renée has crafted a must-read for anyone facing organizational change and the accompanying conflicts. Her years of experience as a subject-matter expert has been captured in the systematic and practical lessons anyone can learn from, regardless of their business experience.

DAN SMITH, Chief Operating Officer, CWPS

Life is all about people, and Verizon—despite its very large size—is no exception. I know that coaching brings out the best in people, not only in their performance but in their caring, in being involved. People want to know that their work is appreciated, not just through monetary rewards, but with personal recognition as well. Coaching does that by dedicating personal attention to good performers. Renée knew this and practiced it in Verizon with passion and conviction.

ALDO FIGUEROA, former Vice President, Operations, Latin America Verizon

It was a truly unique experience to be a Senior Leadership Development Consultant on Renée's team, comprised of people with amazing talent and unique strengths. Our roles expanded from leadership coaching and facilitation to organizational development in order to meet the ever-changing needs of the leadership and the company. We truly had the chance to partner with our HR Business Partners and the heads of our assigned functional organizations to translate business objectives into recommendations that drove business results. Internal coaching remains a missing link to success in so many organizations. No Talent Management organization is complete without it.

LINDA DOLCEAMORE, Leadership Development Consultant

I met Renée 12 years ago and this young lady had a dream—she wanted to coach and help others reach their big dreams. She did all of it with study, perseverance, being true to herself and always living her life with integrity and a passion for helping others who simply wanted the same things for their life—purpose, fulfillment and living a life with integrity. Renée has truly modeled the very things we all strive for.

PETER KUNK, Partner, Built to Lead

Renée Robertson delivers the inside story of internal coaching with passion and practical guidance. Organizations need cultures of coaching to bring forth the best in their people. This book is a must-read for practitioners wanting to nurture and develop extraordinary human capital.

DON MARUSKA, winner of National Innovator Award and co-author of *Take Charge of Your Talent: Three Keys to Thriving in Your Career, Organization, and Life*

Renée has tackled the concept of internal coaching from the perspective of one who has been there, in a variety of circumstances. The book marries two key concepts— the importance of well-designed coaching and making that coaching process part of the organization. Those who are building an internal coaching program will find valuable recommendations. Also, much of Renée's counsel can be applied by coaches themselves, and indeed those seeking a coach relationship, whether internal or external.

WILLIAM A. SCHIEMANN, Chief Executive Officer, Metrus Group, Inc.

I started working with Renée when she was promoted into a newly created position and tasked with restructuring and expanding the MCI New York City Field Marketing Teams. Not only did she ensure that we supported our sales branches well in order to meet our clients' needs and achieve our results, she also encouraged all team members to set and reach career and performance milestones. Once our goals were established, Renée utilized her coaching skills to develop us each individually and as a team, resulting in a best-in-class program that was subsequently modeled and implemented around the country. For me personally, working with Renée was a highlight of my career.

NORI INSLER, former Field Marketing Manager, MCI Telecommunications

It was a privilege to have Renée as a coach for many years. Her thoughtful coaching and honest advice have had a profound and enduring impact on my professional development. In addition, Renée's coaching programs have had a real and measurable impact on business results.

BECKY CARR, Chief Marketing Officer, CenturyLink

Renée is a tenacious yet passionate professional with a thirst for her profession and the drive to help others excel. She is a caring person, but also at the same time a tough and disciplined business woman. The combination of her skills, experience and knowledge that make up her story, plus her coaching philosophy and principles—when put into practice—will help every individual and team to become more successful.

DAVID GRAY, former Vice President, Strategic Initiatives,
MCI Telecommunications

After Renée asked that I write a short testimonial for her book, I took some time to gather my thoughts and memories of the time past when we first met and the evolution of our relationship. For many years I climbed corporate ladders, along the way completing tasks and reaping rewards. Yet the most important lessons I learned, I learned from Renée. Renée is a top salesperson who knows how to engage a customer and navigate a company. What differentiated Renée was that she realized that the path she had initially taken was not the path she wanted to continue on (as you will read about in the book), and that transformation is not about changing yourself but rather about getting to the place where you can be yourself. One of the chapters in Renée's book is called "Finding the Leader Within." Renée found the leader within herself, and I would suggest to the readers of this book that she help you to do the same.

JIM KNEGO, former Vice President of Sales, MCI

The Coaching Solution provides great insight and practical advice to anyone who aspires to be a coach in the Talent, Change and OD space. Renée has captured the essence of what is mission critical in the change and transformation process through the eyes of a talent management executive, experienced coach, and trusted advisor to senior leadership at Fortune 100 companies.

KAREN PINKS, former Accenture Managing Director,
Talent and Organization Performance

Both inspirational and practical, Renée Robertson clearly articulates the value add of comprehensive, holistic coaching—and why coaching is an essential ingredient in the recipe for change and key to increasing ROI (in the "numbers realm" and in a "people context"). The business case for introducing and embedding coaching into one's enterprise has never been more compelling!

TOM ZAHAY, Vice President, Human Resources,
smartShift Technologies

Having been one of the many beneficiaries of Renée's leadership programs at MCI and Verizon, I continue to leverage the many tools of her leadership program, including strategy development; maximizing organizational efficiency and productivity; continually adapting and succeeding in a high-performance organization; and finding better ways to serve customers. Every manager should have this book in their office.

BRUCE ROSEN, Executive Vice President of Global Sales and Marketing,
Landmark Dividend LLC

Renée's experience as a business leader gives her an intuitive understanding of business dynamics and drivers. Her experience as a coach and integral part of developing future leaders gives her the unique ability and experience of helping leaders to leverage their skills and achieve their aspirations.

Vice President, Talent Management, Fortune 500 firm

I was fortunate to work alongside Renée during the integration of Verizon Business with Verizon Telecommunications described in Chapter 19 of this book, and witnessed her strong leadership and coaching abilities firsthand. Renée's comprehensive approach guided a very complex organization successfully through a time of significant change, including streamlining operations, reducing costs and enhancing customer experience. Renée was focused on the desired outcome of the organization but never lost sight of the needs of the individual. I personally value Renée's coaching and continue to learn from her insights.

TARA BRIGGS, former Senior Manager, Accenture

Renée understands organizations and has a passion for the people who desire to make them work. That desire fuels the internal coaching programs she creates—she brings the experience of someone who has been there and done that—brilliantly.

JAY PERRY, Master Certified Coach and co-author of *Take Charge of Your Talent*

Organizations worldwide are facing challenges that coaching is uniquely suited to address. In addition to providing everything you'll need to know about how to create and run a successful program, Renée teaches you how to sell it! Her sales experience is invaluable as she relays how to position the program internally for maximum success.

SIOBHAN MURPHY, MCC

At Montblanc, North America, we have been partnering with Renée and her company in a number of consultative areas, including executive coaching, integration consulting, and change management. It is a pleasure to collaborate with a professional who understands and values the Montblanc brand and practices within its culture and ethos.

MARY GORMAN, Director Human Resources, Mountblanc, North America

Bookshelves and online bookstores are overflowing with books about leadership, employee development, driving results and business success. One could spend two lifetimes absorbing the available content. Renée Robertson's *The Coaching Solution* rises above all the noise and wide variety of methodologies, systems and theories, and gets right to the bottom line of why coaching is a pivotal leadership learning and development strategy for everyone in your company. Renée delivers the message from a real-world and totally transparent perspective. That, coupled with the detailed roadmap on how to leverage coaching in your organization, makes this a must-read for every leader.

FRANK TRADITI, Regional Sales Learning Manager, XO Communications

In all my years of experience as a business leader, the most effective and enduring partnership I've enjoyed with my HR partner is one built on serving as my conscience. Not the "yes" person, not the "no" person—just my conscience. Renée exemplifies this with great finesse.

JEANNIE DIEFENDERFER, former Senior Vice President, Verizon Communications, and Founder & CEO, courageNpurpose LLC

The Coaching Solution

How to Drive Talent Development, Organizational Change, and Business Results

Renée Robertson

**Two-Time Winner, Prism Award,
International Coach Federation**

The Coaching Solution
Copyright © 2015 by Renée Robertson
All rights reserved.

Care has been taken to trace ownership of copyright material contained in this book. The publisher will gladly receive any information that will enable it to rectify any references or credit line in subsequent editions.

This publication is designed to provide accurate and authoritative information in regard to the subject matter covered. It is sold in the understanding that the publisher is not engaged in rendered professional services. If professional advice or other expert assistance is required, the services of a competent professional should be sought. The publisher and author specifically disclaim any implied warranties of merchantability or fitness for a particular purpose.

Secant Publishing, LLC
615 N. Pinehurst Ave., Salisbury MD 21801
www.secantpublishing.com
ISBN **978-0-9909380-4-0**

Library of Congress Control Number: 2014957473
Printed in the United States of America

Interior design and formatting: Ruth Dwight Graphics
Cover design: Rebecca Finkel, F + P Graphic Design

Editorial Services:
Project Manager: Don Loney, Loney Publishing Group Ltd.
Production Editor: Pamela Vokey
Copy Editor: Lindsay Humphreys
Indexer: Dan Liebman

To my family: Gregor, Nicole and Rémi.

Thank you for being incredibly supportive and by my side
during this journey.

To each and every one of my clients who place their trust in me
to be their business and career partner.
Namaste.

Table of Contents

FOREWORD BY MERYL MORITZ

Crack open the Introduction to the *The Coaching Solution* and you will find it reads a bit like the history of a pioneer of the American West: the terrain is rocky, unchartered; the people—faced with seemingly insurmountable obstacles—are headstrong, possessing a fierce desire for something better and willing to risk a lot for that chance.

Renée Robertson is such a pioneer of organizational coaching. A former sales director and talent development director of two telecommunications firms, she revolutionized the way those firms related to customers. How? That is the subject of her book.

Have other, bigger names preceded hers? Yes. For decades, management consultants as well as industrial and organizational psychologists have been supporting executives at the top of major companies to keep their leadership journeys and the health of the companies they lead on track. But much of that work was carried out one-to-one, behind closed doors. Little got cascaded into the system except, perhaps by osmosis, if the leader emulated his coach's approach when addressing his own lieutenants.

Professional coaching started making headlines only a generation or so ago. Life coaching became a tremendous fad in the mid-1990s, riding on the earlier popularity of large group awareness training (LGAT) interventions like Werner Erhard's EST in the US.[1] As early as the 1970s, sports coaching had begun to insinuate itself into major companies to support performance improvement, according to Reinhard Stelter, professor of Sport and Coaching Psychology at the University of Copenhagen.[2]

Initially, management and leadership development were largely the domain of training entities; however, in the late 1990s, studies attempting to measure the return on investment and return on expectations of training versus other disciplines showed some thought-provoking results. For example, a study presented in 1997 by Olivera, Bane and Kopelman in *Public Personnel Management* found that conventional manager training produced a 22.4 percent increase in productivity in one group in a public sector municipal agency, while another group that experienced training plus coaching enjoyed an 88 percent increase in productivity. Human resources and learning & development professionals began commissioning coaches to help employees translate

---

[1] Vicki *Brock*, Ph.D., *Sourcebook of Coaching History,* 2d ed. (n.p., 2014).
[2] Ibid.

learning into development plans. Soon, coaches were engaged to help employees interpret findings of formal feedback surveys and identify new behaviors and actions to embrace the findings and allow them to inform the employees' path ahead.

Organizations in Australia, Western Europe, South America and the United States started to recognize the impact of one-on-one coaching on their executives and chose to extend coaching's reach into other layers of management.

Despite the widespread acceptance of coaching as an integral part of organizational life in some countries, introducing coaching into the organizational system is not for the faint of heart. So when I broached the topic to Renée about starting a coaching initiative inside MCI to leverage her newly completed coach education, she resisted, saying, "It isn't a coaching culture." My retort was simply, "Could you be mistaken?" You will read just how mistaken that belief was and how one pivotal, well-connected person can help transform a system to one that sees every person in it as creative and resourceful, just awaiting support and direction.

As a leadership coach and coach educator for over twenty-one years, I've had the privilege of accompanying many change agents like Renée on their journeys. However, Renée's journey has been unique from its outset to today, as she sharpened her saw, articulated her dream, passed it on and excelled in developing internal coaching in two companies. Both companies' programs went on to win the prestigious Prism Award of the International Coach Federation for the best internal coaching program. Other winners include the British Broadcasting Corporation (BBC), Deloitte & Touche, Genentech, IBM, NASA and the United Nations Secretariat, to name a few.

Not content to enjoy the fruits of her labors with this recognition in the field of coaching, Renée has chosen to write the seminal text on how to divine and then design an internal coaching program that works. I'm keen to be able to refer people to this book, people, who like Renée, want to bring the prodigious benefits of professional coaching inside their organizations. Many authors around the globe have focused on how to bring out the best of people who lead and manage in institutions. I've benefitted, as have my clients, from reading these books (in English or in the best translations possible). But reading and implementing are two wildly different activities. *The Coaching Solution* is an implementation primer. A thought leader, a team of like-minded development professionals, a CEO and her direct reports could bring coaching to life by studying and acting upon the recommendations in this book.

INTRODUCTION

I have spent over twenty years working inside organizations in a variety of functional areas, including Sales, Marketing, Human Resources and Talent Management. Each position I held provided an opportunity for me to work with different types of employees, and to learn how to manage change, how to deal with adversity and uncertainty, and how to embrace opportunities, challenges and change. Very quickly I learned to be flexible and adaptable, and I found ways to take a positive view, lightening the mood for the leaders and employees who were affected by the stress in an environment full of change.

Throughout my journey, I've met many wonderful people who were my peers, employees, managers, mentors and clients. Each person, in their own way, wished to make greater contributions, to constantly do better and make a difference. I share these aspirations, and they have become the foundation of my mission to support others in achieving their personal and professional success as well as, of course, the goals of their business.

I first had the notion of becoming an internal coach when I was at an International Coach Federation (ICF) conference in Scottsdale, Arizona. I was sitting in a breakout session with approximately fifty coaches listening to a coach, who was with IBM at the time. She was telling her story about how she became a coach at IBM and how she started the company's internal coaching program. I was completely intrigued with the coach's leadership, her courage and the risk she took in becoming the first internal coach at IBM. The thought of becoming an internal coach truly resonated with me. I was so moved and inspired by her story that I decided that she would become my new role model and I would aspire to become an internal coach at my company, which at the time was MCI.

This was the first ICF conference that I had attended. My desire to go had resulted from my own work with my first coach, Laura Berman-Fortgang (or LBF, as she is known), which I had found life changing. It made me curious about coaching and I wondered if there could be a career in coaching for me. (The ICF is the leading global organization dedicated to coaching. Its members look to the ICF for exceptional education, networking opportunities and the latest research on industry trends. ICF does not accredit/approve coach-training schools; it only accredits/approves training programs and provides a process for coaches to become credentialed. As of January 2015, more than 13,000 professional coaches held an ICF Credential.)

Most of the coaches at the conference were life coaches and the breakout group presentation topics were about coaching schools and life coaching, which didn't interest me. But when I heard the IBM coach speak about internal coaching, everything changed—I could see myself being an internal coach, and I saw the possibility of doing it as a full-time job at MCI. This became my dream and my passion. I decided that becoming an internal coach was my destiny, and I began to do the work and take the training to become a coach.

Fast-forward ten years later, to July 2005. I am standing on the general session stage in San Jose, California, with Steve Young, senior vice president of Sales at MCI, being presented with the 1st Annual International Coach Federation's Prism Award. This award honors organizations that have achieved a standard of excellence in the implementation of coaching programs for culture change, leadership development, and productivity and performance improvement. In the words of ICF President and Master Certified Coach Dr. Damian Goldvarg:

> The ICF International Prism Award celebrates those organizations that have achieved the highest standards of excellence both in and through coaching. Prism Award recipients exemplify how coaching can develop an organization's human capital by maximizing individuals' potential, leading to high returns on investment (ROI) and expectations (ROE) from coaching interactions.

The Prism Award was initially created by the ICF Greater Toronto chapter, with ICF Global adopting the concept in 2005. Since 2005, nineteen companies or government organizations have received the award. Prism Award winners include: JK Organisation (India), Banner Health, United Nations Secretariat and Roche Turkey, BC Housing, British Broadcasting Corporation (BBC), Genentech, ibm.com North America, JOEY Restaurant Groups, MCI, NASA, Solaglas Windowcare, Sysco Canada, Deloitte & Touche, IBM, TINE Group, Turkey's Isikkent Schools, University of Texas at Dallas and Verizon Business. Honorable Mentions have gone to the Royal Australian Navy, the United States' Defense Acquisition University and Caresource (USA).

In being selected for the award, MCI was being recognized for its ability to strategically design and integrate an internal coaching program inside a corporation. It was an incredible experience standing before over 1,000 of my peers being honored for my work and making my dream a reality.

2005 International Coach Federation Annual Conference in San Jose, California: Steve Mitten, President of the ICF (far left) presenting the International Prism Award to Steve Young, Senior Vice President (middle), and Renée Robertson, Internal Coaching Program Manager (right), MCI Telecommunications.

In the beginning though, fulfilling my coaching aspirations was quite an undertaking, as I was one person and those who sought me out for counsel were many. This inspired my vision to build one of the first and most sophisticated teams of internal coaches who would support leaders and their employees during times of transition and change, to assist them in achieving their goals and succeeding. Over time, these programs proved invaluable to our participants in their personal and professional development, and the impact on our business goals was undeniable.

When we received the Prism Award, it was six months before Verizon acquired MCI, in turn becoming Verizon Business. Shortly after this merger, I was tasked with taking our award-winning coaching program across Verizon Business. This was a huge undertaking in light of the challenging circumstances of a large-scale merger. But thanks to our exceptional team collaboration and partnership with our clients, the program saw great success over the first six months (details on our results can be found in Chapter 18), which put us in the running for the ICF's International Prism Award in 2006. The coaching team worked together to complete the application process and we were thrilled to learn of our second award. I accepted the award at the ICF's annual conference hosted in St. Louis, Missouri. We were so proud of our accomplishment. We were doing great work and making a difference, and it was such an honor to be presented with our second Prism Award in front of my peers.

2006 International Coach Federation Annual Conference in St. Louis, Missouri: Pamela Richarde, President of the ICF (left), presenting the International Prism Award to Renée Robertson (right).

We would continue to develop our coaches and play an integral role in Verizon Business's talent and organizational development initiatives for four more years. We would have continued to apply for the Prism Award, however, the ICF placed a limit on Prism Award applicants (specifically, no one company that was awarded the Prism Award would be eligible to receive the award in two consecutive years).

I feel incredibly proud that the ICF honored the coaching program at Verizon Business and at MCI—one of the first companies recognized for excellence in internal coaching. I remember the first time that I applied for the Prism Award. I was sitting at my desk filling in the application and thinking to myself, Who would have thought . . . I started with a dream to become a coach and build a team of coaches inside MCI, and today I am a possible contender for the prestigious award that honors best-in-class internal coaching programs. I remember thinking that even if I didn't win the award, the fact that I was in a position to submit an application was an indication of my success and a very real reminder that my dream had become a reality.

My first coaching lesson learned was that a well-selected, trained and experienced team of internal coaches can bring significant and measurable value to an organization. I have experienced this firsthand, and I want to share the value proposition of an internal coaching program with business, human resources and talent management leaders. I also wish to share with coaches the many opportunities and applications for coaching inside organizations and how best to prepare oneself to work with clients in a positive, engaging and thoughtful manner. Sharing my learnings about the powerful impact that coaching programs have inside organizations became my next dream, and now it is time to make this dream a reality.

My vision for this book dates back to 2008, when I first brought pen to paper. I had a strong desire to share my experiences with anyone who wished to leave a legacy at work and in their personal life. Although it has taken some time to make this dream a reality, it has been well worth it. I hope you find this book helpful and inspiring in the journey to fulfilling your coaching goals.

Renée Robertson
April 2015

HOW TO USE THIS BOOK

The following provides an outline for each section of the book—what you can expect to learn about how coaching inside organizations can be a key part of your talent development program as well as an excellent tool for achieving business goals and managing through change. You may skip around to the parts that are of most relevance and interest to you, but you will get the most out of the book by reading it linearly, start to finish.

PART 1: MERGER & CRISES

This section portrays my own career path that led me to becoming a coach. I share a true story about how I partnered with executive leadership to retain and develop a sales force in order to help save a company that was in bankruptcy and crisis. It's the story of how one voice became the voice of many as the company dealt with and overcame the many challenges imposed on it as a consequence of the WorldCom crisis. My hope is that you find this section inspiring and leave with an understanding that we each own our career destiny and have the ability to lead—no matter where we sit within an organization or on a team. Please note the time line of events that occurred during the MCI-WorldCom years, as this can be confusing. Specifically, MCI was acquired by WorldCom in 1998 and the company was named MCI-WorldCom. In 2000, the name changed to simply WorldCom. In July 2002, WorldCom filed for bankruptcy and at the time became the largest case of corporate fraud in the United States. Emerging from bankruptcy in 2004, the name was changed back to MCI Inc.

PART 2: COACHING AND CULTURE

The chapters within this part of the book describe how to take the concept of instituting internal coaching to the next step: designing a winning proposal. It explains the distinctions between coaching, counseling and mentoring, and how they're all so much more than simply giving someone "feedback." You'll learn about the importance of having International Coach Federation (ICF) credentialed coaches and the benefits of having internal coaches that abide by the ICF's Code of Ethics. Insight is offered on how to gain buy-in and alignment, including a proposal outline with real content that demonstrates how to construct a winning proposal. An Internal Coaching Program Readiness

Assessment is provided, as well as key questions on how to determine if your company is "ready" for an internal coaching program. Questions are also provided to help you determine how to shape the actual role of the internal coach. The primary goal of this section is to help you assess whether or not internal coaching is a viable solution for your organization and its environment and to help you get started designing your internal coaching program.

PART 3: LAUNCHING THE INTERNAL COACHING INITIATIVE

The key criteria to be used in the selection of internal coaches—and how to select the best coaches for your company, its culture and its client base—are discussed in this section of the book. An approach for writing an internal coach job description and setting performance goals is provided, including an actual description template that you can readily use when designing your position. Advice is also given on how to scale a program according to company size and need, and how to flex the program according to organizational change, especially in the face of culture friction. This is the "how to" section of the book and its purpose is to describe the essential elements of a successful internal coaching program. In addition to guidelines on how to select and hire coaches, information is provided regarding each resource that you might need to build a program and suggestions are offered on how to market a strong and sustainable program.

PART 4: THE TALENT MANAGEMENT LIFE CYCLE: INTEGRATING INTERNAL COACHING WITH YOUR OVERALL TALENT MANAGEMENT STRATEGY

This section walks through the Talent Management Life Cycle, offering a step-by-step approach and providing all relevant templates for the selection and onboarding of coaching program participants and their management while in the coaching program. I explain how to utilize coaching throughout the employee life cycle, from acquisition through to succession planning and retirement. I also share how to design systems and processes that can be used to measure your overall program activities, participant engagement and coaches' actions. A perspective on how to handle confidentiality is offered, as well as criteria to determine what constitutes a successful program and how long program participants should be coached. This section makes clear the value of having coaches inside your organizations, whether it is on a project basis, part-time or full-time. There are many applications for the use of coaches inside organizations, and my goal is to share these applications with all communities of practice—coaches, consultants, human resources, talent management and business leaders. It is through these coaching applications that coaching can become integrated within an organization, leading to a culture of "coaching" or of learning whereby professional development can be established, integrated and sustained.

Also included in this section is an approach to creating a buzz around the program and building a culture based on coaching that fosters learning and development, as well as views on the benefits of building a coaching culture. You will gain insight on how to build internal partnerships with executives and, subsequently, how to market your program and build a successful internal coaching brand. I examine the differing views on partnerships with Human Resources and business leaders and where internal coaching programs should reside inside organizations. You will learn how to incorporate competency models, training curriculums, mentoring, rotational assignments and other developmental activities and planning into your coaching initiative, with a primary outcome to build a sustainable program. In addition, you will have the opportunity to see how coaching is applied in several different scenarios, from coaching within Sales organizations, to training applications, executive development and career transitions.

PART 5: HOW TO MEASURE THE IMPACT OF AN INTERNAL COACHING PROGRAM

The final section of the book discusses how to leverage coaching and use a coach approach during times of change and transformation. I explain how the success of an internal coaching program can be measured and offer my views and experiences with return on investment (ROI) and return on engagement (ROE). I also discuss the advantages and disadvantages of trying to measure such programs, offering real-life examples, and I look at the impact of specific internal coaching programs on engagement, productivity and customer satisfaction. In addition to measurement, this section offers a chapter on change management and how to use coaches and a coach approach to support and accelerate change for individuals, leaders and organizations.

COACHING AND LEADERSHIP INSIGHT

Each chapter concludes with an insight about internal coaching programs based on the chapter's content—specifically, an insight, experience or lesson learned. Insights include tips on topics such as how and when to start coaching; making certain your clients are engaged and satisfied; creating alignment and integration of your coaching with your organizational capabilities and Talent Management Life Cycle; and how to build sustainable programs in order to create positive and winning cultures that drive engagement and business results.

APPENDIX

An appendix can be found at www.robertsoncoachinstitute.com. Here you can find and download all support documents referenced throughout the book.

Whether you are a new coach, an experienced coach, a corporate employee looking to become a coach, or a business leader or human resources/talent management professional looking to increase engagement and positively impact results, there are aspects of this book that you may find inspiring, informative or enlightening, which may guide you in seeing coaching through a new lens. For experienced coaches and talent management professionals, some of the ideas in this book may act as a refresher or a simple reminder of why you do what you do—to create awareness and demonstrate the power of coaching inside organizations. No matter who you are and why you are reading this book, I wish you all the best in your journey and look forward to hearing about your success.

Part 1:

MERGER AND CRISES

The Coaching Solution

1 My Path to Coaching

I am often asked about my path to becoming a coach. Each time I'm asked, I am delighted to share my story. And I'm very pleased now to have the opportunity to share it with you.

My story starts in the fall of 1995. My husband, Gregor, and I were thinking about starting a family. We wanted to sell our starter house in Rockaway, New Jersey, and build a house in Bernardsville, New Jersey. I was with MCI Communications at the time, in sales, and having a very successful run. I had recently won two global clients, American International Group, Inc. (AIG) and Becton, Dickinson and Company (BD), through our joint venture with British Telecom, Concert Communications Services. Fortunately, or unfortunately, depending on how you look at it, winning these contracts increased my business travel time from approximately 10 percent a year to approximately 50 percent a year. Needless to say, it was a high-pressure and fast-paced time as these companies were implementing new services around the world and the amount of effort required to successfully install these new networks, equipment and managed services was incredibly intense (both for the client and for MCI). I thrived on the challenges associated with implementing these networks and the incredible amount of learning it offered, not only to me but to the entire team connected to these customers.

I learned very early in my career that a happy client usually means relationships are more easily built, problems are more easily rectified, and a positive impact on one's business is more likely to be realized. Happy clients lead to incentive targets being met and commissions and bonuses being earned. These were major contributing factors to rationalizing my time away from my husband, and postponing our new home and starting a family.

As I said, winning the BD and AIG accounts increased my travel, especially on behalf of AIG, as its international data center was located outside of London, England. Given that we were awarded its global network, much of my travel was back and forth to the United Kingdom. To help pass the time on one of my flights from the Newark airport, my home away from home, to Heathrow Airport (my third home), I picked up a magazine entitled *Executive Female Magazine*. The feature story was about the success that a female executive had had from working with a "coach." Intrigued, I flipped to the article and began reading. It described coaching and shared this executive's story about how previously she had been struggling with balancing her life—her career, family and health and well-being. The article had an immediate impact on me. I thought to myself, "I am going to get myself a coach and have her solve my work–life balance challenges." Now, this was 1995 so it wasn't like I could pick up my smartphone and google "professional coach." I would have to wait until I was back home in New Jersey to begin my research. When I did return home, my research project was delayed a few more weeks by business, holidays and just general "life," when an interesting opportunity presented itself.

I was on my way to a meeting in New York City with a colleague and friend. We stopped at a quaint café for lunch in Montclair, New Jersey, where we ran into Laura Berman-Fortgang, her close friend. We joined Laura for lunch, and as we were chatting I discovered the close friend was a coach.

I liked Laura's energy and I could feel that we had good chemistry. She also came highly recommended, so I hired her to be my coach shortly after this encounter. While this worked out wonderfully for me, I highly recommend that, before hiring a coach, a client should interview at least two or three potential coaches. The purpose is to vet the coach for their training and experience, and to ensure that the chemistry between the coach and client is positive. Remember, the client will be sharing personal thoughts and experiences, so it is important that they can place their trust in their coach.

WHAT COACHING TOLD ME ABOUT MYSELF

I worked with Laura over the next six months to be coached through what I thought would be just a job change, but it turned out to be so much more than that. With coaching, I discovered my true self, my passions and, truly, what I was born to "do." My coach helped me to get clear on my values, the vision I had for my life and what type of career would support this life vision while playing to my strengths and maintaining my level of compensation. She also helped me to discover that I had become driven primarily by external motivations such as special bonuses, monthly commissions, sales contests and the adrenaline rush of winning new clients or a large deal. What I began learning in my work with my coach is that I defined myself by these external motivators, and everything that I did was focused on winning, getting to the next level, making more money, but all at a cost: being away from my home and my husband and losing sight of what was truly important to me—starting a family and building a legacy.

I realized that it was time to make a change away from sales and begin to honor the intrinsic values that were most important to me. I began researching several different opportunities, both inside and outside of MCI. However, I knew that I wanted to stay at MCI ideally, as the culture was fast and fun—and we were building something. We were building our future, a legacy that would be remembered by many. We were the catalyst for change as we took on the AT&T Corporation and triggered the divestiture of "Ma Bell."

During my search, I found the perfect position—a branch marketing manager position located in New York City, at MCI. It was a management position and I would be located in two offices—one at 100 Wall Street and the other at 757 3rd Avenue. I would be commuting three to four hours a day; however, this position meant no more international travel! The position was two levels higher than my current one, which helped me to maintain my present level of sales compensation. More importantly, as this was a newly created position, it would require creativity and the capability to build not only marketing programs but also people development and training programs.

I knew this position would be very competitive, but I wanted it and went for it. With my coach's brilliant coaching and my hard work (I was doing all of this and still keeping pace with my sales role and demanding clients), I completed eight interviews and was selected for the role.

COACHING MY TEAM DELIVERS RETURNS

A few weeks into the position, I realized how different being an independent salesperson was from being a manager—I needed to learn some new skills. As I thought about the challenges of my new role, I realized I already had insight into some techniques that could work. But I would need to learn more and master what I already knew. It is at this point in my life that I discovered one of the secrets to being a successful manager and getting results—and it's how I became an internal corporate coach.

I realized the impact that working with a coach had on me, and it caused me to reflect: *If only I could have that degree of impact on my team—what could our success look like?* So, while continuing to work with my own coach at the time, I prepared and presented a proposal to my new boss, requesting that the company support my pursuit of becoming a trained coach. My new boss, who is a huge supporter of learning and development, liked the idea and subsequently met with our Human Resources business partner. The proposal received their blessing and I enrolled into Coach University's coaching program in 1997, attending classes in the evenings and on the weekends. After taking thirty classes and completing 120 hours of training, I graduated in April 1999.

In my new role as branch marketing manager, I quickly applied my new coaching skills and, as a result, my team designed specialized educational programs to support our business partners at the Wall Street Telecommunications Association (WSTA) and the Security & Investments Association (SIA). We hosted twenty-two C-level clients from leading Wall Street and international companies, flying them to Washington, D.C., where we briefed them on new offerings and breaking news about our partnership with British Telecom. As a result of this effort, the very next day we were awarded over US$1 million in new business, and, shortly thereafter, a high-potential team member designed a six-month new-hire program targeted to bring in over thirty new sales and service employees per year to fill our talent pipeline. These are just a couple of highlights of this team's inspired work. Through the process of being coached, these employees developed into my top performers and became high-potential individual contributors and managers, resulting in an overall high-performing team. As for me, I am grateful to have had the opportunity to work with this group of incredibly talented people and that they afforded me the opportunity to coach them.

It is important to point out that during the experience I just described, I understood that not everyone could be coached or would want to be coached. Coaching is a technique where optimum benefits are realized with employees who are able to think strategically and deliver results. If members of my team were not executing on their responsibilities or interested in their professional development, especially when their colleagues were counting on them to grow and adapt with the business (this was telecommunications—where change occurs daily), they were released and replaced with more positive team members. This is a simple lesson and Basic Management 101: non-performers need to be managed accordingly.

After our first year, our team received an award for being MCI's best-in-class branch marketing team in the country. As a result, we were asked to document our organizational structure, roles and responsibilities, as well as the services that were offered to the sales and support teams, which included marketing, technical, product and training services. We were asked to work with other branches that wanted to implement a successful Branch Marketing department, and our work became the prototype for the design of an entire organization. Components of the model are still in place today.

The branch marketing manager position was one of the most gratifying assignments of my career. Taking on the role was truly a career-defining moment for me. It gave me the opportunity to develop as a manager, building my self-confidence and self-esteem while also developing my coaching skills and enjoying the benefits that come with great success. With this growing self-confidence and the support from my leaders and my coach, I decided to take my little coaching experiment further. However, before the opportunity to build an internal coaching program presented itself, I achieved one of my biggest life goals: on October 28, 1997, I gave birth to Nicole Jeanne Robertson. She, in many respects, was a miracle baby, as I had suffered numerous health challenges and for a while I was uncertain if children would ever be possible. Nicole arrived and the way I saw the world, my career and what was truly important to me shifted.

2 Finding the Leader Within

After Nicole was born, which was coincidentally at the onset of the MCI Communications and WorldCom merger, the branch marketing manager position and my team were being wound down, with positions being absorbed into other groups inside the organization. I was offered the opportunity to be a field-marketing specialist (FMS) or a global account manager (GAM) in New York City. I remember looking at my daughter, who was only a month old at the time, and thinking that spending three to four hours a day commuting would mean less time and energy for her. Therefore, neither position was acceptable to me. I decided to accept a severance package and look for something that would keep me closer to home and allow me to continue to coach, manage and develop people. I'd had a taste of what it was like to be a manager and I wished to continue contributing to the success of others.

Shortly after I left the company, I accepted a position as a sales manager at a small telecommunications company called LCI. The position was based in New Jersey, and several of my MCI colleagues were working at LCI. The culture seemed vibrant, energetic and entrepreneurial, and it didn't take much to convince me to join the team. Within six months of joining the company, however, Qwest Communications International, Inc. acquired LCI and, as with most mergers, change inevitably followed. I observed management behaviors negatively impacting the once-vibrant collegial culture, and so I decided it was time to leave.

RETURNING TO MCI

As I was a relatively new coach and quite early in my career, building a coaching practice was a challenge. It was the 90s and I was completing my training, and many clients looked to me for "life coaching," which was not exactly what I wanted to do. During this time I was contacted by my former boss and mentor at MCI, which post-merger was now called MCI WorldCom. He'd had his responsibilities expanded and was now responsible for sales in New Jersey. He told me that he needed someone with the requisite experience to take over the New Jersey–based team. We met for lunch one day in October along with some former business colleagues. Over lunch they offered me the position and convinced me to accept it. We all thought about how great it would be to work together again, and that in and of itself was motivation for me. I rejoined the company in November 1998 and we were off to the races!

But we had our work cut out for us. It was January 1999; WorldCom had acquired MCI the prior year and it was a tough integration. The cultures of the two companies were very different: how we approached business, how we treated and compensated our employees, how our systems worked, not to mention our products and services and networks—all were extremely different. One of the greatest challenges we faced was the lack of integration of our systems and networks. Despite all the years that had passed and the amount of acquisitions over that time, WorldCom had not properly integrated many of the acquired companies' networks, systems, processes and, well, people. There were silos all over the place, process and documentation was absent, and installing new services for our clients was a nightmare. Our clients and our employees were truly struggling. These times brought long hours, extra client attention and care, and a lot of pressure to perform. It would take the pure will and the absolute best of our employees to turn this situation around. (Little did we know what the future would bring, despite our efforts.)

One of the traits that MCIers were best known for was a "do whatever it takes attitude." Our goal was to ensure that our customers received the best customer experience possible. So, we did what every great team would do in a tough situation—we united and made things happen. Employees from all departments and from around the world collaborated for the sake of the customer. In many cases, you would not even know the person that you were reaching out to, nor would they know you. However, we all had one common goal—to serve the customer—and it was this emphasis on the customer that taught me to view all situations through the customer's lens and to develop solutions with the customer in mind. This is an attribute that I am very proud of and to which I credit much of my success.

I have always had a positive attitude as well; I'm a glass-half-full type and I love to solve problems. In the situation at the time, despite all of our collaboration, employees were unhappy working in the new culture. The company was slowly making some progress with its networks and services; however, employees were still unhappy. I thought if we could further strengthen our communication and improve our teamwork and leadership capabilities, we could begin to turn things around. As I continued to witness the distress that the organization and its employees were in, I reflected on how I might be able to help solve this problem. I asked myself, "What experiences have I had that could be shared with the organization that could help our situation?" I felt that if we could create a better culture, we could increase employee engagement, innovate and become more proactive, and positively impact our customers' satisfaction. Happy customers are more likely to buy more services, and selling more services would mean an increase in revenue.

Engaged employees provide top-notch customer service and aim to create an amazing experience for customers. Customers will take notice and repurchase from you as a result. In John Goodman's book, *Strategic Customer Service*, he found that customers who are delighted by proactive education or superior service are 10 percent to 30 percent more loyal than customers who don't receive the same quality of attention from a customer service provider.[1] Improved business results lead to happier employees and leaders, and happier employees experience less stress and work in a more relaxed atmosphere. But such a notion seems pie-in-the-sky when one looks at the current state of the workplace:

> For more than a decade, and however you slice it through whatever external consulting firm's data points, roughly 70 percent to 80 percent of any organization has effectively acted in a practice of workplace ambivalence. The employees would rather not be at work, or worse, they're simply participating in some form of corporate coma—a catatonic catastrophe in the organization. . . .
>
> [W]hy aren't leaders actually doing something about the data that haunts their every move? In a report entitled "Global Leadership Forecast" conducted by Development Dimensions International (DDI) with over 14,000 global leaders, DDI's research indicates that "organizations with the highest quality leaders [are] more likely to outperform their competition in key bottom-line

---

[1] John A. Goodman, *Strategic Customer Service* (New York: AMACOM, 2009)

metrics such as financial performance, quality of products and services, employee engagement, and customer satisfaction.[2]

These thoughts are always in the back of my mind, especially when I build a plan or program for employees. The question I ask myself is, "How can I create an engaging and positive experience for my employees that will flow forward to our clients?" Every time I accept a new role, I envision myself providing a positive experience with each and every person I meet and interact with. My goal is for that person to have a good experience and then take that experience and pay-it-forward, thereby building positivity and momentum for all. When it came to building the coaching program concept and proposal, I thought about these things and how I could incorporate them in order to positively influence a work environment. I began to reflect on what I had learned over the past eleven years in sales.

I thought about the greatest career change for me personally—the transition into the branch marketing role. I reflected on the best practices and the lessons that I'd learned, and thought about how they could be adapted at the organizational level. And then it hit me: establish a coaching program for managers and leaders to help them get unstuck, feel empowered, develop solutions and accelerate through challenges. Our goal was to build a better work environment and positively impact the customer.

I was energized by my new idea and set up a call with my coach at the time, Meryl Moritz. Meryl was my advocate and was instrumental in helping me, especially in times when my vision appeared likely to be compromised by fear and bureaucracy. She coached me as I fleshed out the proposal and then navigated the organizational and political waters. (No small task, given the business and customer challenges and the amount of change everyone was experiencing.)

Next, I met with my manager. I shared my idea with him and secured his support. (At this point, I was running strategic account sales for New Jersey. My manager had overall responsibility for New York and New Jersey and soon he would have Pennsylvania.) The next step was to gain the support of Human Resources, so I met with our HR director, and asked him if he would be willing to help me, too. He agreed, although it took a while to figure out the right process and to whom to present the business case. Building a coach

---

[2] Jazmine Boatman, et. al., *Global Leadership Forecast 2011* (Development Dimensions International, 2011). www.ddiworld.com/DDIWorld/media/trend-research/global leadership forecast 2011_ukhighlights_tr_ddi.pdf.

position and program meant going into unchartered territory, which at that time would prove to be a monumental task.

I also knew that I needed to complete my coach training and meet my sales objectives. (No one wants to get behind someone who can't achieve their goals.) So I continued to work hard to be successful in my role while I designed the future internal coaching program. This took time and patience, which at the time was a skill I had to learn.

POST-MERGER CHALLENGES

At the beginning of 2000, my responsibilities were expanded and I was asked to take over the strategic accounts program in Pennsylvania. It was underperforming and needed to be turned around. The new team would require a lot of my time and attention, but I didn't give up on pursuing the vision of an internal coaching program. I coached my new team to success and continued to keep my finger on the pulse of the organization. In early 2001, my new organization started to stabilize and my leadership was happy with my organization's success. We were achieving our objectives despite the significant challenges with the systems, networks, communications and collaboration across the company. However, the cultures of both companies were still very different, which presented several other challenges. My peers and I would experience daily issues with communications, the fallout from inexperienced managers and differences in general business practices. These were just a few additional challenges that created tension in an already tense environment.

When you are living in a merger situation, it is difficult to analyze and understand the impact of the change on your organization, department, its employees and even yourself. However, during times of change, there is a tendency for everyone involved to experience a wide array of emotions and behaviors from others and themselves. And quite frankly, some of these feelings and experiences can be good and, well, some not so good. For example, you may see information being withheld or too much information being shared in the wrong forums. You may observe a wide variety of communication styles along with mixed messages about a project or strategic direction. Unfortunately, during mergers, everyone involved is typically focused on getting their part of the transaction completed and neglect the soft skills that go along with executing the merger. In an article posted in the *Deloitte*

Review, the results of a comprehensive empirical analysis on post-integration data were published:

> . . . based on an evaluation of one of the world's largest PMI (post-merger integration) databases, built up over a period of six years by the authors in a joint research effort with the University of Muenster, a leading university in Germany. . . .
>
> Containing more than 45,000 data points from post-merger transactions in all important sectors worldwide, the database uses a representative global sample—from Europe (61 percent), Americas (28 percent) and the Asia Pacific region (11 percent)—of all key industries: services and manufacturing, comprising both large enterprises and mid-sized companies. . . .
>
> Forty-six percent of the management interviewed share the opinion that soft factors like motivating people are more essential to merger success than hard factors like project management. Our analysis suggests that it is important to address both soft and hard factors. Even if a merger appears to pose little risk in terms of synergy, structure or people, project risks can still undermine a PMI.[3]

Note: Providing coaching for those responsible for post-merger integration (PMI) projects as well as the multiple facets of a merger, including organizational design, achieving a new culture and building collaboration across new teams to name a few, can be beneficial not only to the project manager but also to all those around the manager who are being impacted by the change. Coaching accelerates the manager's ability to adapt to the change, and that behavior is modeled for others, who upon seeing the behavioral change in the manager also begin to adapt, thereby creating momentum and a shift for all.

Now, back at WorldCom, there was tremendous focus on the hard skills or projects related to the merger such as managing the network, meeting financials goals and so on; however, there was practically no attention given to soft skills or support for the managers and employees going through the changes. In addition and unfortunately, the encouragement I had been receiving from my Human Resources business partner to pursue becoming an internal coach and build an internal coaching program slowly began to wane. He has a remarkable ability to truly understand how organizations function—to work within the "unspoken rules" and make smart decisions that positively impact employees and the business. My business partner suggested that I reconsider

---

[3] Johannes Gerds, Freddy Strottmann, and Pakshalika Jayaprakash, "Post Merger Integration: Hard Data, Hard Truths," *Deloitte Review*, 6 (2010).

taking my proposal any further at this point in time. He felt that the organization was volatile and that there might be some unexpected consequences resulting from my innovative proposal. Despite his warnings, I maintained my commitment to it. Employee morale was at an all-time low; someone needed to do something and, well, I decided it would be me.

As we were waiting for the assignment of a new vice president, my patience was subsiding. I requested a meeting with our senior vice president of Sales and the executive director of Sales Operations, to discuss my plan. By going straight to the decision makers, I was able to secure a meeting and place the coaching proposal on the agenda. When the new vice president was assigned, my manager then spoke with him on my behalf about my coaching proposal and the upcoming meeting.

As you can imagine, I was very excited about this meeting. It took place in Ryebrook, New York, where I met with our executive director of Sales Operations who was prepared (as he always is) with his feedback and feedback from our senior vice president. They were both impressed with the time and energy I'd invested in my professional development and the proposal. However—and here comes the "but"—they indicated that the business was about to face a significant downturn and several thousand employees would be losing their jobs in the following month. It was going to be an extremely difficult time and I could understand why launching a program to invest in the development of your employees, when thousands of employees were about to lose their jobs, would not be a priority. But, on the other hand, there were going to be several thousand employees that would have to survive this reduction and cope with the impact it would have on their clients, themselves and their lives. Everyone was already working so hard and were overloaded with customer issues; how were we going to manage the increasing needs of our clients, deliver positive customer experiences and meet our objectives in this stressful environment while also dealing with dramatic change?

As these thoughts were firing in my brain, our director of Sales Operations made it clear that they would like me to remain in sales. The company needed my expertise and leadership, and my teams were known to deliver results and achieve their targets. The trusted relationships I had with our clients were of great value, and my experience and knowledge of our business were going to be called upon now more than ever. What could I say? These were difficult times and they were about to become even more difficult. So I continued in my role, achieved my targets and near the end of 2001 was faced with yet another change: our head of Sales announced that he would be leaving the company. Shortly after this, we learned that his replacement as senior vice president of Sales would be Mr. Stephen Young, a vice president from Marketing.

Positive Changes

For as long as I live, I will never forget the day that I met Steve. Our first encounter was an operations review meeting held in December 2001. Operations reviews are an opportunity for your boss, and perhaps his manager, to conduct deep dives into your business, your customers and your results. They are typically intense meetings and can be very stressful for the person being reviewed; it's an arduous question and inspection process. Therefore, I always took these meetings seriously, as everyone should.

I truly thought that I was thoroughly prepared for this review. Like I always do for operations reviews, I spend hours upon hours preparing. I knew my business, my clients, my metrics and my team better than anyone. And then, on the night before my review, my peers and I received a several-hundred-page file of all of our clients, their services and their monthly billing for each service in each month of the past year. We knew Steve had a reputation for holding tough operations reviews. I must say though, that he practices what he preaches and truly "inspects what he expects." Throughout my review, he would go to the file and ask very targeted questions about specific accounts—an excellent management tactic and there are many of us who are much better business managers because of it. I was able to field all of his questions, except for one. I asked if I could get back to him with an answer and he said, "Yes, of course." Overall, the review went well and the feedback that I received was very positive. I would live to see another review.

Soon after my review, I received an invitation to the first session of World-Com's (they'd removed "MCI" from the company name in late 2000) newly formed Leadership School. The class was to be held in Dallas, Texas, in January 2002. At this point, I was eight months pregnant with my second child and my due date was just around the corner, on March 9. I knew my doctor would not be happy about me traveling, but I also knew that, based on the agenda, the participants and the opportunity to receive a comprehensive assessment and work with a professional coach, this would be an incredible experience. It would give me the chance to connect with my peers from around the country and accelerate my professional development by learning more about coaching and leadership development. The sales professional in me also knew that this was an ideal opportunity to network with those executives and external coaches who might be interested in and supportive of my internal coaching proposal. I pleaded with my doctor and secured his approval.

The program was less than three days in length, but we made use of every minute. It started on a Sunday evening with a reception, followed by a dinner then a working session that went until 11 P.M. The next two days would begin each morning with breakfast at 7 A.M. and then continue through dinner, and we'd wrap up with a working session that would end, again, around 11 P.M. The program was rigorous, especially for an eight-month-pregnant woman to say the least.

Attending the Leadership School was one of the best decisions I have ever made. During the process, a 360-degree assessment was administered and I was assigned a coach. As my assigned coach and I were reviewing the results of my 360-degree assessment, he shared with me that many of the people who had rated me (my peers, employees and colleagues) had provided additional feedback on my abilities as a manager, partner and coach, and that it was all positive. He mentioned that they had all referred to me as "coach," which prompted him to ask what that was about, so I shared my story, the whole thing. He was so interested—I couldn't believe it! My assigned coach asked if I had shared my story with the head of the Leadership School and Steve. I replied "no" and asked him why he had asked me this question—would they be interested? He strongly encouraged me to share my proposal with them. So, during a break-out session, I took advantage of an opportunity to speak with the head of our Leadership School. He was surprised to learn of my coach training and my passion for leadership development, and suggested I share my story with Steve. After I returned from the leadership session, I sent them both a copy of my proposal, following up with a phone call to Steve. I talked to him about my vision, and he said he would give it some thought and get back to me. In the meantime, my daughter, Remi Noel, decided to arrive three weeks early on February 17, and I went on family leave for the next three months.

THE BREAKTHROUGH

Fast-forward to May 2002. I received a call from my manager. He wanted to let me know that Steve Young had called him about my proposal and that he was interested in having me become a "coach" for the organization. This assignment meant that I would be responsible for all leadership development, sales force performance and executive coaching. I couldn't believe what I was hearing—was this true? I was thrilled and immediately jumped on the opportunity.

Looking back, this time of my life is a blur to me. Frankly, I was exhausted and had a two-month-old baby who did not sleep through the night (until she was four years old!). One of my main memories of those days is going to the local supermarket to get two Krispy Kreme donuts and a super-large hazelnut coffee loaded with raw sugar. I would see the same gal at the register each morning and she would say to me, "So, I see we have another Red Cross Special." I would smile with baby in her carrier and say, "Yes, another sleepless night!" (By the way, the carrier was a very thoughtful gift from everyone who attended the Leadership School conference in January, in recognition of my good sportsmanship and staying power.) With this in mind, I suspect Steve's recall of those days is superior to mine, and so below I offer you his narrative. He had this to say when I asked him about our meeting and how the coaching program came to be:

> Renée was a sales manager in New Jersey at the time. I had met her previously during several operations reviews and I'd identified her as a future high-potential (HiPo) employee. I was always on the lookout for HiPos, especially women and minorities, as it was my personal objective, as well as that of MCI, to build a diverse management team. Renée had been on maternity leave with her second child, and Human Resources had notified me that she was about to return to the workforce. My plan was to re-engage her as a sales manager in New Jersey, giving her a similar territory as [she'd had] before her leave to take advantage of her relationships with certain customers. However, Renée, being a "Jersey girl," had her own ideas that I learned about on an unsolicited phone call she made to me. I always preached my availability to any of the 3,200 employees on the team, so the call was not totally out of the normal sphere of events, but it did show a certain assertiveness on Renée's part, as there were two levels (branch director and regional vice president) between us.
>
> Renée waited patiently as I explained our plans for her return, referring her to the appropriate channels and Human Resources for more details. When I was finished, she told me that while she appreciated the new assignment, she was calling to tell me that she was a "certified coach" and wanted to serve in that role on the team. As the father of two children who had done the "soccer thing," I immediately thought, "Cool, Renée is a soccer coach too, but what does that have to do with WorldCom and her career?" (Sad but true, I was

clueless about coaching.) Was she telling me she wasn't coming back? I was concerned. She had a great job and made a good deal of money due to her success. A soccer coach couldn't make that much money, even in Bernardsville, New Jersey. And more to the point, what were we going to do to backfill her [position]?

Thus began my education on the value of coaching to an organization, as Renée began to explain her plans. As it worked out, Renée's coaching ideas fit in perfectly as a potential solution to the biggest challenges in the organization: keeping the sales force ahead of the curve of a massively changing marketplace, the imminent introduction of new strategic products and the urgent need to move to a new sales methodology. The telecom industry was in decline in 2002, having suffered through the Internet bust of 1999/2000. As dot-com companies went bankrupt, demand for network decreased across the board. Competition between WorldCom, AT&T and Sprint reached new heights as earnings forecasts to Wall Street [still] had to be met.

We needed to find new sources of revenue in new product and service areas, which required our sales teams to mature and stretch themselves. In turn, we as management needed to provide them with the tools to meet these new challenges. And Renée's pitch on coaching held promise. I asked her to prepare a formal presentation, detailing exactly how she would implement the program, including budget and return on investment. Renée [did this] and presented her proposal to me and two of my critical team members, the head of Sales Operations (including budgeting) and the vice president of Strategic Initiatives. Renée delivered a well-thought-out proposal, and after the meeting the three of us discussed the proposal and agreed this was something we would like to implement in the organization.

We decided that Renée would report into our vice president of Strategic Initiatives, as this was a strategic initiative and he would be an ideal person to give her day-to-day support as she built our coaching program. However, it would also be made clear that I was going to be her first customer and seek her coaching. I would never ask any member of my organization to do anything that I wouldn't do, and more importantly, I believe in the benefits of learning and professional development and I wanted to make certain that my organization knew that this was a program that if you were invited into it, you were to take it seriously.

THE WORST NEWS

Within two weeks of returning to work and figuring out my new role while managing my sales manager responsibilities and developing a succession plan,

I received a call from one of my best sales managers (whom I had chosen as my replacement candidate and who backfilled my position). He asked me to turn on the news and sit down. It was at this moment I learned that World-Com had announced that it had overstated its earnings by $3.8 billion—and this was only the beginning. On July 21, WorldCom declared bankruptcy and, on August 8, the company announced that it had also manipulated its reserve accounts in recent years, affecting an additional $3.8 billion. At this point in time, this was the largest fraud to have ever occurred in U.S. corporate history. I sat in my family room as the feeling of loss and devastation washed over me. This news was incomprehensible—what did it mean? What would be the impact?

My husband arrived home from work and saw me just sitting there, staring at the television with a blank look on my face. I was feeling overwhelmed, fearful and concerned about my employees, their families and the overall well-being of our company. I, like many, felt passionate about what we'd created at MCI and what we'd brought to the telecommunications industry. It was heartbreaking to see our efforts threatened and potentially destroyed. I felt sick to my stomach.

Gregor asked me what had happened. When I explained the situation, he said, "Let me get this straight. You left your sales manager position, where you dealt directly with clients and were responsible for hundreds of millions of dollars, for a staff job a.k.a. "coaching" position, in which you do not have a title nor a job description and the compensation is still not worked out, and your company just announced the largest case of fraud in U.S. history." I paused and thought about me specifically, and as various thoughts raced through my brain, I replied, "Yes, I did, and you know what? This company, my colleagues and our employees are going to need what I have to offer now more than ever." He looked at me and said, "This is one of the many reasons why I married you—you always do the right thing because it's the right thing to do. I trust your judgment and you have 100 percent of my support."

Leaders come in all shapes, sizes, races and genders from all over the world. I believe that there is a leader in all of us and that it's incumbent upon each of us to take responsibility for our own personal leadership, to embrace it and to have the courage to stand up for what we believe in.

According to Gallup's 2013 *State of the Global Workforce* report, 80 percent of people globally never use their greatest gifts at work, which means that only 13 percent of workers worldwide are engaged at work, with Canada and the United States holding at about 29 percent engagement. I find these numbers disheartening, and I will be forever grateful to all of the mentors, champions and coaches who put me in a position where I could use my gift and passion for people development to make a living.

I felt a significant increase in responsibility when I assumed the role of coach, and I've made it my personal mission to provide support to those who reach out to me about business decisions and career planning. I know it's not always possible to use your natural gifts to make a living, but I'm committed to doing the best I can to help those who want to try. My thinking here goes back to employee engagement and the thought that if you can do what comes naturally to you, what you enjoy doing, you will be happier and more engaged; therefore, creating a win–win for all—you, your organization and your company.

I was a top-performing sales manager, responsible for $150 million-plus in annual revenue, working in a company with annual revenue of approximately $40 billion. I had a vision for that company, made up of tens of thousands of employees worldwide, to become a place where employees would thrive as they developed professionally. No one gave me this vision. No one held my hand as I voiced my ideas. I saw a bigger picture and I had the passion to see it come to fruition. Despite the challenges that I faced, I never gave up, and for that I became a better manager, leader and role model for my employees, colleagues and most importantly, my daughters. I encourage each of you to find the leader within you and embrace it. Have the courage to pursue your own passions.

Part 2:

COACHING AND CULTURE

The Coaching Solution

CHAPTER 5: BUILDING THE BUSINESS CASE FOR AN INTERNAL COACHING PROGRAM

3   The Coaching Imperative

I have learned that coaching means many things to many people. I often see a certain technique in practice that is referred to as "coaching" among managers and executives, when really, all that is happening in these instances is that counseling or feedback is being supplied. For example, on several occasions I have heard a manager say, "Let me give you some coaching around ABC," and they proceed to explain to an employee why the employee failed to accomplish a task. The manager then explains the way ABC needs to be done and sometimes will provide an example of how ABC has been accomplished in the past. More times than not, I have seen the recipient of this so-called "coaching" walk away disillusioned by what they think was a coaching experience. As a result, coaching can get a bad rap and be misunderstood.

So what does a real coaching conversation look like? Well, something more like this: "So, how do you think your presentation on ABC went?" The employee is given time to reflect, respond and be an active participant in the conversation. The manager continues to ask thoughtful questions of the employee and gives them ample time to respond. Such questions may include the following: What do you think went well and/or not so well? What would you have done differently? How can you prepare better for next time? What steps will you take between now and then to do so? How would you like to be held accountable for your actions? What can I do to support you?

Do you notice the difference? This is a true coaching conversation! The employee is empowered to act, and with the support of his manager he gains clarity regarding the situation and comes up with an action plan to resolve it. The employee gains confidence knowing that there's a viable solution that can be carried out, and he feels acknowledged and supported by his manager.

Unfortunately though, in some corporate cultures, you would be hard pressed to find these types of coaching conversations. Some managers believe that it's faster to get something done by telling employees what to do rather than having them work out a solution themselves. This may be especially true if an employee is new to their role or to the company or has never done a certain task before. However, if this behavior is endemic and repeated, both the employees and the company can suffer in the long run.

This is a great place to pause for a moment and reflect. Ask yourself: *How many times in my career have I been told what to do? What would be different if I had been given the opportunity during these situations to solve things myself?* Now ask yourself: *How much more quickly do my problem-solving skills improve when I'm allowed to resolve situations myself? Because of this, when similar situations come along, how much better prepared am I to handle them myself?*

Now imagine that genuine coaching conversations are the norm throughout an organization and employees are asked to solve problems, be innovative and think critically and strategically. These are exactly the types of capabilities we will require more of, especially as the technology, engineering and science industries become leaders in the world economy. Each time a manager misses out on the opportunity to have a coaching conversation with an employee, he or she risks losing this opportunity for development and potentially negatively impacting that employee's engagement and motivation to do their job. When this happens, productivity can decrease and the customer experience can be adversely affected, which will have a similar impact on business results. It's a vicious cycle. In the chapters to come, you will see how implementing internal coaching programs are a major contributor to improved corporate culture, employee engagement, customer satisfaction, company performance and, therefore, results.

THE INTRODUCTION OF COACHING AT VERIZON

In 2006, MCI was acquired by Verizon. The merger between Verizon Enterprise Services Group (ESG) and MCI became Verizon Business. It was an exciting time for the internal coaching program, as it was expanded to other functional groups and to legacy Verizon leaders and managers who had previously never been exposed to such a program. They were thrilled with the idea of having a coach and having the opportunity to participate in our award-winning program. So it was then that the internal coaching program at

Verizon Business became even more robust and successful. We continually received positive feedback from participants and their managers, as well as from the executives in the company. The program was so successful that leaders would actually fund headcount so they would be able to have coaches dedicated to their organizations.

In one such instance, a sales vice president who was extremely supportive of the program transferred headcount to my department in order to enable me to hire a coach to support his region. He was so delighted with the coaching program and its impact on developing high potentials that during his operations review he mentioned the fact that he'd funded headcount in order to have a dedicated coach for his region. While many of his peers thought this was a terrific investment of resources (and they had done the same), the new-to-role (and also new to Verizon Business) senior executive hosting the review thought differently. In his view, the vice president had abdicated his responsibilities. There could not have been a greater disconnect. The senior executive perceived coaching as a form of counseling you received from your manager, which was very unlike the highly respected way of coaching at Verizon Business—a strategic approach designed to develop a manager's or leader's business and leadership capabilities.

This was quite a lesson for all of us that day, and especially for the brave sales leader who stood so proudly before a large audience and presented the positive results and the success he was having in developing a strong team because of coaching. It was clear that at the senior-most levels of the organization, coaching was still in the wilderness, and that in order to keep the coaching program alive, we would have to keep it under the radar. Happily, the program continued to thrive well past the eighteen months that the senior executive held reign at Verizon Business.

COACHING AS A METHODOLOGY

Let's pause my story here for a moment and discuss coaching as a methodology. Here, according to *Merriam-Webster,* are some definitions of coaching and related concepts to get us started:

Coach (*verb*)
1. to instruct, direct, or prompt as a coach
2. to train intensively (as by instruction and demonstration)
   <*coach* pupils>

3. to act as coach of <coach tennis> <coach a team>

Mentor (*noun*)
1. a trusted counselor or guide;
2. tutor, coach

Counselor (*noun*)—a person who gives advice or counseling <*marriage counselor*>

Counsel (*noun*)
1. a: advice given especially as a result of consultation

   b: a policy or plan of action or behavior

Feedback (*noun*)
1. the transmission of evaluative or corrective information about an action, event, or process to the original or controlling source; also: the information so transmitted[1]

Now, let's look at how the International Coach Federation describes coaching. (This is stated in its Code of Ethics, which can be found online at www.coachfederation.org/ethics/)

> **Coaching**: Coaching is partnering with clients in a thought-provoking and creative process that inspires them to maximize their personal and professional potential.
>
> **A professional coaching relationship:** A professional coaching relationship exists when coaching includes a business agreement or contract that defines the responsibilities of each party.
>
> **An ICF Professional Coach:** An ICF Professional Coach also agrees to practice the ICF Professional Core Competencies and pledges accountability to the ICF Code of Ethics.[2]

Let's reflect on the two scenarios presented earlier in this chapter. Can you see the difference in the definitions and why confusion exists around the understanding and process of coaching? Take a moment and think about what you may want as an experience for yourself, your employees and the organization. Capture your thoughts in the box below:

---

[1] URL: m-w.com
[2] ©2015. International Coach Federation. All rights reserved.

Let me highlight some of the key reasons why I lean toward the ICF's definition of coaching and why I have always made it a requirement to hire ICF-credentialed coaches, or coaches who are in the process of securing their credentials. First, the ICF's philosophy of coaching describes a collaborative approach that fosters innovation, action and empowerment. In essence, it teaches problem solving and accountability in the simplest form. Second, the credentialing process, in and of itself, demonstrates one's commitment to his or her own professional development and it speaks to a person's level of professionalism. In addition, ICF-credentialed coaches agree to and sign a code of ethics. The code of ethics is exactly that—an agreement that the coach will abide by a set of professional standards and ethical practices in his or her coaching practice. I recall an instance at Verizon when an external consultant/coach who was hired (not by me) as a coach disclosed confidential information that she acquired through a coaching conversation. I checked her credentials and discovered that she had received no coach training, nor was she a credentialed coach. I strongly advise you to check the credentials of coaches you intend to hire as well as conduct reference checks.

Trust me, you do not want to have a situation on your hands where you have someone functioning in a coach role who cannot maintain the confidentiality of the coaching conversation or what they might learn and disclose about your business while they are working within your organization. This may not only jeopardize your business initiatives, it can foster mistrust among your employees, and this mistrust can spread across your organization, negatively affecting your coaching program and perhaps the overall culture.

COACHING TERMS

Now, let's clarify the different roles and responsibilities of those involved in the coaching process. In doing so, we'll explore a couple of other key terms that will be used in describing your program, especially if your proposal will be for a coaching program that will live inside your organization.

First we must distinguish between the client and the sponsor. For purposes of identification, the ICF defines these roles as follows:

Client: The "client" is the person(s) being coached.

Sponsor: The "sponsor" is the entity (including its representatives) paying for and/or arranging for coaching services to be provided. This could be the Human Resources department, the head of Human Resources or Talent Management, a Human Resources business partner, or sometimes the chief financial officer or chief sales officer. In these types of situations, the department or individual could also be known as the executive sponsor, as they are the executive sponsoring the program and providing the funding. Human Resources could also be the executive sponsor if they are setting the strategy and design, and providing the funding for the program. In my experience, I have been hired or sponsored more often by executives such as presidents, strategy and change leaders, global heads of Sales and chief financial officers rather than traditional human resources executives.

Sometimes, Human Resources may not be involved at all, depending on the goals of the executive sponsor and the organization in which the coaching is going to occur. In addition, the integrity of the Human Resources staff and how much employees trust them can be a determining factor in the role that HR plays. When we designed the internal coaching program at WorldCom, the executive sponsor was the head of Sales. At that time, Human Resources had been primarily a provider of transactional services (compensation, benefits and managing workforce reductions), and the head of the Leadership School reported directly to the chief operating officer. Human Resources didn't have the resources or funding to deliver leadership development programs, nor did they have the expertise in sales that was critical (in terms of ability as well as credibility) to coach inside a Sales organization. Therefore, it made sense to house the program within the Sales organization but with the support of Human Resources.

I have experienced this exclusion of Human Resources from the coaching initiative in other companies as well. When I've questioned the missing collaboration, the response was usually based on a perception that HR wouldn't add any additional value and may in fact slow the program's progress. This perspective stems from the belief that HR's role is solely "transactional," and it continues to be a major challenge for some Human Resources organizations. When I uncover these situations, I work with the HR teams to coach and counsel them on how to be a more strategic partner. Having had experience in multiple roles, I find that I can add value in developing HR professionals by helping to bridge the gap and foster better understanding between their organization and their client organizations.

Other key players in coaching programs include the actual coach and the client's manager/supervisor. The manager or supervisor of the employee being coached plays an active role in helping their employee throughout the coaching process. They set appropriate coaching goals for the employee and, ideally, provide the employee with feedback at the beginning, middle and end of the coaching process, and support the employee as they work on their professional development.

A couple of other terms that you will most likely use when describing your internal coaching initiative are "engagement" and "program." Engagements are the one-to-one pairings of a coach and a client and the scope of work involved in that coach–client dyad. The term "program" encompasses all of the engagements, activities and results that occur across the entire initiative or organization that are considered part of your scope of work. The terms of the coach–client partnership are communicated and mutually signed in a "coaching contract" or "coaching agreement." Coaching agreements or contracts clearly establish the roles and responsibilities of the client and of the coach. (**Note:** The above terms apply whether it is an internal or external coach who is working with the employees/clients in a coaching role.)

In our situation at MCI and Verizon Business, we were clear on the roles of our coaches and clients and this was communicated through our agreements. In addition, we wrote a very specific job description for our internal coaches, clearly articulating the desired background and qualifications we were looking for in a coach. (See www.robertsoncoachinstitute.com for a sample job description.) We worked with Human Resources to create a job title and determine the appropriate compensation, and together we wrote the internal coach job description. The job was categorized as a senior consultant position. We set a base salary range that hinged on experience, education and training. Additionally, there was a bonus component as part of the overall compensation. The goal of the bonus was to provide an incentive to ensure that our coaches were achieving their objectives as well as supporting their clients' objectives.

RESPONDING TO CRISIS AT WORLDCOM

From my vantage point during the period of time following the MCI–WorldCom merger, I could see challenges facing the company that were, in turn, affecting our overall performance and our ability to achieve our targets. Back then, WorldCom was a darling on Wall Street. (In hindsight—wow. We have to ask, how was that possible?) I was running a Sales organization and was four levels away from the now infamous CEO at the time. It was a funny thing: many of the sales managers would wonder why certain compensation plans were designed the way they were. Higher compensation was paid to legacy WorldCom sales representatives who sold wholesale products, which typically produced lower profits, while the legacy MCI sales representatives had lower base salaries and a lower commissions and bonus structure despite the fact that the legacy MCI services involved a more complex sales process and, in fact, the products were more profitable. As you can imagine, this was fodder for many heated water-cooler conversations and it made it difficult to keep salespeople motivated. Those of us from the MCI camp felt that there wasn't much that could be done to change this inequality. We would write it off as TBU—*they* bought *us*—and dismiss it as part of WorldCom's domination of MCI culture.

During this time, my vice president would invite me to listen in on the quarterly phone calls with a Wall Street analyst. I remember how these calls amazed me; how casual and confident the CEO sounded as he answered the analyst's questions. I also noticed how he would deflect certain questions to other members of his leadership team—questions that in my mind he should have answered himself. We had so many challenges in the company and he made it sound like everything was as perfect and sweet-smelling as homemade apple pie!

The truth was—as is now well known—the company's culture was crippling employees, many of whom were fearful of losing their jobs. Many managers and leaders reporting into legacy WorldCom leaders have since shared their experiences about verbal abuse and unfair treatment. But at the time, Human Resources was virtually unresponsive, as the head of HR had strong ties to the CEO. Therefore, our cries for help fell on deaf ears or else made one a target for reduction or demotion.

It all contributed to a dismal culture at WorldCom, and the CEO's ego and his greed ultimately led to the company's demise. The criminal activity cost thousands of employees their livelihood and retirement plans. However, thanks in large part to the strong will of the remaining employees, coupled with a resilient executive leadership team and the guidance of our court monitor, we would emerge once again, as MCI, Inc.—a serious competitor in the telecommunications industry and a company that still had enough fight in it to win a war.

COACHING & LEADERSHIP INSIGHT:
It's about People and Principles

So how does one secure the support and funding for an internal coaching program? Well, like everything else in business, it begins with having an insight into what is happening in the company: discovering areas of opportunity, recognizing challenges and having the desire to be part of a solution. When I would talk with my peers, my manager and other leaders at WorldCom, everyone would tell me how much they were struggling with the integration of the two companies, especially around the differences in leadership styles and cultures. There was a lot of speculation that very talented leaders were thinking about leaving the company.

This is when I decided to take action and try to come up with a solution. Initially, I pinpointed our challenges and thought about potential solutions. Coaching and leadership development initiatives would be two critical components of the program I envisioned as having the potential to solve some of the major challenges the company was facing, one of which was that we were going through significant changes related to our shift in our sales methodology. Next, I needed to gain executive sponsorship, support and funding. Initiatives like this require strong executive support and, of course, money. The most important aspect of designing our coaching program was ensuring that it was aligned with the company's overall business goals; we had to demonstrate that the program would achieve positive results, a return on investment. (More specifics will be disclosed later in the book, when we discuss measurement and success in Chapter 18.) It was at this point that I began to formulate my plan.

Is an Internal Coaching Program the Right Solution for Your Company?

It took me two attempts and two years to secure the support for an internal coaching program. In hindsight, I see that I was swimming against a strong "anti-coaching" political current. My Human Resources business partner must have sensed this at the time. He would repeatedly ask me if I was sure I wanted to go through with my proposal. Had I thought through what the consequences might be of having the proposal accepted or declined? My response remained, "Yes, we need to do something. Our employees and managers deserve such a program, and we need to develop our talent and achieve our targets. Doing nothing is not an option." He told me, "Okay, then I will support you. However, I am not sure where this will go and how I will be able to help you if things go wrong."

That's when I had the experience I talked about in Chapter 2, when I pitched my proposal to the executive director of Sales Operations. I believed that if I could secure his support (he controlled the Sales organization's budgets), then I would be able to secure support from his boss, the senior vice president, and implement the program.

I was pretty nervous going in to the meeting with the executive director, but his warmth and open-mindedness soon put me at ease. He was very supportive of my proposal and we discussed it at length. I learned that both he and the head of Sales were in favor of the initiative; however, he told me that the much more urgent priority was overseeing the departure of thousands of employees. The company needed me to keep running Sales in New Jersey and take over the strategic accounts program in Pennsylvania. As much as they would have given their serious consideration to launching an internal coaching program, the immediate business need called for my sales experience and leadership so that we could continue to make our numbers—not to mention, launching the program would have sent a mixed message at a time when we were sending so many employees home. The timing was just not right.

I understood why the program couldn't be implemented at this time, but I couldn't believe what happened next. My new vice president reprimanded me for not following protocol (he claimed that I had gone over his head in meeting with the executive director of Sales Operations, despite the fact that he had been briefed on the proposal and invited to the meeting), and as a result the title and compensation associated with my management level would be stripped from me. I was an account manager left with nineteen direct reports and not eligible for stock options, whereas before I was a manager with seven direct reports and was eligible for stock options. Well, what could I do . . . Welcome to WorldCom!

I was devastated. I should have listened to my Human Resources business partner and heeded the warning he was trying to give me, but I'd been too focused on the goal. I didn't take the appropriate time to fully understand the organizational changes that were underway.

I continued to function in my role and I delivered the results expected of me. The good news is that six months later there was an organizational change and my regional leader was replaced. A review of the organization and its business revealed that my title and compensation had been changed and both were reinstated immediately.

The lesson here is about knowing whether your organization is ready for a large-scale internal coaching program. Coaching is typically used as a single-point solution or one-time event to support a leader in becoming a better leader or to prepare them for succession; or it is initiated at the beginning of a transition such as a new position, or an expatriate or relocation assignment. Internal coaching programs, on the other hand, can be used in all of those situations in addition to many others. They can be integrated with leadership development programs; they can offer support during a merger or acquisition; they can be part of a culture change initiative; they can be used to reinforce a training program; and they can support and accelerate a business transformation. Internal coaching programs achieve optimum results when they are integrated into the overall talent management strategy and are aligned with the objectives and goals of the business. This is why it is critical to know if your company is ready for an internal coaching program and, just as important, where the program should reside inside the organization.

IS YOUR COMPANY READY?

Let's examine whether your company or organization is ready for an internal coaching program. To help you determine this, I've provided an Environmental Assessment that will help you take an external look at your industry and its competitive environment, as well as your company's performance, plans for the future and ability to manage change. The second assessment, the Internal Coaching Readiness Assessment, will assist you in determining if your culture and talent management strategy is set up to incorporate an internal coaching program. Completing the assessment questions will provide insight on whether or not coaching is a viable option for your company.

Note: You may wish to take breaks between each assessment or each question, but do not skip ahead! Thoroughly complete each assessment in order, as understanding each component will be critical to the overall success of your positioning and your internal coaching program. Securing the external and 30,000-foot view first will help you connect the business opportunities with the talent development opportunities and, therefore, create a winning proposal. In order to complete the assessment you may need to interview members of your leadership team and Human Resources organization and/or conduct some external research, such as reading your company's annual report and any recent press releases, or viewing company broadcasts where executives talk about the business, results and future direction. It is important to treat your research and preparation work as if you were preparing to write a thesis in graduate school. Having a deep understanding of your business and how it intersects with your human capital to achieve business results will better position your proposal—and you—for success.

ASSESSMENT AND VISION EXERCISE

Step 1: Internal Coaching Program Environmental Assessment and Visioning Exercise

Take a high-level view of your company and the state of the industry it's in and answer these questions:

1.   **What industry are you in? How is that sector performing?**
     Can you envision a coaching conversation about your industry
     and its performance? With whom would you have this conversation?

_____

_____

_____

2. **What is the environment in which your company must compete and win?**

   Can you envision a coaching conversation about your company, its position in the marketplace and designing competitive strategies? With whom would you have this conversation?

   _____

   _____

   _____

3. **What critical areas must your company be competitive in to be successful at the highest level?**

   Can you envision a coaching conversation about these critical areas and what it will take for your company to achieve the desired results? With whom would you have this conversation?

   _____

   _____

   _____

4. **How does your company organize to implement change in order to be better than its competitors?**

   What do you know about your company and change? Does it embrace change or resist it? How can you see coaching playing a role in implementing change?

   _____

   _____

   _____

5. **How successful has your company been in making changes and adapting to change in the past?**
    How can coaching play a role in accelerating change within your company and enabling employees to embrace change and adapt quickly?

    _____

    _____

    _____

6. **How would you describe your company's culture?**
    Where do you see coaching playing a role with regard to company culture?

    _____

    _____

    _____

7. **What are your company's strategic initiatives or goals? How are they measured?**
    What would a coaching conversation about performance be like? Who are candidates for this conversation within your company?

    _____

    _____

    _____

8. **Looking at your company's strategy and its alignment to organizational design and talent, where can you see applications for coaching? How could a coaching program support organizational changes; the future state of business; and the leaders, managers and employees who are the company's greatest asset?**
    Where could a pilot coaching program potentially be tested?

_____

_____

_____

9. **Where do you see coaching playing a role in creating and maintaining a competitive advantage for your company?**
    What would this type of coaching conversation sound like? Who are candidates to have this conversation with at your company?

_____

_____

_____

10. **Which business leader (or leaders) do you feel would be the best champions and/or sponsors of coaching in the organization?**
    How well do you know this individual? How receptive do you think he or she would be to coaching?

_____

_____

_____

Self-Reflection & Coaching Questions: What have you learned? What is the state of your industry? Company? How much change is expected? Are some areas faced with more change than others? What will the future look like? What gaps can you begin to see in your company's talent capabilities, if any? Consider writing an executive summary on your findings, and if they lead you to believe that there are opportunities for coaching applications within your company, proceed to Step 2 and complete the Internal Coaching Program Readiness Assessment. The purpose of this assessment is that the output will guide you to the openness of having an internal coaching program, what types of applications may exist for coaching and where and how to position your program.

Step 2: Internal Coaching Program Readiness Assessment

Please answer the following questions/statements with True or False.

1. Your company/firm has a culture of learning and development. Employees receive on average a minimum of 35 hours of learning and professional development annually. (Technical training or training required to do one's job is a component of time allocated.)

2. Your company's talent management strategy and tactics are directly aligned to business objectives and tied to results.

3. Your company's competency models are fundamental to its learning strategy and aligned to the future of the business.

4. Your organization holds people accountable for their development and measures their progress.

5. Your organization measures the impact of its leadership development programs regularly.

6. Coaching/mentoring/teaching employees is a key component of every manager's job description. They have specific performance management objectives (PMOs) and are measured against them in their reviews.

7. Employees know the difference between technical training and professional development.

8. Employees believe they receive the appropriate level of professional development annually and communicate this to their management or Human Resources via employee engagement surveys.

9. When employees are asked in their employee surveys about opportunities for career advancement, their responses are positive as they are indeed provided with opportunities to advance.

10. When asked via an employee engagement survey about their readiness to accept another position or promotion, employees indicate that they have the professional development capabilities to accept the position today.

11. Your company has a deep bench of talent for all critical positions.

12. Your company experiences high employee retention commensurate with your industry.

13. When asked about their ability to be productive, your company's employees' responses are extremely positive.

14. When your company's employees are asked about their manager's professional capabilities, they indicate that their management and leadership across the board are fully proficient in their emotional intelligence and social intelligence capabilities.

15. Your company's employees embrace change and are flexible and agile.

Your Score

The more True responses you have, the higher probability that your organization and its culture is ready for coaching, but it doesn't mean that if you have more False statements your organization is not ready. Whatever your score, I recommend that you allocate some quiet time for reflection and think through the questions that follow below. In addition, review the Environmental Assessment and Visioning Exercise results to help you determine your next steps. If you are not already working with a coach who has experience designing internal coaching initiatives at this point, I strongly encourage you to do so.

Self-Reflection & Coaching Questions: What have you learned? What is happening inside your company? How engaged are your employees? What do they say about their managers? How well does your company perform in the areas of talent retention, development, building a sustainable pipeline of talent? What gaps can you begin to see in your company's talent capabilities? Obtain a summary of your company's most recent employee survey. If a survey has not been conducted within the past year, consider contacting an employee survey company to discuss the possibility of having one done. Once you have clear insight into your company's talent development strategies, consider writing an executive summary on your findings. This summary, as well as the summary from the Internal Coaching Program Environmental Assessment, can be utilized in the preparation of your proposal for an internal coaching program.

Having determined what coaching applications could be helpful to your organization, you need to look at where and how to position a program within your company.

WHERE SHOULD AN INTERNAL COACHING PROGRAM LIVE?

Let's explore where coaching programs can potentially reside inside an organization. This is a topic that can cause debate, as it is not always clear where an internal coaching program and its coaches should be housed. My view is this: house the program where it makes the most sense for your employees and your budget, and where it will be best aligned with the goals of the organization and have the greatest level of executive sponsorship and support. Also, keep in mind that coaching is a personal and private engagement between a professional coach and a member of your organization. Think about where your employees will feel most comfortable engaging with a coach who is sponsored by _____ (Human Resources, Sales, Talent Management and so on).

Now, Human Resources organizations are typically responsible for programs that develop employees. Sometimes, however, they are set up to focus solely on the more process-oriented activities that need to occur on the talent front. Think about it: Human Resources developed out of personnel departments that were focused on hiring and firing, and making sure compensation was paid, benefits were administered, and performance reviews and pay increases were processed. Therefore, if your Human Resources department has this legacy, continues to function in this manner and the talent management capability is low or absent, you should consider whether Human Resources is the optimum location for your program, or if there is another department that would be a better sponsor. It may be the case that there is an alternative organizational design that could support your program through your Human Resources organization. The most important piece here is to make certain that the sponsor organization has the highest level of credibility with their employees (your clients).

Another factor to consider is, what is the "brand" or reputation of the organization that could potentially house the internal coaching program? If you are in Human Resources and want to build an internal coaching program, you especially need to ask yourself this question. Every function within the organization, as well as its leader, has a "brand" associated with it. If your human resources function has a brand built on trust, credibility and reliability; is one that honors confidentiality; advocates and provides programs for leadership and employee development; and its actions truly align with programs focused on development, supporting the business and achieving results, then Human Resources could be a natural location for your internal coaching program. But if your human resources function has a reputation of "policing" employee behavior and activities, or if trust is low or absent between employees and those within Human Resources, I would strongly encourage you to consider an alternate organization to house your internal coaching program.

For example, the internal coaching program can have its coaches based inside specific organizations that would like to a) have coaching inside their functional area and b) are willing to fund the headcount, while the manager of the coaching program is based in Human Resources or Talent Management. In this way, the program manager is able to set the strategy for the internal coaching and leadership development programs, engaging the coaches as delivery vehicles for their initiatives. With this option, the business maintains control over headcount, and the employees may feel more at ease to openly engage in the coaching.

An alternative plan is to have the internal coaching program reside within the sponsor organization and allocate resources to that organization only. For example, if the goal of the internal coaching program is to support a sales transformation and shift in sales methodology while still achieving business objectives, then it may make sense to have the program report to the Sales organization. In terms of to whom the coaching program leader should report, specifically on paper, I would encourage you to put this position on the organizational chart as close as possible to the leader of the sponsor organization. Executive sponsorship is key to the success of any strategic initiative, and I would consider an internal coaching program strategic. Moreover, the fact is that if your managers and employees see that the leader of the organization is involved and has direct insight into the program, they will be more apt to take the program seriously and engage at a higher level.

Now, let's explore the reason we are having this conversation about where to locate an internal coaching program on an organizational chart. Many of us automatically think that an internal coaching program would be in the wheelhouse of talent development, and typically Human Resources is responsible for this type of work. However, the reality of the matter is that coaching requires a certain type of environment, and coaches require a certain set of capabilities. Sometimes these skillsets can be difficult to find in human resources professionals. I am not knocking these types of professionals; however, I am suggesting quite honestly that this is one of the biggest complaints that business leaders have about their human resources colleagues.

Think about your own situation—do the business organizations view your Human Resources organizations as strategic and adding value? Do your Human Resources counterparts understand the big picture and align with it and design talent solutions to achieve success? Or do they excel more at managing transactional activities? If you are a human resources professional, think about how you support your clients, how and where you spend your time. Is your approach (or the approach of your human resources professionals) strategic or transactional? To help determine this, answer the following questions:

STRATEGIC VS. TRANSACTIONAL HUMAN RESOURCES QUESTIONNAIRE

1. How would your clients, colleagues and manager describe you? How would you describe yourself? Choose one of the following:

   a. Strategic

   b. Transactional

   c. Both

2. How would you characterize HR's activity at client–staff meetings?

   a. The focus is on providing talent solutions to business problems.

   b. Human Resources results are reported (e.g., number of reviews completed) and/or updates are given on Human Resources activities that employees need to be doing.

   c. Both.

3. How knowledgeable is your Human Resources contact about talent management programs with respect to succession planning, leadership and organizational development?

   a. Extremely knowledgeable—I have a resource dedicated to talent development or my Human Resources personnel are well trained in these areas.

b. Some knowledge—I have/am a human resources generalist with some training in order to implement the process.

c. Not sure.

If you answered with the letter "a" across the three questions, this indicates that you (or your HR personnel) provide strategic thinking and true value to employees. This may be a great opening to engage them and secure their thoughts on implementing internal coaching.

If you answered with a "b" or "c" to any questions, you (or your HR personnel) have room to improve. I would encourage you to ask employees how they view the services and performance of Human Resources. What would they like to see more of? Less of? Is there anything they'd like done differently? Perhaps, together, you can go to your leadership and have a conversation about the future of talent in the company. Could this be an opportunity for an internal coaching program for human resources professionals?

Also, it may be time for you (or your HR personnel) to engage a coach to explore your career choice and/or enroll in some talent management and organizational development training programs. Consider having a conversation with your manager or Human Resources leadership about its charter in order to determine if the plan is to become more strategic. It is important to note that sometimes the business calls for a transactional Human Resources department and a coaching program just may not be in the cards.

I have been in situations where I've worked with strategic human resources leaders, and other times I've worked with transactional human resources leaders. Occasionally, there have been times when the individuals that I worked with excelled in both capacities. As a former Human Resources business partner, I can tell you this: my clients preferred my ability to be a strategic business partner, advisor and coach and they understood that there are some transactional components required. However, they much preferred that their business partner and managers accomplished the transactional exercises efficiently and allocated more time thinking strategically about their talent and their future. If this is the case for your situation, consider working with a coach to further develop your coaching capabilities, enroll in a coach training program or consider bringing coaching skills and an internal coaching program to your Human Resources organization. For more information about becoming a coach or coaching for human resources professionals, please go to www.robertsoncoachinstitute.com.

FINDING A SUITABLE INTERNAL COACHING PROGRAM LEADER

Crucial to the success of your internal coaching program is a suitable leader, someone who has a strong knowledge of business and talent development and who has a solid professional reputation. Personal strengths that contributed to the success of the internal coaching programs I designed were my business savvy, my proficiency for developing people, my ability to problem solve and find innovative solutions, and my strong relationship and execution skills.

Now, when it comes to those who work in Human Resources, there are typically two types of individuals: talent management and organizational development professionals and human resources professionals. (The latter would be known as a human resources generalist or business partner.) Each position has distinct responsibilities that require different competencies, and not everyone may be strong in both areas. In my experience, human resources generalists are very good at managing the activities that occur in the Talent Management Life Cycle (see Part 4 for more on coaching talent throughout the life cycle), as these individuals are adept at delivering and managing a process. Individuals in talent management are typically strong at designing talent management strategies and building talent acquisition and development solutions. Such solutions may include succession plans, leadership development programs, internal coaching programs and organizational development engagements and interventions. Both roles require strong business acumen and skills including critical thinking, strategic business planning and complex problem solving, and there is no doubt that both functions are necessary in order to execute an effective human capital strategy.

I have designed and led multiple award-winning internal coaching programs within a Sales organization and within a Human Resources organization under the auspices of talent management. I have learned that the most successful programs are those whose program leader and coaches have the following characteristics:

- They are passionate about talent development.

- They are strong leaders who are adept at business.

- They are credible and have a strong "brand" amongst their peers and colleagues.

- They are experts at execution.

  I have also learned that the most successful internal coaching programs are:

- supported by executive sponsors

- well-integrated into the corporate culture

- aligned with the objectives of the business

- composed of talented and highly engaged program participants committed to their professional development

The more you and your program have of these characteristics and components, the more likely you are to be successful in developing, implementing and integrating an internal coaching program into the fabric of your company. If any of these attributes are missing, determine how you can close the gap. Capture your missing attributes and actions in the box below:

The probability of your program's success will also be increased with the more business experience you have and the more understanding you have of your role as a coach and how you can impact the performance of your client. Depending on where you house or position your internal coaching program, your program's approach can be different. For example, if your company is focused on performance management, and that is the functional area that will house your internal coaching program, then your program may be designed with an eye toward performance. If your program is based in an organization that is focused on building bench strength for its management ranks, then your design will be focused on management and leadership development. Use your findings from the assessments you completed earlier in this chapter to determine what kind of approach would best work in your situation. The location of an internal coaching program within a company should be reflective of the company's focus and its needs.

MOVING FORWARD

If, after considering all of the information in this chapter and completing the assessments, you feel that your company really is ready for an internal coaching program and you have a good idea about where the program should be housed, you'll need to design a plan to help you achieve your goal. Fundamental to this will be creating an effective proposal, which I cover in detail in Chapter 5. In preparation for this, please complete the checklist below. Remember, this is no small undertaking and Rome wasn't built in a day—ask for help and enroll the resources you need up front to help you build your program. Now, if you find that your company isn't ready for a fully realized internal coaching program, perhaps there are areas in the company's talent management strategy or within its training or management development programs where you can begin to introduce the concept of coaching. Again, Rome was not built in a day. It took me two years to get leadership to say "yes" to internal coaching. Have faith and work with a coach yourself to assist you in this process.

Setting Up for an Internal Coaching Program

- ❏ Get clear on why you want to establish an internal coaching program. Work with a coach who has experience designing internal coaching programs. In detail, describe in writing your purpose and values and how implementing such a program aligns with your personal purpose and values. Repeat this exercise using your company's mission and values and show how the program will align with them.

- ❏ Research your company's industry, strategy and goals, and determine if you can see opportunities for coaching.

- [ ] Assess your organization's culture. Complete the Internal Coaching Program Environmental Assessment and Internal Coaching Program Readiness Assessment. If the score is unsatisfactory, design an action plan to close the gaps. Identify who you will need to secure support from and to whom you will be selling the program.

- [ ] Design a positioning matrix or a heat map and take the appropriate actions to enhance your position. (A heat map is a graphical representation of data, in which the individual values, in this case relationships, are represented in colors. For example, red may mean "no good," green may mean "go" or positive, and yellow may mean "proceed with caution" or "uncertain.")

- [ ] Align the internal coaching program to business and talent objectives.

- [ ] Integrate coaching with the company's overall leadership development strategy, programs, training and culture, and change initiatives.

- [ ] Define the program objectives and determine how you will measure success.

- [ ] Research and prepare your internal coaching program business case.

- [ ] Practice, practice, practice your presentation and anticipated questions.

- [ ] Secure support from business leaders and human resources/talent management leadership and build momentum.

COACHING & LEADERSHIP INSIGHT:
Lobby Hard for Executive Sponsorship

Human Resources can be an advocate and supportive partner for you and your program, but that is not always the case, unfortunately. If you already work within the company, your Human Resources colleagues may present an obstacle, especially if you are perceived as a threat to their livelihood. I strongly encourage you to form alliances with your Human Resources colleagues in order to ensure that you have the appropriate executive support and sponsorship for getting the program off the ground. The same goes if you are in Human Resources—make certain you have the executive sponsorship as well as support from your business clients to make this initiative a success. In either case, if you don't have the support you need, you'll need to determine the best way to secure it.

Remember, an internal coaching program is about leveraging your human capital to achieve business success. This is about partnership, collaboration and commitment. It may take a couple of sponsors and flag-bearers to get the program off the ground, and that's okay. As more leaders and managers get involved and help wave the flag, the easier it will be to build a program and create a coaching culture.

5 Building the Business Case for an Internal Coaching Program

When I set out to design the WorldCom internal coaching program, I had to take into consideration several things: what was happening in our industry on the whole as well as inside our company specifically, and how it all was affecting our employees. There was an urgent need to retain sales talent, who now had a much tougher job in selling our products and services to skeptical customers. Retaining them would be no small task, due to the likelihood that they'd be making fewer commissions and the stigma of working for a company that had just committed the largest fraud in U.S. history at that point. Hence why, retaining and investing in our sales talent was a number-one priority. Our top talent was being recruited by AT&T and other competitors, and it would have been easy for those employees to leave if we didn't make their development a priority. If we lost our talented sales force, we would have been doomed! By investing in their professional development through the coaching program, we would have a distinct advantage not offered by the competition. Therefore, the goals of our program were to:

1. Retain and develop our sales talent, specifically managers and top talent employees, while building a deep and sustainable bench strength.

2. Facilitate and support our sales force transformation and the shift in sales methodology.

3. Accelerate the integration of two companies that possessed distinct cultures.

4. Achieve all of the above *while at all times meeting our business objectives.*

As any good salesperson would do, I identified the greatest pain points for the organization, and then I identified the target audience for the program, estimating the number of participants and the funding that would be needed. I then assessed the political waters (much more wisely this second time around) and secured the necessary support as I prepared the business case for the program.

The information provided in this chapter will help you to build your proposal or business case. Before creating it, I encourage you to identify the audience that you will be presenting your business case to, as knowing the "who" will help you focus your goals and key points. Specifically, you will want to identify the key influencers and decision makers, and you'll want to understand the decision-making process and whom the decision will impact.

IDENTIFY THE KEY STAKEHOLDERS

Let's get started. First you will need to determine who your key stakeholders are and then come up with an approach to rally their support. To help you do this, ask yourself the "self-coaching" questions listed below. If at any point you get stuck, ask yourself, "Who can help me get unstuck?" Your manager, Human Resources business partner or business operations contact may be able to assist you. Another resource could be a coach who has experience building these types of programs.

The material below is adapted from a stakeholder positioning approach and assessment that I created to identify obstacles and solutions when building your program. The Stakeholder Positioning Matrix can be found on my website at www.robertsoncoachinstitute.com.

STAKEHOLDER POSITIONING: SELF-COACHING QUESTIONS

1. Whose support will I need to secure in order to get this program off the ground? Do I know who will be the ultimate decision maker?

Response: _____
_____
_____

2. Who are the key influencers (the individuals who may have some influence over the stakeholders)? What are their roles and how large is the audience that they influence? Do they have a relationship with the ultimate decision maker? If so, what is that relationship?

Response: _____

_____

_____

3. Who (of the identified above) might benefit from an internal coaching program? What information or ideas about an internal coaching program might they have? If their perspectives are helpful, what else will I want to ask them? How can they support my proposal?

Response: _____

_____

_____

4. What is the final decision maker's experience with coaching, and what are his or her views on coaching and talent development? On a scale of 1–10 (1 being the lowest), how supportive are they of developing the company's talent? Can I identify and point to a program that they created or supported in the areas of training and talent development?

Response: _____

_____

_____

5. Who needs to implement the decision once it is made? Who will be responsible for the execution of the program? What are they responsible for today? On a scale of 1–10 (1 being the lowest), how supportive are they of talent development programs?

Response: _____

_____

_____

6. Whom will the decision of putting an internal coaching program in place ultimately impact? How will their roles and responsibilities change? Will this mean more work for those affected? How will this decision benefit them?

Response: _____

_____

_____

7. What is my relationship like with each of the influencers and decision makers?

Note: To answer this question, complete the "Key Influencer and Decision-Maker Matrix," which can be found at www.robertsoncoachinstitute. com. To complete this positioning matrix, you'll need to get a solid handle on everyone's goals for the internal coaching program, issues anyone might have and all possible applications for the program. You'll need to listen carefully to each individual you speak with, especially as they share their goals and concerns, which will require thoughtful inquiry and consideration so that you can design creative solutions.

Response: _____

_____

_____

8. What steps will I need to take to secure the support of the key influencers and final decision maker(s)? Can the beneficiaries help in any way?

Response: _____

_____

_____

9. What is the decision-making process? What steps need to be taken and what obstacles do I need to anticipate? What can I do to prevent obstacles or overcome them quickly? How would I describe the decision-making process?

Response: _____

_____

_____

10. What type of decision-making style will be used in making a final determination about my proposal? (**Note:** Before answering this question, review the section below regarding the different decision-making styles of leaders.)

Response: _____

_____

_____

THE DECISION-MAKING STYLES OF LEADERS

Your response to question 10 will help you navigate the decision-making and organizational waters as you begin the sales process for your internal coaching program. A leader is there to provide guidance to her organization. She is responsible for their decisions—decisions that steer the organization and align its overall goals. Different leaders have different styles of decision making, such as:

Authoritative — The leader is the sole decision maker and her decisions are intended to be followed by subordinates.

Self-Coaching Thought and Questions: It can be difficult to sell to this type of decision maker, as you will need to sell to her agenda. This person will be solely responsible for deciding your program's fate. Also, the authoritative style can create disenfranchisement among the employees, those who accept her orders and must do the work. If you are able to secure a pilot coaching program under this type of leadership style (more on pilot programs later in this chapter), be aware that the participants may be acting in compliance with your program but may not necessarily be committed to coaching. How can you find ways to quickly secure their trust, demonstrate their potential for success and gain their support? Is it possible to coach the leader on the benefit of having multiple leadership styles and demonstrate how to use them in different situations in order to create more positive outcomes? How might employees react to a less authoritative leadership style? How can this approach make others more apt to engage in coaching themselves?

Facilitative — The leader and her subordinates work together to arrive at a decision. The subordinates should have the requisite expertise as well as access to information required to make the decisions.

Self-Coaching Thought & Questions: If the people who'll be making the decision about your proposal use this approach, is there an opportunity for you to coach individuals on this team? Would it be possible to provide each of them with their own personal coaching experience in order for them to have enough knowledge to effectively contribute to the decision-making process?

Consultative — Similar to the facilitative decision-making style; however, a leader who uses the consultative style will take into consideration a subordinate's opinion but is ultimately the sole decision maker.

Self-Coaching Thought & Questions: Refer also to the facilitative thoughts and questions for guidance. Additionally, can you request to coach the ultimate decision maker or secure an alternative coach for that individual? How can you demonstrate the power of coaching to the decision maker and his or her key influencers?

Delegative — The leader passes on the responsibility of making decisions to one or more of her subordinates. This decision-making style can be exercised when the leader has considerable confidence in her direct reports.

Self-Coaching Thought & Questions: If you're facing this type of decision-making style, how can you be certain who is making the ultimate decision? What information do you need, and how will you secure it? What steps can you take to position yourself and your concept for a pilot coaching program with this team?[1]

Note: Be sure to identify the type of decision maker that characterizes the key stakeholder and/or influencer in your positioning matrix from question 7 above. This will help you determine the approach you should use to present the proposal and close the sale of your internal coaching program.

IDENTIFYING OBSTACLES AND FINDING SOLUTIONS

Once you have identified all of the stakeholders and completed the positioning matrix, the next step is to consider the possible obstacles and then brainstorm various solutions to overcome them. Creating an "obstacle chart" will

---

[1] Adapted from: www.buzzle.com/articles/types-of-decision-making.html

help you to design actions to prevent anticipated obstacles and gather information that will enable you to overcome hurdles more quickly.

After you have completed your obstacle chart, you'll want to build an applications chart, which will capture all of the potential internal coaching program applications. This chart will house your original applications for coaching as well as any other applications you may have picked up in speaking with the stakeholders, influencers and beneficiaries. You can download the obstacle and application charts from www.robertsoncoachinstitute.com.

The goal of completing these charts is to help you gather as much information as possible in order to build a strong proposal and sales strategy. A strong proposal will demonstrate your expertise and your commitment to building and maintaining an internal coaching program, thereby increasing your probability of success in getting to the next stage: implementation. Preparing an accurate sales strategy allows you to clearly identify your client's (or the organization's) pain points and sell to your client's or sponsor's agenda, eliminating their pain with a thoughtful coaching solution.

APPROACHING THE KEY STAKEHOLDERS

At this stage, the stakeholders, influencers, beneficiaries, potential obstacles and applications of your internal coaching program should be identified, as well as where the program should live within the company. Let's now talk about your approach to each of the key stakeholders. Determining the best approach will not come to you via osmosis; you may need to meet with leaders in Sales, Human Resources or other groups, depending on where you are looking to build your internal coaching program.

I suggest that you start with an introductory e-mail, which you can use to secure a meeting with the targeted individual. If you don't know the person to whom you're reaching out, you may want to consider having someone else refer you. If possible, have the referral send an e-mail and copy you. (If you choose this route, be considerate of your referral's time and draft the e-mail for them, so that they'll just need to modify it slightly before sending.) If the individual you're contacting has an assistant, be sure to copy that person on the e-mail and contact him or her for follow up. The assistant is the gatekeeper to the executive and can be instrumental in setting up your meeting. If you don't hear back within twenty-four to forty-eight hours, I encourage you to make a direct call to the person you want to meet with.

When the meeting is secured and you are preparing for it, keep in mind that these individuals are usually very busy, so you will need to be efficient in your meeting with them. In addition, think of this information-gathering interview also as a sales call. This may be the stakeholder's first and only interaction with you. Therefore, you must show up with an expert understanding of the business and its talent challenges, and how coaching could be a solution. Lastly, I suggest that you prepare for this interview as you would if you were going to be interviewed for a new job. Be prepared to ask questions that will showcase the strengths and benefits of your proposal as well as you as a coach, and conversely, be prepared to answer questions that the stakeholder you are meeting with may have for you. Listed below are some suggestions for questions you should prepare to ask, followed by some questions that you should be prepared to answer.

Questions You Should Ask

- How familiar are you with coaching? If familiar, please describe your definition of coaching.

- Have you, personally, ever worked with a professional coach? If so, what was your experience and the outcome?

- Where do you see possibilities for coaching in your organization? What types of resources might you have available for such a program? How would you like to see the effectiveness or impact of such a program measured?

- What are some of your greatest business challenges and how are you working toward solving them today?

- When you look at your workforce, where are the gaps in talent? Are there specific capabilities missing? Do you wish your employees and managers were stronger? Please share how you develop your managers and leaders in order for them to be better in their roles and allow you to fill your talent pipeline. How ready is your talent pipeline for management and leadership opportunities when they become available?

- When you look out five to ten years, where will the business be? What skills and capabilities will your employees, managers and leaders require? How are you preparing them? How are you readying them for this change?

- On a scale of 1–10 (1 being the lowest), how likely would you be to support coaching inside your organization?

- What types of applications do you see for coaching inside your organization? What obstacles do you feel might hinder the introduction of an internal coaching program? Who would present the greatest obstacle to the program, and what would we need to do to get them on board?

- If I were to present you with a proposal for a coaching program, how would you go about making a decision on whether to implement the program?

- What information would be helpful to you in making such a decision?

- What question have I not asked that you would have liked me to ask? What questions do you have for me?

Questions You Should Be Prepared to Answer

- What is driving you to want to build this program?

- Where do you see the greatest need, and where can we see the greatest benefit?

- What makes you qualified to coach and build such a program?

- If you were me, why would I hire you to be my coach?

- How will you measure the program's success and the program participants' success?

- What will you do if the program is not successful?

- How will you secure the necessary resources and budget for this type of program? What is the budget you will need to get the program off the ground?

- How will you market and maintain the program?

- Who will be your target audience? What will they say about their coaching experience after six months in the program?

- What else would you like me to know about you, and why I should sponsor such a program?

Note: After the meeting, be sure to send a thank-you note and provide some research on internal coaching programs. (See www.robertsoncoachinstitute. com for papers and links to additional research.)

LAYING OUT THE INTERNAL COACHING PROGRAM

Now that you have the lay of the land in terms of who's who and what the decision-making process will be for the internal coaching program you're proposing, it's time to create the proposal, or business case. Regardless of what you call it, a good proposal will include the components outlined in the template on the following pages. (Please note, depending on your organization's culture, you may want to prepare this as a Word document or as a PowerPoint presentation, or both. Consider the audience and the format in which they are accustomed to seeing proposals or new information, and create your presentation in a similar manner.)

INTERNAL COACHING PROGRAM TEMPLATE

The first element of the proposal is the executive summary. It should provide a concise summary of the highlights of the program, emphasizing the company's need for the program and the objectives it will meet. The summary should also outline the strategy of the internal coaching program you're proposing and the financial details. Present key points from the research that you gathered during your informational interviews. Here is a sample executive summary:

EXECUTIVE SUMMARY:
Internal Coaching Program Highlights

The internal coaching program being proposed has been designed to solve several business and talent challenges. One of the main challenges is that the integration of the two companies has been slow and challenging due to the distinct cultures. This slowdown is beginning to negatively impact our company's performance, results and customer experience. (Leaders are being faced with new challenges daily.) A well-designed internal coaching program could accelerate integration and uncover hidden and/or cross-organizational obstacles while developing and retaining leadership talent. The program can be utilized as a talent acquisition strategy in order to compete with and distinguish our company from major competitors in our industry.

The next section of the proposal should include an overview of the current state of the business. The description should include the challenges the organization is facing, the opportunities it has for growth or improvement, and how the proposed initiative would align to the organization's business objectives. (You can include statistics found in your research, your company's annual report or recent quarterly reports.) Here is an example:

Key Business Challenges

- Organizational integration and adaptation is slow, which is negatively impacting our customer experience and the ability to achieve our goals.

- Our professional service expansion is creating "frenemies" as well as creating a war for the best talent.

Key Business Opportunity

- Achieve our #1 growth strategy: the expansion of our business into consultative and professional services.

Next, describe the business and/or talent goals you would like to accomplish through an internal coaching program. For example:

Goals of the Internal Coaching Program

1. Accelerate the integration of our two companies and drive one culture of collaboration and learning.

2. Provide a coach for new hire professional services consultants, which will result in rapid assimilation.

3. Achieving goals #1 and #2 will lead to meeting sales and revenue targets in addition to heightening customer satisfaction.

Your proposal should include your desired results of the internal coaching program and how it will address the company's challenges and opportunities that you identified earlier in the proposal. Ideally, it should outline the program's objectives in measurable terms. For example, it might say something like, "Through coaching we will increase employee engagement and productivity, thereby positively impacting the customer experience."

Desired Results of the Internal Coaching Program

1. Identify key succession-planning candidates. Design development plans and develop, promote and rotate talent accordingly.

2. Build a strong and talented professional services organization.

3. Increase sales and improve our customer experience by X%.

The next section should provide the audience with a range of possibilities to be considered as potential actions to address the company's challenges and/or take advantage of its opportunities. It should also provide the possible outcomes from each potential action. The purpose of this section is for your audience to be able to evaluate the options, eliminate some of them, determine the best solution and to take action. A description should be included of the viable options under consideration, and one of the options should be "do nothing."

Options for Consideration

1. **Do nothing and jeopardize:**

   a. talent retention

   b. sales and revenue growth

   c. expansion into new markets

   d. customer experience

2. **Continue with technical training only and establish our brand for technical competence and risk aversion, which means risking opportunity to:**

   a. build a brand that will attract new talent

   b. achieve our goals to build leadership bench strength and an effective talent pipeline

   c. retain top talent

   d. achieve the company's strategic objectives

3. **Deploy a comprehensive and integrated internal coaching program:**
    a. include competencies based on future business skills and capabilities requirements
    b. establish measurable objectives aligned to business goals
    c. integrate with leadership development and succession planning
    d. leverage to reinforce training initiatives and make learning sustainable

Note: Emotional intelligence and interpersonal skills (necessary for effective relationships and personal development) are excellent areas for coaches to work with clients in order to enhance their leadership and sales competencies, thereby building more engaged and effective organizations.

The final section of your proposal or presentation should be a cost–benefit analysis. This will help you understand the economics of the investment opportunity as indicated by a financial analysis of project costs and benefits. Such an analysis is imperative for making an informed decision about whether to proceed with a program.

The example is for descriptive purposes only. Depending on the country and sponsoring organization (for example, corporation, government, non-profit) internal coaching fees will vary.

The prospect for producing a return on effort and investment will only be verifiable well into project implementation. However, you can reference research and statistics that support the benefits of coaching and include the research in your proposal. A good source is the Human Capital Institute's *Building a Coaching Culture* study published in 2014 or *Measuring the Success of Coaching* by Phillips, Phillips and Edwards. Also, please see www.robertsoncoachinstitute.com for additional sources and research.

COST–BENEFIT ANALYSIS

Annual Costs

One full-time coach @ $125,000 base salary

+ 20% bonus based on objectives = $150,000

+ 10% × base salary (or $12,500) to cover the cost of benefits*

Sub-Total = $162,500 per coach

Total for 2 Full-Time Coaches = $325,000

*Given all the changes in healthcare and associated costs, this percentage and cost may vary depending on type of employee, geographic location and benefits selected. Consider this a placeholder as a cost that should be included in your headcount expense calculation.

Coach Duties Include:

- Coach 25–30 managers/directors for 12 months annually

- Design and facilitate management development programs

- Conduct high-performance team workshops

- Manage or participate in special projects, i.e., competency and curriculum designs

Benefits:

- Ability to insource workshops and management training programs

- Leverage knowledge of the culture and corporate savvy

- Internal coaches have a personal connection and commitment to the performance of the company

- When leaders are coached, they are more apt to coach; therefore, creating a coaching culture

- Coaching fosters trust; trust fosters collaboration and innovation; and collaboration and innovation can be a competitive advantage in the marketplace

For your consideration: You may also wish to engage external coaches for targeted executive coaching needs. If that is the case, those services would be complementary to your internal coaching program. Please note that you will want to make certain the external coach is well briefed about your company, its culture and the client, and the coach's capabilities are aligned with your coach approach.

An additional option for your consideration would be to pay a retainer fee to secure a coach or coaches. For example, for a lesser fee you may be able to keep a coach on retainer and have them coach, consult or facilitate leadership, or additionally change programs. You may wish to hire a coach on a part-time basis and save the costs of benefits.

Please note that the external coaching fees can vary significantly depending on the scope of the engagement, level of the individual being coached as well as the experience, training and credentials of the external coach.

Lastly, if you have any additional documentation that supports your business case, you can include it in an appendix to the proposal. Such documents may include organizational charts, annual reports, sales results, talent management objectives and results. You may also want to include a copy of a job description for an internal coach or a draft description of the position. This may require you to work with Human Resources and your compensation team. Following are some questions to think about when creating the description.

QUESTIONS TO CONSIDER WHEN DESIGNING A COACH JOB DESCRIPTION

1. What will be the scope of the coaching position?

2. What other areas of responsibility will be included in this position? Will this individual be responsible for organizational development? Leadership development? Competency modeling? Workshop design? Facilitation?

3. Who will be the individuals coached? What level are they within the organization? What functional area(s) are they a part of?

4. Given #1 and #2, will the position be full-time or part-time?

5. Which department will fund the program headcount or be responsible for the costs?

6. What key attributes would you like this individual to have?

7. What work experiences would be beneficial for the person filling this role to have, particularly with regard to working with their clients?

8. What type of formal education would you like to be a requirement for this position? What type of coach training and certifications would you like candidates to have?

Answering these questions will help you construct a preliminary job description. I go into much more detail about job descriptions in Chapter 7, and you can find further resources online at www.robertsoncoachinstitute. com. (Note: I strongly encourage you to draft your version before reviewing our sample. This will ensure that you maintain the focus on your own business and talent requirements, and you won't be influenced by what you read in our sample.)

Once you have completed your proposal, answer the questions below, taking into consideration all of your research. Be honest with yourself: Does your organization truly have the scope of work and the type of environment that would support an internal coaching program? Or would working with external coaches be a better fit to accomplish the company's objectives? (We will discuss the use of external coaches in Chapter 6, but please note that you can certainly use the same approach and proposal format to build a business case for utilizing external coaches to achieve talent and business goals.)

FOR YOUR FURTHER CONSIDERATION

1. Reflect on your decision-making process that led you to take on this initiative. Do you see or anticipate any hidden barriers or obstacles?

2. Stand in the shoes of each key influencer and decision maker. How does this program support them? How might it threaten them?

3. How can you rally the support of the key influencers or decision makers for your program? Is there anyone else you need to enlist in your efforts? Who are they? What is your relationship with them and how can they help you?

4. What are the next steps? Design your action plan and execute.

Please note that starting an internal coaching program from the ground up is a tremendous undertaking and I strongly encourage anyone considering it to work with a coach that has had experience in doing so. The same goes for anyone wishing to coach inside organizations.

Let me also say that for any new coaching initiative, I recommend you begin with a pilot. It is much easier to test a new coaching program with a small group of participants in order to assess interest and engagement. This will allow you to determine what works and doesn't work in your organization before implementing the program on a larger scale. Pilot programs also give you the opportunity to determine how to scale your program to fit the needs of its participants, identify the applications for coaching and figure out how you will manage the program as your business expands and contracts. Additionally, as was the case at WorldCom, sometimes one needs to fly under the radar until a concept is developed and proven. When I spoke with Steve Young about how we approached our coaching program, he believes there is no doubt that if we had trumpeted it in the early days we would have lost funding and it may never have even taken off at WorldCom. The fact that we built it small and grew it from there, funding it from current budget within his organization, is what gave the program the time to mature, establish success and build momentum.

COACHING & LEADERSHIP INSIGHT: Be Prepared to Course-Correct as You Launch Your Program

Creating an internal coaching program and preparing to "sell" it is a large and complex undertaking, and I encourage you to establish a project plan for yourself as well as consider hiring a coach-consultant who has expertise in building internal coaching programs. Getting coaching programs off the ground can take time, and it is helpful to have a coach who can hold your vision and also function as an advisor as you move through the stages of research, proposal and implementation.

As part of your project plan, be sure to set daily and weekly goals for yourself. Regularly review each document that you completed in this chapter, measuring your progress against the activities that result from this part of your project. Keep in mind that organizations are fluid, and along the way you may gather additional information or experience an organizational change or a delay. Whatever the case, account for any adjustment in your program and course-correct as needed, and do so quickly. The one thing you can always count on is change. Therefore, expect it and plan for it and you will never be disappointed, nor will your proposal experience too much of a delay.

Politics exist in all organizations, both large and small. The key is to uncover and learn as much as you can about the influencers and decision makers. Build relationships, gain as much support as you can, and ask your sponsors and anyone else involved in the process to be honest with you and help you navigate the waters to your goal.

Part 3:

LAUNCHING THE INTERNAL COACHING INITIATIVE

The Coaching Solution

6 Selecting Top-Talent Coaches

When it comes time to select a coach or coaches, the first step is to assess your clients in terms of the scope of the challenges that need to be addressed. It's important that you be aware of any professional development objectives that will require certain capabilities of the coaches. The following questions will help you with this initial part of the coach selection process—ascertaining what capabilities and attributes you will need in your coaches.

- Have you identified your potential clients?
- At what level are they in the organization?
- What are their functional responsibilities?
- What types of budget, profit and loss statement, headcount and decision-making responsibilities do they have?
- What are their business objectives and professional goals?
- What do they want to accomplish, and by when?
- What are their expectations of a coach, and how can you help to manage those expectations?
- How would you describe their leadership styles?
- What is their "brand" inside the organization? Are they aware of their brand and its impact—either good or bad—on the organization?
- What are the knowledge gaps or skills gaps that need to be addressed?
- Are the coaching expectations of the clients aligned with the knowledge gaps or skills gaps?
- How are these gaps validated?

INTERNAL OR EXTERNAL EXPERTISE?

Once you've determined the needs of your potential clients, you will want to consider how those needs will best be met: by establishing an internal coaching program, by utilizing coaches that are employed by the organization or by bringing in external coaches.

If your intention is to have coaches in order to provide one-on-one coaching to a small number of individuals over a finite period of time, and your coaches' sole responsibility is to fulfill this imperative, then I would suggest you explore using external coaches.

If you are looking to integrate your coaching program with other areas of the Talent Management Life Cycle—such as training and development, leadership, organizational and management development, succession planning, capabilities modeling, change management, employee engagement, or culture programs—and you can see this work continuing year-over-year as the Talent Management Life Cycle renews, then you should consider establishing at least some of the coaching positions internally.

The questionnaire that follows will help you determine which of the two types of coaching programs (internal or external) would be more appropriate for your potential clients. Whichever it is, answering the questions will also assist you in identifying the challenge areas and opportunities where coaching may be an excellent solution.

INTERNAL COACH VS. EXTERNAL COACH QUESTIONNAIRE

Please respond to the following questions with Yes or No.

1. Your industry is evolving and external threats are placing increased demands on your company.

2. Your company's leaders and employees are under constant pressure to improve results.

3. Organizational change and development require your leaders to adapt at accelerated speeds.

4. Your leaders are required to be adept at change management and organizational planning.

5. Your company has gaps in its talent pipeline.

6. It is difficult for your company to retain talent.

7. It is difficult for your company to attract and secure the right talent.

8. There are gaps in your company's succession plans.

9. Your company acquires, integrates and then sells parts of its business at a rate that appears to be inconsistent with company goals.

10. There are different subcultures in place and the company is striving to have one single, collective culture.

11. Collaboration challenges exist within your company.

12. Innovation is stifled within your company.

Tallying Your Questionnaire Results

If you responded in the affirmative for more than nine questions, your company is unquestionably faced with talent and change challenges. Employees are stressed and pushed to the maximum. Providing an internal coaching program to support them as they deal with constant change and the increased demands of the business will demonstrate the company's support for the employees, thereby enhancing engagement, productivity and results.

If you responded in the affirmative for three to eight questions, there is an opportunity to explore coaching programs for your company. Depending on the coaching applications, the amount of change at the company and its talent goals, the program could comprise internal (full- or part-time) coaches or a cadre of external coaches who can engage, exit and re-engage as needed.

If you responded in the affirmative to fewer than three questions, the opportunities for a coaching program may be limited or nonexistent. You'll want to further investigate your company's current talent development and business needs, inquire about the anticipated business activities and talent needs for the next one to three years, and be on the lookout for coaching applications. Your company may not be ready for a large-scale internal coaching program; however, you may uncover other opportunities in the talent management and business life cycle that may be ideal applications to introduce external coaching into your organization.

Note: If you determine that internal coaches are the way to go, I suggest hiring coaches who come from outside the particular organization that will house the program, and perhaps even outside the company. These individuals will have no history with the organization and as a result can offer a fresh perspective; they don't have a personal agenda or preconceived notions to overcome. The opposite is true of the leader of the internal coaching program, as he or she needs to have a track record of credibility and trust in the organization. But the coaches need to build their own trust with their clients, so it's best if they're not associated with the executive team in the organization or else they could be perceived as having a bias toward the executive team, and this perception could impact the effectiveness of their coaching.

KEY CRITERIA FOR COACHES

When looking to fill a full-time internal coaching position, you should seek candidates who are willing and able to do more than just coach. In order to justify a full-time position, coaches need to be versatile enough to work on different projects and programs. Therefore, internal coaches should be skilled in multiple talent development disciplines. For example, they should be willing and able to:

- deliver assessments (e.g., EQ, 360, Hogan, The Birkman Method, DiSC)
- conduct stakeholder assessments and deliver feedback and recommendations
- conduct shadow-coaching
- develop and facilitate leadership development programs, team-building sessions and change management programs
- teach management development skills
- facilitate action-learning projects

If your internal coaching needs are for employees within a corporation, you should seek a coach who has some corporate experience in his or her background. With respect to coaching managers and executives, it is particularly helpful for a coach to have either some type of management or leadership experience, or a strong knowledge of business and an understanding of the challenges that potential clients may face on a day-to-day basis. Business savviness is important when coaching inside an organization, especially when the organization has the attention of Wall Street and must maintain a performance-oriented approach to its business.

Having management and/or leadership experience, or a background in similar industries or business situations will help the coach gain the trust of those being coached, particularly when it's business leaders and executives who are being coached. It will also help the coach hold her own in a room full of executives discussing topics like business and investment strategies, forecasts and transformation initiatives. For these reasons, business knowledge and experience is one of the first traits you should be looking for in a person you are considering hiring as a coach, whether it be for an internal or an external coach position.

Similarly, the other key criteria I'd like to share with you applies to both internal and external coaches. If you want to have a top-talent coach or coaching team, these are the traits you should look for:

Passion and authenticity: A coach should be passionate about her work and truly believe in the talent development and coaching process. These are characteristics that potential clients will want to see in their coach. Be aware that these clients may be suspicious about coaching and tentative to give up their precious time and trust a stranger assigned to "coach" them. Therefore, what they'll be looking for isn't a supercharged cheerleader but, rather, someone with expertise and knowledge who is sincere about their work.

Coaching credentials: I strongly encourage you to seek coaches who have completed extensive coach training and, ideally, have been certified to coach by the International Coach Federation (ICF). Hiring an ICF-credentialed coach provides consistency in the level of competency and the overall methodology of the coaching at your company, and it ensures a similar experience for each of the clients.

Credentialing by the International Coach Federation was a factor that was of great help to me during the selection process of internal coaches when I was a hiring manager, because it's a signal of the commitment that a coach has made to their professional development and it shows a willingness to abide by the ICF's Code of Ethics. In addition, being ICF-certified means that the individual has completed a rigorous training curriculum of over 120 hours and has completed over 750 hours of live coaching in order to meet the certification requirements and receive the Personal Certified Coach (PCC) designation or 2,500 hours of live coaching to receive a Master Certified Coach (MCC) designation.

A side note: While credentialed coaches are indisputably of great value, clients may not care a great deal about a coach's credentials, as was found to be the case in coaching expert Brian Underhill's research, which was presented at the 2013 Worldwide Business and Executive Coach Summit (WBECS). Underhill's findings showed that recipients of coaching are most interested in the following when it comes to selecting a coach: the coach's a) ability to build rapport, b) experience and skills, and c) experience dealing with specific leadership challenges.

Commitment to professional development: A coach should be committed to continuous learning and be willing to maintain his certifications. An internal coach is a role model for his clients, so the more committed the coach is to his professional development, the more he will inspire clients to commit to the coaching process and their own professional development. Such commitment is an important trait to have as a lifelong learner. If a person is always open to learning and developing, then growth can always happen.

Highly adaptable and comfortable with change: Organizations change more frequently today than ever before; one day you may have one set of clients, and the next you may be assigned to a whole new set. It is imperative that a coach—especially an internal coach—be adaptable and model this capability for those being coached. Change is one of the most difficult challenges that we as humans have to deal with in our lives. In organizations today, higher levels of performance are required and leaders are looking for more efficient ways to achieve their rigorous objectives. Organizations have had to become more fluid as change occurs more rapidly. Therefore, sometimes there is very little time for an individual, leader or department to process the change, make the proper adjustments and adapt. This is a new reality of the business world, and one in which skilled coaches adept at dealing with change can be extremely valuable.

CAPABILITIES OF A SUCCESSFUL COACH

A coach who will be working inside a company in any kind of capacity (be it on a full-time or a part-time basis on an internal coaching team, or as an external coach working in one-to-one situations or as part of a cadre of coaches) should have the capabilities outlined on the following pages. While it is possible to be an effective coach without possessing all of the capabilities I outline, at minimum I recommend you look for candidates who are strong in coaching knowledge and business acumen and who also possess well-developed professional attributes. Depending on your requirements, you can determine what is needed in the areas of organizational knowledge and leadership.

Figure 6.1: Capabilities of an Internal Coach

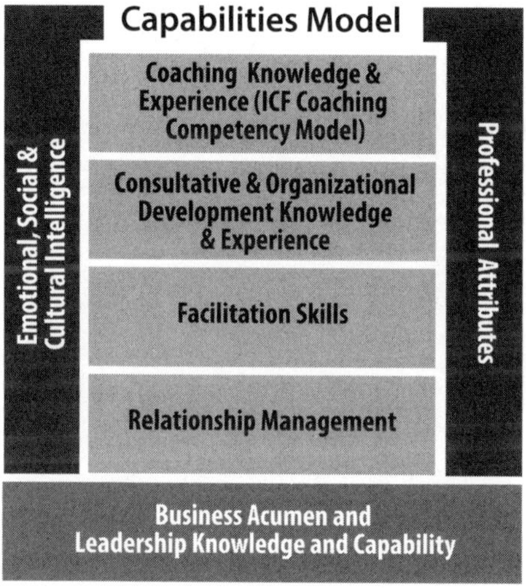

Capabilities Model

- Coaching Knowledge & Experience (ICF Coaching Competency Model)
- Consultative & Organizational Development Knowledge & Experience
- Facilitation Skills
- Relationship Management

Emotional, Social & Cultural Intelligence

Professional Attributes

Business Acumen and Leadership Knowledge and Capability

The general capabilities of a successful internal coach include:

- coaching knowledge, experience and using the ICF Competency Model

- consultative and organizational development knowledge and experience

- facilitation skills

- relationship management

- professional attributes

- emotional, social and cultural intelligence

- business acumen and leadership knowledge and capability (mandatory for internal coach managers)

Note: It can be difficult to find coaches with all of the capabilities listed here. If you are fortunate enough to have one of these coaches on your team, they are worth their weight in gold.

Let's explore in further detail the different capabilities required of coaches and how having experience and knowledge in these areas will benefit both coach and client. Keep in mind that these skills can always be developed and improved upon. After all, it is often through experience that we learn best. As Geoff Colvin writes in *Talent Is Overrated*, "The impression that emerges most strongly from the research on great creators is that of their enthusiastic immersion in their domain and their resulting deep knowledge of it. Since organizations are not innovative—only people are innovative—it follows that the most effective steps an organization can take to build innovation will include helping people expand and deepen their knowledge of their field."[1] Therefore, as coaches work with business leaders and managers on their professional development, the coaches will be constantly developing and growing as well.

INTERNAL COACHING CAPABILITY MODEL

The Internal Coaching Capability Model incorporates components of various "Best-In-Class" capabilities models from the ICF, ASTD and SHRM. I believe that coaches need to be highly adaptable and willing to take on various roles such as coach, consultant, facilitator and business partner. By doing so, they make themselves highly valuable and also sustainable. When new programs are offered or perhaps during a lull in the coaching program, there is an abundance of areas that they can work within and continue making great contributions to the company. Let's begin by looking at the actual Coaching Capability components of our model.

Coaching Knowledge and Skills: A coach must have knowledge of the theory, research and practice of internal coaching and, most importantly, have strong coaching skills. Ideally, your internal coaches have been trained or are in the process of being trained through an ICF-accredited program. A coach who completes an ICF-accredited training program and the other credential requirements will secure an ICF coaching credential.

If you include the ICF's credential as part of your criteria for filling an internal coach position, you will know that the coach candidate has completed the ICF's credentialing process and has demonstrated a comprehensive knowledge and application of the eleven competencies. Depending on the level of credential that is acceptable to you (ACC, PCC or MCC), you will be able to more easily vet the candidate.

See the "ICF Core Coaching Competencies" outline that follows.

---

1. Geoff Colvin, *Talent Is Overrated: What Really Separates World-Class Performers from Everybody Else* (New York: Portfolio, 2010).

The content, which is published on the ICF's website (www.coachfederation. org/icfcredentials/core-competencies/) and used here by permission, describes the eleven competencies.

ICF Core Coaching Competencies

The following eleven core coaching competencies were developed to support greater understanding about the skills and approaches used within today's coaching profession as defined by the International Coach Federation. They will also support you in calibrating the level of alignment between the coach-specific training expected and the training you have experienced.

A. SETTING THE FOUNDATION

1. Meeting Ethical Guidelines and Professional Standards
2. Establishing the Coaching Agreement

B. CO-CREATING THE RELATIONSHIP

3. Establishing Trust and Intimacy with the Client
4. Coaching Presence

C. COMMUNICATING EFFECTIVELY

5. Active Listening
6. Powerful Questioning
7. Direct Communication

D. FACILITATING LEARNING AND RESULTS

8. Creating Awareness
9. Designing Actions
10. Planning and Goal Setting
11. Managing Progress and Accountability

A. SETTING THE FOUNDATION

1. Meeting Ethical Guidelines and Professional Standards—
Understanding of coaching ethics and standards and ability to apply them appropriately in all coaching situations.

1. Understands and exhibits in own behaviors the ICF Standards of Conduct (see list, Part III of ICF Code of Ethics).
2. Understands and follows all ICF Ethical Guidelines (see list).
3. Clearly communicates the distinctions between coaching, consulting, psychotherapy and other support professions.
4. Refers client to another support professional as needed, knowing when this is needed and the available resources.

2. Establishing the Coaching Agreement—Ability to understand what is required in the specific coaching interaction and to come to agreement with the prospective and new client about the coaching process and relationship.

1. Understands and effectively discusses with the client the guidelines and specific parameters of the coaching relationship (e.g., logistics, fees, scheduling, inclusion of others if appropriate).
2. Reaches agreement about what is appropriate in the relationship and what is not, what is and is not being offered, and about the client's and coach's responsibilities.
3. Determines whether there is an effective match between his/her coaching method and the needs of the prospective client.

B. CO-CREATING THE RELATIONSHIP

3. Establishing Trust and Intimacy with the Client—Ability to create a safe, supportive environment that produces ongoing mutual respect and trust.

1. Shows genuine concern for the client's welfare and future.
2. Continuously demonstrates personal integrity, honesty and sincerity.
3. Establishes clear agreements and keeps promises.
4. Demonstrates respect for client's perceptions, learning style, personal being.
5. Provides ongoing support for and champions new behaviors and actions, including those involving risk taking and fear of failure.
6. Asks permission to coach client in sensitive, new areas.

4. Coaching Presence—Ability to be fully conscious and create spontaneous relationship with the client, employing a style that is open, flexible and confident.

1. Is present and flexible during the coaching process, dancing in the moment.

2. Accesses own intuition and trusts one's inner knowing—"goes with the gut."

3. Is open to not knowing and takes risks.

4. Sees many ways to work with the client and chooses in the moment what is most effective.

5. Uses humor effectively to create lightness and energy.

6. Confidently shifts perspectives and experiments with new possibilities for own action.

7. Demonstrates confidence in working with strong emotions and can self-manage and not be overpowered or enmeshed by client's emotions.

C. COMMUNICATING EFFECTIVELY

5. Active Listening—Ability to focus completely on what the client is saying and is not saying, to understand the meaning of what is said in the context of the client's desires, and to support client self-expression.

1. Attends to the client and the client's agenda and not to the coach's agenda for the client.

2. Hears the client's concerns, goals, values and beliefs about what is and is not possible.

3. Distinguishes between the words, the tone of voice, and the body language.

4. Summarizes, paraphrases, reiterates, and mirrors back what client has said to ensure clarity and understanding.

5. Encourages, accepts, explores and reinforces the client's expression of feelings, perceptions, concerns, beliefs, suggestions, etc.

6. Integrates and builds on client's ideas and suggestions.

7. "Bottom-lines" or understands the essence of the client's communication and helps the client get there rather than engaging in long, descriptive stories.

8. Allows the client to vent or "clear" the situation without judgment or attachment in order to move on to next steps.

6. Powerful Questioning—Ability to ask questions that reveal the information needed for maximum benefit to the coaching relationship and the client.

1. Asks questions that reflect active listening and an understanding of the client's perspective.

2. Asks questions that evoke discovery, insight, commitment or action (e.g., those that challenge the client's assumptions).

3. Asks open-ended questions that create greater clarity, possibility or new learning.

4. Asks questions that move the client toward what they desire, not questions that ask for the client to justify or look backward.

7. Direct Communication—Ability to communicate effectively during coaching sessions, and to use language that has the greatest positive impact on the client.

1. Is clear, articulate and direct in sharing and providing feedback.

2. Reframes and articulates to help the client understand from another perspective what he/she wants or is uncertain about.

3. Clearly states coaching objectives, meeting agenda, and purpose of techniques or exercises.

4. Uses language appropriate and respectful to the client (e.g., non-sexist, non-racist, non-technical, non-jargon).

5. Uses metaphor and analogy to help to illustrate a point or paint a verbal picture.

D. FACILITATING LEARNING AND RESULTS

8. Creating Awareness—Ability to integrate and accurately evaluate multiple sources of information and to make interpretations that help the client to gain awareness and thereby achieve agreed-upon results.

1. Goes beyond what is said in assessing client's concerns, not getting hooked by the client's description.

2. Invokes inquiry for greater understanding, awareness, and clarity.

3. Identifies for the client his/her underlying concerns; typical and fixed ways of perceiving himself/herself and the world; differences between the facts and the interpretation; and disparities between thoughts, feelings, and action.

4. Helps clients to discover for themselves the new thoughts, beliefs, perceptions, emotions, moods, etc., that strengthen their ability to take action and achieve what is important to them.

5. Communicates broader perspectives to clients and inspires commitment to shift their viewpoints and find new possibilities for action.

6. Helps clients to see the different, interrelated factors that affect them and their behaviors (e.g., thoughts, emotions, body, and background).

7. Expresses insights to clients in ways that are useful and meaningful for the client.

8. Identifies major strengths vs. major areas for learning and growth, and what is most important to address during coaching.

9. Asks the client to distinguish between trivial and significant issues, situational vs. recurring behaviors, when detecting a separation between what is being stated and what is being done.

9. Designing Actions—Ability to create with the client opportunities for ongoing learning, during coaching and in work/life situations, and for taking new actions that will most effectively lead to agreed-upon coaching results.

1. Brainstorms and assists the client to define actions that will enable the client to demonstrate, practice, and deepen new learning.

2. Helps the client to focus on and systematically explore specific concerns and opportunities that are central to agreed-upon coaching goals.

3. Engages the client to explore alternative ideas and solutions, to evaluate options, and to make related decisions.

4. Promotes active experimentation and self-discovery, where the client applies what has been discussed and learned during sessions immediately afterward in his/her work or life setting.

5. Celebrates client successes and capabilities for future growth.

6. Challenges client's assumptions and perspectives to provoke new ideas and find new possibilities for action.

7. Advocates or brings forward points of view that are aligned with client goals and, without attachment, engages the client to consider them.

8. Helps the client "Do It Now" during the coaching session, providing immediate support.

9. Encourages stretches and challenges but also a comfortable pace of learning.

10. Planning and Goal Setting—Ability to develop and maintain an effective coaching plan with the client.

1. Consolidates collected information and establishes a coaching plan and development goals with the client that address concerns and major areas for learning and development.

2. Creates a plan with results that are attainable, measurable, specific, and have target dates.

3. Makes plan adjustments as warranted by the coaching process and by changes in the situation.

4. Helps the client identify and access different resources for learning (e.g., books, other professionals).

5. Identifies and targets early successes that are important to the client.

11. Managing Progress and Accountability—Ability to hold attention on what is important for the client, and to leave responsibility with the client to take action.

1. Clearly requests of the client actions that will move the client toward his/her stated goals.

2. Demonstrates follow-through by asking the client about those actions that the client committed to during the previous session(s).

3. Acknowledges the client for what they have done, not done, learned or become aware of since the previous coaching session(s).

4. Effectively prepares, organizes, and reviews with client information obtained during sessions.

5. Keeps the client on track between sessions by holding attention on the coaching plan and outcomes, agreed-upon courses of action, and topics for future session(s).

6. Focuses on the coaching plan but is also open to adjusting behaviors and actions based on the coaching process and shifts in direction during sessions.

7. Is able to move back and forth between the big picture of where the client is heading, setting a context for what is being discussed and where the client wishes to go.

8. Promotes client's self-discipline and holds the client accountable for what they say they are going to do, for the results of an intended action, or for a specific plan with related time frames.

9. Develops the client's ability to make decisions, address key concerns, and develop himself/herself (to get feedback, to determine priorities and set the pace of learning, to reflect on and learn from experiences).

10. Positively confronts the client with the fact that he/she did not take agreed-upon actions.

Consultative and Organizational Development Knowledge and Experience: An internal coach should have an understanding of organizational structures, systems and processes, and she should be able to assess these elements within an organization. Coaches with this capability are particularly ideal when change is a common occurrence. If your environment is being affected or will be affected by change, you should look for coaching candidates who are adaptable and who have a demonstrated ability to be a change agent. Key knowledge areas of this capability include:

- organizational assessment and diagnosis
- organizational design and development
- culture and leadership models
- the nature and role of politics in an organization
- organizational change management
- succession planning and leadership transition

Facilitation Skills and Experience: This is the art of bringing adults together and helping them learn through self-discovery. Possessing strong facilitation skills allows your coaches to deliver customized workshops, management training programs and more. Facilitation skills are similar to coaching skills in the sense that the emphasis is on the coaching client/participant or learner; the facilitator, like a coach, will use self-discovery as an approach. The following list of facilitator competencies have been selected from the list provided in *Facilitation Basics*.[2]

- Models appropriate communication skills: listening, repeating and summarizing
- Ensures a safe and conducive learning environment for all participants
- Helps participants apply content to their jobs
- Provides complete feedback during discussions and activities
- Manages group involvement processes
- Promotes the development of action plans
- Asks in-depth questions
- Shares relevant knowledge
- Helps participants understand and apply the concepts
- Identifies environmental factors that support (or hinder) knowledge-transfer to the participant's job
- Helps learners manage the above factors to ensure transfer

Note: Also similar to coaches, facilitators are guides in the learning process. They are responsible and accountable to the group and have the goal of preparing the learners for self-development and continual learning.

Relationship Management: Internal coaches are responsible for the day-to-day relationships with their client groups. Developing trust with their clients and client group is critical to creating the coach–client relationship (as addressed above in the ICF's Core Coaching Competencies). The Society for Human Resource Professionals (SHRM) is the world's largest membership organization dedicated to Human Resource Management. Its competency model is

---

[2] *Facilitation Basics* (ASTD Press: ASTD Speaker Orientation, May 2007).

designed as the foundation for human resource professionals in support of their professional development. As it relates to internal coaching, I particularly like its Relationship Management competency. It truly speaks to attributes of a good internal coach on how coaches should manage their relationships with their clients. SHRM's Relationship Management definition is, "The ability to manage interactions to provide service and to support the organization." According to the SHRM model, when it comes to relationship management, these behaviors are also highly desirable in an internal coach:

- Establishes credibility in all interactions
- Treats all stakeholders with respect and dignity
- Builds engaging relationships with all organizational stakeholders through trust, teamwork and direct communication
- Demonstrates approachability and openness
- Ensures alignment with HR when delivering services and information to the organization while discussing HR positions, programs and perspectives
- Delivers exceptional customer service to organizational stakeholders
- Manages internal and external relationships in ways that promote the best interests of all parties
- Champions the view that organizational effectiveness benefits all stakeholders
- Serves as an advocate when appropriate
- Demonstrates an ability to build a network of contacts within HR and the business at all levels[3]

Professional Attributes: These are the common professional qualities that I have observed in successful internal coaches:

- self-confidence and executive presence
- positivity
- assertiveness
- interpersonal awareness
- approachability

---

[3] ©2012 Society for Human Resource Management

- adaptability
- goal and results-driven
- collaborative and influential
- open to continually learning
- confidentiality, integrity and respectability

Emotional, Social and Cultural Intelligence: An internal coach should have a strong understanding of how emotional, social and cultural intelligence works among individuals and across organizations. This knowledge is a critical component in enabling a coach to understand the organization, the culture and how managers and employees behave within the company. By having this level of awareness, the coach is in a better position to support clients' professional development.

Business Acumen and Leadership Experience:* In order to be successful, an internal coach must have an understanding of general business, possess a proficient knowledge of financial terms, and be aware of how a company works. This knowledge is crucial to the coach's credibility, which is a key quality that executives look for when selecting a coach. Within the purview of business acumen, there are specific challenges that may surface for a client that they will request to be coached on. As such, it's recommended that your internal coaches possess these qualities:

- executive-level thinking
- business savviness
- financial literacy

A critical component of business acumen is not only having a basic knowledge of business but also exhibiting the behaviors that are necessary to being a good leader. The ability to coach on leadership capabilities is what some executives may look for in their coach, especially at the senior executive level. This does not mean the coach needs to be fully competent in all of the leadership areas, but they must at least have experience coaching on these competencies:

- strategic focus
- dealing with ambiguity

---

*These capabilities are especially required for the internal coaching program manager; a well-developed knowledge of business and experience with coaching around the leadership capabilities is required for individual coaches.

- communications
- collaboration
- leading change
- critical thinking and problem solving
- customer focus and quality assurance
- decision making
- initiative, execution and results
- innovation

I understand this list of competencies is long and comprehensive; however, if you want to build a sustainable program, it is important to have well-trained coaches with expertise in various areas. It is also imperative that you understand what your core competencies are, which competencies can be developed on your team and which competencies are not in your wheelhouse and that you may wish to outsource. For example, you may have excellent coaches for your manager population, but you may have a gap in facilitators for management training or coaching at the C-Suite or executive level. If that is the case, do not hesitate to consider external sourcing of the capabilities you need because your clients expect no less than excellence. Prepare to consider a hybrid model where both internal and external coaches are deployed. The goal is to provide the best service and experience for your customers because they are your advocates and will support you in making your internal coaching program sustainable.

COACHING & LEADERSHIP INSIGHT:
Get Clear on Accountabilities in Order to
Identify the Required Coaching Capabilities

If you feel that the list of coaching capabilities in this chapter is overwhelming and you aren't sure where to go next, ask yourself these questions: What is required for the position that needs to be filled? What skills and capabilities would the individual in the position need in order to be effective and successful as an internal coach? What is the best way to ascertain if a person is the best candidate for the position? For example, it may be important for a coach to have significant strength in coaching, customer service and sales because the targeted clients are mostly coming from those organizations and are facing challenges associated with Sales and Service organizations. Therefore, it is important that your coach be "wired" and familiar with the sales process and customer satisfaction, and that she be a strong coach and facilitator. My point is, draw from this chapter whatever applies to your particular situation. You can access the entire list of capabilities as well as a list of related interview questions at www.robertsoncoachinstitute.com.

In order to ensure that you select coaches who are the best fit for your clients, you need to begin with a clear description of the coach's role, responsibilities and day-to-day duties and objectives. This requires having a well-defined and well-written job description. In the next chapter, I will discuss how to write an internal coach job description and I'll provide a sample to help you get started. In Chapter 7 you will find an approach for selecting coaches.

The Internal Coach Position: Designing It, Filling It and Assessing It

When creating the job description for your internal coach, I recommend that you begin with a Position Evaluation Form (PEF). This is a document that will assist Human Resources in determining the level/band of the position, the compensation, and the functional area or job family in which to place the position. Your human resources representative should be able to provide you with this form (or something similar), if not, you can download one from www.robertsoncoachinstitute.com. The sample PEF below will get you started on the right foot.

SAMPLE POSITION EVALUATION FORM

DATE: 5/22/2015

NAME OF INDIVIDUAL SUBMITTING THE REQUEST: Samantha Smith

SUPERVISOR'S NAME: Linda Jones

PROPOSED TITLE: Internal Sales Coach

PROPOSED LEVEL: Band # 6 (Sr. Consultant or Manager level)

Section A: *General Information—Reporting structure, current title (if candidate is internal), proposed title, current and proposed grade/band levels.*

This position will report to the director of Talent Development and hold the title of internal coach (Band 6).

Section B: *Purpose of Request—Is this a new position or an existing position? List the purposes of the position. If this is a pilot and had success, reference this success here or in your business case.*

This is a new position that is being created to support the significant changes that the Sales organization will face over the next three years. The nature of the work will require that the coach have an in-depth understanding of our business; a strong business and sales acumen; a commanding executive presence; and excellent communication, presentation and influencing skills. We would like this individual to have completed an ICF-accredited coach training program (and hold an ICF credential of PCC, at minimum) and to be skilled at coaching, facilitation and change management. The coach will be interacting with and supporting the Sales organization, specifically the managers and their organizations, in order to:

» professionally develop sales managers and their employees

» support them through sales transformation initiatives

» help them resolve sales challenges

We would like to begin with one headcount and pilot the position for six months. Based on our research, we anticipate that a total of five coaches will need to be hired within the subsequent six months. In total, there will be a team of six coaches (including one manager). Each will be assigned to a region and be responsible for the development and the delivering of sales transformation and change management programs to support that region over the next three years. After the business of the sales transformation initiative is completed, the coaches will either continue to support their client base or be rotated to support other change initiatives or leadership development programs within the company.

The position being proposed at this time will be responsible for:

» the coaching and change strategy

» recruiting the team of coaches

» the delivery and facilitation of new sales methodology, leadership development and change management programs

» providing coaching to the directors and vice presidents in their regions and key managers as identified

Section C: *Scope of the Position—Full-time/part-time; budget allocation or source of funding*

This is a full-time position. We will be using an open headcount from the Southeast Region that was vacated when one of the team members chose not to return from a leave of absence.

Section D: *Responsibilities—Key areas of responsibility and percentage of the coach's time that will be allocated to these areas.*

» Recruitment, training and development of internal coaches: 15%

» Delivery and development of internal coaching, sales methodology, leadership development and change management programs: 30%

» Executive coaching—Responsible for coaching members of the leadership team and other nominated directors and managers: 50%

» Administrative duties—Supporting coaching and leadership and organizational development initiatives: 5%

Section E: *Complexity of the Position and Its Impact on Business*

We see this role as having a tremendous impact on our sales business. This individual will work on problems diverse in scope and, therefore, needs to have knowledge of our industry, business and organization. The coach will be empowered to determine the appropriate course of action that is required to develop talent and to support our employees in solving business challenges while they are adapting to the multitude of changes that result from the company's many business and sales transformation initiatives. The coach may come across opportunities to recommend changes to policies, procedures and processes that affect immediate operations, which could have corporate-wide impact.

The following is an example of how, through coaching, a business challenge can be identified and resolved. A coach working inside an organization, having multiple coaching conversations that occur throughout the organization and at multiple levels, is able to identify issues with, for example, a business process. Individually, each instance may appear isolated; however, to the internal coach, it can become apparent that the issue is more widespread and significantly impacts the amount of time it was taking to complete the process.

Section F: *Knowledge/Education Requirements*

» Bachelor's degree required—master's degree (general) or MBA preferred

» Graduate of an International Coach Federation–accredited coaching program

» International Coach Federation certification—PCC designation preferred, or at minimum enrollment in the program

» Minimum three years of experience coaching managers and/or executives

» Minimum five years in a functional area (e.g., Sales and Marketing, Finance) at a manager level

» Strong communication, presentation and negotiation skills

The reporting structure of this position depends on the needs of the business, the objectives of the internal coach and what makes the most sense for the client group. It is important to consider which organization is funding the headcount and which organization controls the headcount. For example, if the Sales organization provides funding for a headcount and the headcount resides in the Human Resources organization, which then experiences a reduction in force (RIF), then the headcount or coach position may be in jeopardy.

RECRUITING AND SELECTING COACH CANDIDATES

There are many places you can find an internal or external coach, such as the resources that are listed here:

- International Coach Federation (ICF)
- European Mentoring & Coaching Council (EMCC)
- Association for Coaching (based in the United Kingdom)
- Human resources and executive recruiting firms
- Boutique coaching and professional development firms
- Word of mouth

In addition, you can consider posting the position(s) on LinkedIn within the many coaching groups, or you can make use of job sites like ExecuNet, Glassdoor, or TheLadders.

The key to selecting an effective coach is to be crystal clear on what your expectations are for the position and how you see it working inside your organization. In particular, how do you envision the coach's degree of engagement with the various functional areas of your company? This is where it is critically important to understand your company's corporate culture, the subculture of the organizations whose employees will be participating in the coaching program, and what the client's pain points are with respect to professional development. When selecting coaches (internal or external), I strongly encourage you to engage the leaders of the participating organization and even some of the top talent who would be working with the coach. These individuals should be active participants in the interview and selection process. Once you've arranged for their participation, I recommend that you prepare for and conduct a rigorous recruiting process that is composed of the following steps:

Step 1 – If you do not have one already, write a clear job description, including title and pay. Ensure that Human Resources has evaluated the position and is supportive of your program, its goals and its objectives.

Step 2 – Ask the leaders and program participants who helped draft the job description to review it and provide you with their feedback, thoughts and recommendations. Ask them what qualities they would like to see in a coach who would be assigned to their organization. What are the skills and capabilities that they consider as requirements (must-haves), and what requirements are optional. **Note:** These requirements should come from the highest level or close to the highest level of the client organization—someone who truly understands the company's strategic vision and key objectives; someone who can articulate what "good" looks like for his or her organization.

Step 3 – Make certain that the requirements identified by the group are covered in the job description and discussed in the interview process. Ensure that your hiring manager as well as the recruiters conducting the search are clear on the requirements in addition to the details of the job (compensation, to whom the position reports, etc.).

Step 4 – Determine your recruiting strategy and tactics. Will you use internal or external recruiters? What job boards are ideal for attracting well-qualified candidates? Where are the best places to find the type of talent you're looking for? How will you use LinkedIn and other social media venues? You should have a session with your recruiters to design your approach and determine the key milestones and deadlines that align to your program's "go live" date.

Step 5 – Establish the recruiting and selection process, including decision-making points and subsequent steps. For example, a possible recruiting and selection workflow for your company might look like this:

Interview & Selection Process

Recruiter Briefing Package Distributed & Briefing Call Completed	Recruiter Interview	Hiring Manager Interview	Human Resources Interview	Client Representative Interview	Candidate De-Brief Call	Internal Offer Process

a. The recruiter builds a position briefing package. In addition to informing the candidates about the position, the package is to be referenced by the individuals conducting the interview. This ensures that all parties are on the same page and are properly informed throughout the interview process. The recruiter distributes the packages and hosts a briefing call with the hiring manager and anyone else identified to be part of the selection process, explaining the interview process and how to use the guide and each interviewer's evaluation matrix.

b. The recruiter posts the position and notifies key external search firms and mines the Internet and social media sites for qualified candidates.

c. Résumés are gathered and the recruiter screens them, prequalifying the candidates who match the key criteria provided by the hiring manager, the clients and Human Resources.

d. The recruiter conducts a prescreening interview (Skype is an ideal medium for this type of interview) to determine if the candidate meets the key criteria for the position's general requirements (qualifications, capabilities, compensation level and educational requirements). If so, the candidate goes on to the next step.

e. The recruiter sets up a face-to-face interview for the hiring manager and the candidate. The hiring manager conducts a much deeper interview in the areas of coaching capabilities, business acumen and interpersonal skills as covered in the Internal Coach Selection Criteria in Chapter 6. If the candidate passes this interview, he or she proceeds to Human Resources.

f. Human Resources (preferably the business partner or generalist who will support the coaching program) interviews the candidate face-to-face and explores his or her capabilities for the job and fit within the culture of the organization. If the candidate passes this interview, he or she proceeds to the final interview.

g. The candidate meets with the primary point of contact for the client group that the coach will be supporting. This individual needs to have in-depth knowledge of their organization—its function, its subculture, the employees' working styles, and in what capacity the coach will be interacting with the organization.

h. Once all parties sign off on the candidate, you can follow your internal offer process.

Note: My recommendation is to use the tools provided in this book and on our website (www.robertsoncoachinstitute.com) to design your interview guides and scoring mechanisms. You want to have a consistent interview and evaluation approach that is used by all parties involved in the selection process. The Recruiter Interview Package (interview guide and evaluation summary) is designed for these purposes.

The Recruiter

The recruiter will make certain that all of the general requirements are met and conduct a pre-screen of the candidate to make certain they are qualified for the position. The recruiter can use the template below to track his evaluation and capture his thoughts, which will be helpful as a recruiter will most likely speak with several candidates. At the end of the process, all of the individuals who were involved in conducting the interview process will re-group and compare their notes and feedback. Each of the following sample templates is designed to assist each individual interviewer with his or her role in the process.

RECRUITER EVALUATION MATRIX (insert candidate's name)			
Requirement	**Requirement Met (yes/no)**	**Level of Requirement – High/Medium/Low**	**Comments**
Education/Training	Yes	High	Meets requirements
Business Experience	Yes	Medium	Has excellent finance leadership experience
Coach Experience	Yes	Medium	Has coached over 100 executives
Compensation	Yes	Medium	Falls within range

Notes: Candidate may not be well qualified for the position. I am not certain if this is the best candidate for the Sales organization position. She has limited experience in sales and with coaching sales leaders, although she has excellent experience in coaching executives in Finance.

The Hiring Manager

The hiring manager will be looking for the capabilities of the candidate. Specifically, the manager will be evaluating skills, abilities and experiences. This matrix can be helpful to the manager for keeping track of his or her feedback on each candidate.

HIRING MANAGER EVALUATION MATRIX (insert candidate's name)			
Requirement	**Requirement Met (yes/no)**	**Level of Requirement – High/Medium/Low**	**Comments**
Coach	Yes	High	Holds PCC credential and coached over 100 executives
Facilitation	Yes	High	Has experience delivering and facilitating sales training, leadership and conflict workshops
Relationship Management	Yes	High	Sales experience managing a base of clients
Organizational Design & Development	No	Low	n/a
Change Management	No	Low	n/a

Notes: Individual exceeds almost all requirements except OD and change management, which are future areas and he can be trained.

Human Resources

The Human Resources interviewer will be looking for cultural fit for the company and the client group that the coach will be supporting. In addition, the interviewer may want to see what additional experiences and interests the candidate may have, as well as the findings of the assessments (if assessments are utilized).

HUMAN RESOURCES EVALUATION MATRIX (insert candidate's name)			
Requirement	**Requirement Met (yes/no)**	**Level of Requirement – High/Medium/Low**	**Comments**
Cultural fit (HR)	Yes	Medium	Similar work style
Cultural fit (Client)	Yes	High	High energy
Talent assessment/ Succession planning	Yes. Ready in the future for additional responsibilities	Medium	Subject Matter Expert (SME)
Overall fit for role	Yes. Excellent Fit	Medium to High	Without a doubt

Notes: This individual is an excellent fit for the Sales organization. Given her marketing knowledge and sales experience, she understands sales and the culture. She would complement the team.

The Client Representative

The client representative will be looking at the industry and business acumen capabilities of the candidate, as well as their cultural fit and working style. Their goal is to see if the candidate would be a good "fit" and make a good team member to the group.

CLIENT REPRESENTATIVE EVALUATION MATRIX (insert candidate's name)			
Requirement	**Requirement Met (yes/no)**	**Level of Requirement – High/Medium/Low**	**Comments**
Industry knowledge	No	Low	Does not have experience in our industry
Business acumen	Yes	High	Has strong business experiences and knowledge, which compensates for lack of industry knowledge
Cultural fit (client organization)	Yes	High	High energy – strong fit
Work style	Yes	High	High energy, performance oriented

Notes: This individual is an excellent fit for the internal sales coach position. His business acumen is a plus; he has strong executive presence and presentation skills, and his working style is collaborative and high energy with an eye toward performance.

Once the interviews are completed, each person who interviewed the candidates can summarize and present their views to the rest of the group. From there, candidates can be rated and ranked or, if a rating approach is not utilized, a rigorous discussion with the group about the candidates may be sufficient. This can be decided up front in the process by the selection team.

THE PERFORMANCE MANAGEMENT PROCESS AND OBJECTIVES FOR INTERNAL COACHES

After you've completed your job description and the position has been filled, the coach will need to be assessed from time to time to ensure that he or she is meeting the performance expectations of the position. The method of evaluation may be given many names—a performance appraisal, performance agreement, performance review or performance evaluation—but they are all technically the same thing. The performance management process is a common vehicle for evaluating on-the-job performance of employees in organizations. Performance appraisals are also typically part of a career development process that is composed of regular reviews of an employee's performance, creating a venue for coaching, counseling and feedback.

The performance management process and the evaluations themselves are a critical component in the Talent Management Life Cycle; unfortunately, however, sometimes the process is undervalued and underutilized, considered more of a "check the box" exercise than an opportunity to identify, retain and develop talent. In my experience, savvy managers take the performance management process very seriously, taking the time to prepare thoughtful and meaningful performance reviews and feedback. They do this in addition to designing a performance appraisal that aligns the employee's objectives to the overall strategy and objectives of the business.

The goal of the performance appraisal is to provide a systematic process that periodically assesses an individual employee's job performance and productivity in relation to certain pre-established criteria and organizational objectives. The essence of each objective requires the employee to establish a goal, choose the requisite course of action, and effectively execute the course of action. An important part of the evaluation process is the means of measurement and the comparison of the employee's actual performance with the standards set. Interestingly, I have found that when employees themselves have been involved with setting the goals and choosing the course(s) of action that they are to follow, they are more likely to fulfill their responsibilities. (**Note:** This is likely to have the opposite effect if taken to the extreme. For example, I have seen managers request that an employee prepare their own evaluation, including inputting all the data for their goals. While this may be a time-saver for the manager, it abdicates one of their most important responsibilities as a manager, which is to oversee the development of their people. Moreover, it becomes cumbersome for the employee and subsequently could demotivate the employee or create a feeling or a culture, if done across the board, in which talent is not considered a valuable asset to be retained and developed.)

The performance objectives established for the employee is their roadmap to success. In addition to making clear what the responsibilities of the job are, it ensures alignment of the employee's actions to the business objectives, which drives momentum across the company to achieve the company's strategic goals or imperatives.

In addition to objectives, other aspects of an individual's contribution to the organization can be evaluated. Such contributions may include "demonstrating organizational citizenship" or "demonstrating our corporate values."

In order to collect meaningful personal evaluation data on the performance of internal coaches, you should focus on three main aspects:

- the results of the coach's measurable objectives

- feedback from the coaching clients and stakeholders

- the return on investment (ROI), return on engagement (ROE) or impact study (more on this topic in Chapter 18)

The performance management process provides measurable results on the coach's performance and their impact on the organization's performance through coaching, program facilitation and interventions that the coach designed and delivered to their clients. Remember, at the highest level, performance management systems are deployed to manage and align an organization's resources in order to achieve the highest possible performance of its strategic objectives. At an individual level, the performance management process can drive the career development of employees as well as their promotion (or termination) and rewards or compensation.

Assessing Coach Performance by Objective

Now we'll explore some possible objectives that can be used to evaluate an internal coach's performance. These objectives can be broken down into four categories:

- A. Program Participation and Utilization
- B. Project and Overall Program Management
- C. Business and Leadership Coaching Capabilities
- D. Professional Coach Development

A. Program Participation and Utilization

It is important to track a coach's level of engagement in the internal coaching program, as well as how valuable a team member he is and how useful a resource he is to his clients. Just as business operations or marketing liaisons are critical to a Sales organization, the coach needs to be onboarded and viewed as a valuable partner to his client group. Some potential performance objectives are:

- The number of participants engaged by the coach vs. target

- The number of coaching hours completed vs. target

- How the coach identifies new ways to serve clients without going over his or her capacity limits as a coach

- How the coach identifies and measures trends/themes occurring in his or her client group that may surface a training requirement or knowledge gap

- How the coach identifies and quantifies gaps or trends in leadership competencies, business trends and other areas of importance that could be relevant to the company, employee engagement and business performance.

- Has the coach obtained an ICF credential (e.g., Professional Coach Certification) and, if so, has he or she completed a minimum of fifteen Coach Continuing Education Units (CCEUs) annually in order to maintain coach certification?

B. Project and Overall Program Management

A key component of an internal coach's role is not to just coach, but also to help manage the internal coaching program; to provide data to demonstrate the continued value of the program; to manage the clients; to ensure the customer experience is exceptional and that expectations are managed; and to see that deadlines are met and that goals, at a minimum, are met, if not exceeded. Some criteria for evaluating performance in these areas include:

- How well does the coach manage his or her clients?

- Was an NPS (Net Promoter Score) survey conducted for each individual coaching engagement? If so, what were the results?

- How well does the coach manage their client's expectations? Meet deadlines?

- How well does the coach manage and deliver programs for their clients?

- What is the overall client feedback about their experience with the coach?

Timely and Effective Reporting, Analytics and Business Impact

A component of the coach's role is to track her time spent coaching and to identify gaps, trends and themes that surface during each and across all coaching conversations. As a result, the coach can identify and offer solutions to help her clients close these gaps and solve their problems. These solutions may include specific training or a workshop on a particular topic. The ability of the coach to help quickly identify problem areas can provide a much deeper value to the individuals being coached, the client group and the company overall.

Timely and Effective Reporting

Therefore, defining and creating reports relevant to your business and the expectations of the business (client groups) and of Human Resources (see Program Participation and Utilization objectives above) allows the coaching program to connect the coaching to the business and to further demonstrate value to their client group. For example, if the coach is keeping track of how many times they hear about a specific business problem, they are able to identify a theme or trend and begin to analyze this information and surface it accordingly to find a solution. In order to do so in a systematic way, some type of reporting system will be needed. Depending on the size of your coaching program, this can be done via an Excel spreadsheet, a software application or a tracking system. Also, the goals/areas of competency must be defined as well as the measurement metrics related to the client's performance and results. Some potential areas the coach's manager may evaluate include:

- How often does the coach update the coaching data system?
- How accurate and complete is the coach's input?
- How does the coach utilize his or her data in order to help clients improve their performance and results?

Analytics

A good coach compares a company's raw data or business imperatives with what is being heard in the coaching conversations. For example, the data might suggest that sales of a new product are exceeding targets; however, the coaching conversations disclose that although sales are being made, the ability to actually deliver the product is a challenge. The coach, in conjunction with his manager and the other coaches, identifies a pattern and sees that there are problems occurring in specific distribution centers, thus creating broader process issues that are inhibiting the organization's ability to turn orders into revenue.

Business Impact and Internal Coaching Program Expansion

A successful coach proactively manages her business and looks for opportunities to expand her coaching and other services. If her clients are meeting or exceeding the coaching hours allocated to them, then this can be an opportunity to grow the coaching practice. In this regard, the coach's manager may want to evaluate the coach on the following:

- The demand for the coach (to do this, compare the number of coaching clients and/or workshops that the coach had anticipated or recommended to the actual number of coaching clients that enrolled in coaching and the actual number of workshops that the coach had delivered)
- The potential to take coaching into new areas of the business
- The impact of coaching programs on the client's business performance and results

C. Business and Leadership Coaching Capabilities

This objective closely examines the coach's ability to coach at a professional standard and provide added value to his or her clients. An internal coach will be onboarded with the expectation that he possesses a certain degree of business acumen, coaching experience and organizational knowledge. Perhaps the coach may possess knowledge about the company, its navigational challenges and how the company's "system" really works. Therefore, the coach cannot hide behind the veil of ignorance and claim that he simply doesn't know. He needs to be active and engaged from the start, and understand the big picture in order to effectively support his clients in achieving their goals. Some potential performance markers are:

- The number of clients that a coach retains
- The number of the coach's clients who are promoted or in rotated positions
- The number of the coach's clients who are identified as high potentials or moved along in succession
- The coach's ability to utilize assessments (360-degree, EQ, etc.) to gather feedback and further his client's professional development
- Customer Experience Rating, which is based on the client's and the stakeholder's satisfaction with the coach's ability to serve them

- The number of client requests for the coach to participate in business meetings, provide additional programs and coach other managers and leaders

D. Professional Coach Development

The following are some sample focus areas that can be used to develop a coach. These may include continuing education programs, certification programs or stretch assignments to help the coach grow professionally.

1. **Collaboration and influence:** Evaluate how your coach partners with his or her business partners and clients. This will be a key area for growing your program and building the program's brand.

2. **Internal exposure:** This occurs as coaches develop capabilities in multiple areas of the business and in other talent development disciplines such as diversity and inclusion, training and facilitation, and change management.

3. **External exposure:** Building coaching programs will attract talent and should be used as a recruiting tactic. In addition, your clients and competitors will see the value you place on investing in your talent. Your coaches should be visible and contribute to the professional development of the coaching industry.

4. **Professional coach credentials:** As an ICF-credentialed coach, it is imperative that the coach maintains his credentials. In order to do this, a coach must complete forty CCEUs over a three-year period or a minimum of fifteen CCEUs each year.

An internal coach is not just a coach working inside an organization, the role is also part sales and marketing professional, part program manager, part strategic partner, part sounding board and part business analyst. Having a coaching practice inside a company is like running a business with an actual profit-and-loss (P&L) operation. If you aren't profitable in terms of your return on human capital (in other words, there isn't a direct linkage between your coaching program and an improvement in the organization's talent development and performance and results), then you will jeopardize the program's brand and its sustainability. Hence, why it is so important to select the best coaches for your company and culture.

COACHING & LEADERSHIP INSIGHT:
Build According to Momentum

A crucial part of coach selection is knowing how large a team of coaches your organization needs. The secret to determining this is to grow your program based on momentum and success. A success-based program, funded through existing headcount and budget, is an excellent approach that allows you to grow and flex with the organization as needed.

When I started the internal coaching program at MCI/WorldCom, I was the only coach. Within six months, enrollment for the program had grown by 115 percent. I had to create a waiting list. From there, I hired one coach, who was an excellent coach and partner. She was a great contributor to the program's success, and together we measured our work over a six-month period and expanded again in the following year. Demand increased—not only for coaching, but for team-building and collaboration engagements, individual and organizational 360-degree assessments, leadership development programs, customer experience workshops and more. At this point, the other business leaders offered to fund the headcount in order to have a coach assigned to their geographic region, and we expanded into functional areas to support our technical services and customer service teams. (**Note:** Even though headcount was funded from within the particular region, we still included the expense of our headcount when analyzing our value and impact.)

8 Building a Sustainable Internal Coaching Program

When I was at Verizon Business and tasked with taking the former MCI internal coaching programs from Sales and delivering coaching across multiple functions, my greatest concern was consistency in our service and our customer experience. In order to make certain that each coach was being consistent in his or her approach and in the services each of them offered, my team and I designed a success plan or "playbook." Today, I refer to this as the Internal Coaching Program Playbook (ICPP). The ICPP houses the processes, procedures, resources, templates and so on that are critical to the internal coaching team's ability to execute their program in a fair and consistent manner that is aligned to the company's objectives.

The playbook includes essential documentation such as the process for selecting and onboarding coaches and clients, templates for all aspects of the coaching process, how to exit clients at the end of a coaching engagement, and how to measure success of the engagement and the overall program. As with any initiative, it is imperative to have consistency in the approach and execution of the coaching program, as this will directly impact your "customer's experience." This, in turn, will directly impact the brand and results for the program and ultimately your clients' customers and their business objectives.

Therefore, when designing any type of coaching engagement or program, the coaching program manager or coach should begin with the end in mind and determine the desired outcomes for the individual being coached as well as the overall coaching program. With this in mind, the most important question that the coaching program manager or coach can ask of their coaching clients is, "What would need to occur in our coaching that would enable you to highly recommend myself as your coach and the coaching program to your peers and others?" The answer to this question is the basis for what is known as the Net Promoter Score (which I discuss in further detail in Chapter 18). "How likely are you to recommend the coaching program to your colleagues?" The coach and/or coaching manager must keep this question in mind when designing the coaching engagement or program. They'll want to create the engagement or program in such a way that would best serve its customers and provide for a "highly recommend" response.

So the goal, really, is for one client to have the same positive experience as the next, at least in terms of coaching procedure. If you are crystal clear on the design of your internal coaching program, the coaching process and the coach selection requirements up front, you will have a greater chance of delivering services in a consistent manner.

In terms of the actual coaching experience, absolute consistency should not be an expectation. This is because each coach brings their own unique personality, background and coaching experiences to the coach–client relationship, and often the training they have received and coaching framework they have been taught to use differs.

THE IMPORTANCE OF THE INTERNATIONAL COACH FEDERATION CREDENTIAL

What I like about the ICF coach-credentialing process is that it ensures coaches undergo a rigorous process to achieve and maintain the credential. There is something about having to study, acquire coaching hours, take a written exam and deliver a live coaching session—in order to qualify for the ICF credential—that fosters a sense of professionalism as well as accomplishment. In addition, in order to maintain your credential, a coach must complete forty Coach Continuing Education Units (CCEUs) every three years. As I am a business leader, and a coach, I believe it is imperative to have professional objectives and always be working toward them. The accomplishment of objectives is a true measure of success.

Another benefit of ICF-credentialed coaches is that they must abide by the ICF's Code of Ethics, which is a set of standards that addresses a coach's professionalism and conduct, and by nature requires the coach to adhere to the code during coaching engagements. If a complaint is made against a coach, the plaintiff can bring the matter to the ICF's Ethical Review Board and the complaint will be addressed in the Ethical Conduct Review (ECR) process. This process is posted on the ICF's website (www.internationalcoachfederation.org).

It is for these reasons that I recommend you choose ICF-credentialed coaches for your internal coaching program. This isn't to say that coaches who aren't ICF-credentialed aren't good coaches; choosing someone with the ICF designation just gives you that added assurance. Because they've met the demands of a rigorous process and must abide by certain coaching standards, you can expect that they will hold themselves to a higher standard. This in and of itself will lead to a higher degree of consistency in the approach your coaching team takes.

THE ELEMENTS OF THE INTERNAL COACHING PROGRAM PLAYBOOK

Now that we have discussed why credentialed coaches are important to the consistency of an internal coaching program, let's take a look at the other areas where consistency plays a role in the success of the program.

The primary purpose of the Internal Coaching Program Playbook (ICPP) is to ensure consistency in your internal coaching program with respect to its approach, coaching model and resources, as well as the templates and processes used for communicating with sponsors and clients, and the processes and guidelines needed for managing the expectations of your sponsors, clients, coaches and your management. More specifically, the playbook is an efficient tool for your coaches to use when delivering their services and when providing the processes and tools (such as assessments) that support your program. You can build all of your program marketing materials and communications from the content of the playbook and know that a) the protocols will be consistent for coaches and clients across the board, and b) the parties on all sides of the program will have realistic expectations. In addition, the playbook becomes an easy reference guide for anyone involved in the program who may need clarification on how to approach a task, handle a client need or manage a client expectation. After all, so much of our life and our success is about how well we communicate and manage expectations.

Alignment to Company Vision, Mission And Values

The first items I suggest placing in your ICPP are your company's values and mission statement, and its strategic and business goals. It is important that you, as the leader of the program, and the coaches can articulate your organization's overall strategic initiatives and its business goals so that the coaches are able to articulate the same to their clients. In addition, it is important for you and the coaching team to understand how the broader business objectives align to the coaching program goals. It is essential and therefore worth mentioning again that your internal coaching program goals must align with your overall strategic business initiatives and business goals. This alignment is critical in setting up your program properly, targeting program participants and working with them to achieve their goals and their business unit's goals.

Internal Coaching Program Objectives

In this section of the ICPP, you should state the goals of the internal coaching program and follow it with the services that are offered by the coaches. The main purpose is to ensure alignment between the goals and the services that are provided. Clients will begin to come to you with all types of requests and you will want to respond positively to each client request; however, this can result in building one-off workshops and, before you know it, your coaches and your program have gone off course. You need to be clear on what the coaching program's objectives are, as going off course can result in spending too much time and money on ancillary programs for one or two groups of employees.

Possible internal coaching program objectives might be as follows:

1. Accelerate leadership development and build our talent pipeline
2. Retain key talent and customers
3. Reinforce sales force transformation and training initiatives
4. Develop a high-performance culture built on pride, professionalism and customer satisfaction
5. Positively impact performance and results

Internal Coaching Program Services

Once you have included the business component in your Internal Coaching Program Playbook (ICPP), the next element to include is a description of the services that you and your team will offer. For example: a menu of services and a description of each, the target audience for each service, and time commitment and budget. (**Note:** The cost for your services may be charged back by your organization or absorbed through your budget, or cost allocation may vary for each service. Your program participants should be made aware of the cost component in advance in order to plan and budget accordingly.)

This section of your playbook should also include the objectives of each service offered through the internal coaching program. List the expected outcomes for the client and coach. Define the step-by-step process for enrollment in each offering and the process for how and when to transition from the engagement. You should include success factors and the standards by which coaching success will be defined. This section is a good place to make a statement about how matters of confidentiality will be handled.

Based on your talent development strategy, program offerings can be designed and integrated into the overall talent development strategy. Make certain that within the ICPP you provide the requisite training materials for your coaches and consultants, and the relevant resources for them to use with their clients, such as a facilitator's guide, presentations and workbooks. The key here, again, is to ensure consistency and to make certain that the program's delivery arm—the coaches—are equally knowledgeable about the offerings, their content and that they are equally equipped to facilitate the program or service being offered. You want to ensure that your clients have a positive and consistent experience no matter who is facilitating the program.

Internal Coach Roles, Responsibilities and Objectives

The next section of your playbook should include the internal coach job description, a profile on the ideal coach, performance management objectives and approximate percentages of the coach's time expected to be spent on each of the programs or services (one-to-one coaching, broad-based leadership development programs, and so on). You should also include information on the distinctions between coaching, mentoring, consulting and counseling. By clearly articulating your definition of coaching—what coaching is and what it isn't—and what is expected inside your organization, your coaches will have a better understanding of their roles and responsibilities, which will help them to deliver optimum levels of coaching, facilitation and mentoring, and avoid scope creep.

Client Engagement

I encourage you to also include in this section of the playbook tips on how coaches can engage their clients and build powerful and bonding relationships, as well as pointers on tricky situations to be aware of when working with upper-level management. For example, you may find that, when it comes to talent development, some managers or even some leaders may not be attuned to the development of their employees, such as when and how to apply coaching programs, or they may not know when the best time is to coach versus mentor versus counsel. In these kinds of situations, in order to support both the employee and the manager in achieving the desired results, the coach may need to provide guidance to the manager as to what approach is best for a specific employee and why, and demonstrate that approach. Following are a couple examples of situations involving upper management that a coach would be wise to look out for.

Outsourcing of People Development

Some managers can get overwhelmed with their workload and, therefore, have limited time to spend on the "people" part of their role, or sometimes managers are simply not comfortable with the people part of their role (I know! Then why be a manager? That is a subject for an entirely different discussion . . .) because they are not spending time developing their people, whatever the reason, the manager may try to shift their responsibilities onto a coach. In an effort to support the manager and win over his or her trust, the coach may be all too willing to take on some of the manager's people development responsibilities, which isn't fair to the coach or the client. When faced with this situation, the coach needs to recognize what is happening and work with the manager to set parameters around their role and the manager's role.

Coaching for Remediation

A manager may ask a coach to focus on an employee who is a low performer. The coach's responsibilities are much more exclusive than this, so the coach must clearly articulate what those responsibilities are to avoid any confusion. More importantly, coaching poor performers can be dangerous territory for many reasons. First of all, the employee could be on or heading toward a performance plan in which coaching isn't intended to play a part, and so introducing coaching may create confusion for the employee and in the actual performance management of the employee. In addition, coaching is designed for a company's high-potentials and strong bench performers—those individuals who are looking to accelerate or enhance their performance. The process requires strategic thinking and action, not always found in situations where individuals are concerned about their performance and perhaps their tenure with the company. If you find yourself in this situation, speak with your manager and/or your Human Resources contact and together formulate a plan to exit the situation respectfully.

Client/Coach Relationships

The relationship that the coach has with the sponsor client is crucial to the overall success of the program. The coach must work toward establishing an honest, open relationship, and one based on mutual trust and respect. In addition, within that approach it is important that the coach clearly sets expectations about what will be kept confidential. A positive environment creates a culture of learning and development. Proactively and collaboratively working in the talent development space will increase productivity, efficiency and engagement. The coach must be certain that the sponsor client believes in this concept. Otherwise it may take some time to win this client over or the coach may need to make a decision to forgo this client for coaching.

In each company that my coaches have coached managers and leaders, we made certain that the executive of that organization was supportive of our work and efforts. Their direct engagement with the coaches and involvement with their team were a ringing endorsement for the coaching program, making it easier for us to work with the organization's managers and leaders. As a manager, you should tell your coaches to let you know when they encounter a situation where support is absent so that together you can determine the best way to proceed.

The Coach Capability Model

Also in the Coach Roles, Responsibilities and Objectives of your playbook, you may want to include the competency model used for your coaches. For example, you may have chosen certain capabilities that you would like your coaches to have strength in and be knowledgeable about. Whatever those capabilities are, this information should be included in the playbook. (Review Chapter 6 for recommended capabilities to seek in a coach.) Making this clear enables the coaches to identify their own areas for professional development, and it enables you to inform your clients about the capabilities of your coaches.

Internal Coach Development Plan Template

In addition, include the coaching plan template that your coaches are to use with their clients. The coaching plan template is the document that coaching program participants use to capture their objectives, actions, progress and overall success.

ICF's Code of Ethics

Be sure to include the ICF's Code of Ethics in your playbook and provide web links to information about ICF's credentialing process. Having your coaches engage in continuous education will keep them focused on their professional development, and it's a great way of modeling the behavior your company would like to see in its culture. If your company has a code of conduct or guiding principles that employees are expected to sign on to and follow, this is an ideal place to include that information.

Internal Coaching Program Measurement

In addition, you will want to include a section on measurement. Depending on your approach, you may want to describe how you plan to measure the success of the program, the success of the individual coaches and/or when the measurement occurs. More information can be found in Chapter 18 on measurement and success.

Supporting Documents

You'll want your playbook to have an appendix (or Resources section), where you can include all of the documents that support the internal coaching program. Ideally, in addition to the hard copies, you would have a SharePoint site, Box application or intranet site where you and your team can access the required documents in electronic form. In the appendix, be certain to include the following:

1. **Coaching enrollment package:** welcome letter to the client, coaching agreement, coaching plan template and list of FAQs.
2. **Assessments:** list of assessments offered, and the fees, training and certifications required for each.
3. **Leadership program information:** description of the program including its length, target audience and modality, as well as what coach training/certification is required in order to deliver the program.
4. **Coach's toolkit:** reading materials, websites and any other resources that should be shared across the team.

5. **Coach training and certification information:** descriptions of the available and recommended options, and a coaching call time-tracking sheet for your coaches to track their time spent coaching, which they can also use for ICF certification.
6. **Measurement tools:** tools for tracking coaching utilization, assessing client engagement, measuring the program's impact, and monitoring business and cultural trends that arise through coaching.
7. **Program marketing materials:** executive briefing presentation; list of coach capabilities; coaching presentations, including PowerPoint and Word presentation templates with program name and logo to support branding; communications pieces, such as letters to executive sponsors; online or printable program brochures; coach bio template; and so on.

MAINTAINING YOUR PLAYBOOK

Your Internal Coaching Program Playbook (ICPP) is a living document and will expand over time. In order to ensure that it is kept relevant and up to date, discuss procedures and approaches with your coaches regularly. Ask your coaches and clients what is working well and what could be working better. Also ask them what suggestions they may have. You will find the playbook to be an invaluable tool for communicating changes and making certain that everyone involved in the coaching program is on the same page. Additionally, you can use the content in the playbook to create your internal web and marketing materials for the coaching program, such as PowerPoint presentations, electronic brochures, and so on.

For more information about building an ICPP or to purchase an ICPP Workbook, please go to www.robertsoncoachinstitute.com. The ICPP is a critical tool in building a sustainable internal coaching program. The following list articulates the recommended steps necessary to build a sustainable coaching program.

Steps for Building a Successful and Sustainable Internal Coaching Program

1. Understand your company's business and talent management goals.

2. Design and align your internal coaching program goals to support your company's business and talent management goals.

3. Identify and secure the coaching talent needed to accelerate the achievement of your internal coaching program's goals in Step 2.

4. Create an Internal Coaching Program Playbook (ICPP) to ensure consistent execution of the coaching program. (Building the ICPP will help the internal coaching program manager to identify all service offerings, process and related training, and communications.)

5. Deliver value-added programs to clients in addition to coaching in order to support their professional development and business success.

6. Create a thoughtful plan to measure the goals set for the program and the contributions and performance of your coaches.

7. Establish a system to track coaching activity and capture trends that can be converted into key data points and utilized with your clients and also used to build programs to meet future professional and business development needs.

8. Commit to continually developing your coaches through ICF credentialing and credential renewal as well as providing other developmental opportunities such as new client groups, facilitating management, leadership programs and more.

SUPPORTING INTERNAL COACHING EFFORTS

Regardless of the size of your client base, you will need to figure out how you're going to track the information reported by all of your coaches, how you're going to analyze that information and how you're going to use the findings in a way that will drive business results and ensure the sustainability of your internal coaching program.

If your program is new, you may want to see what themes surface in the coaching conversation and then share those themes with your peer coaches. Establish some type of criteria. For example, if a certain issue comes up more than three times from three different coaches, and it's an issue that could negatively impact the business goals of the organization, then it's an issue that may be shared with the other coaches on the team (in a confidential way). Collectively, the coaching manager and the team can determine if there is a need for a specific solution or intervention to address the issue. Depending on the nature or severity of the issue, you may want to bring the concern forward to the business leader (again, in a way that protects the individuals involved). **Note:** Such issues need to be validated with the client organization or with leadership, depending on the issue. Do this prior to expending resources to design solutions.

Let me emphasize the significance of being an internal coach. As an internal coach, you are in a position where you can navigate the company's inner landscape effectively. You also should have a deeper understanding of the true business challenges and employee engagement issues versus noise in the system; therefore, not only making you a valuable contributor to achieving solutions but also a critical member of the client's team. Recognize your role and be aware of your responses and proceed accordingly.

Also, when identifying organizational issues, you will need to attune your listening skills and be able to distinguish between whining or venting and a real issue. Also, you will need to use strong inquiry skills in order to determine if the issue being raised is a local one or more global in nature, and if it's a localized issue or a deep, systemic problem that needs to be addressed in order to achieve the organization's goal.

Leadership Support

If you are trying to develop specific leadership capabilities in your client group, then you may want to track how much coaching time is being devoted to developing those capabilities, and the effectiveness of the approach. Again, bring your findings back to the team and collectively determine if an issue is systemic and requires additional solutions in order to resolve and/or enhance a specific business area or leadership competency.

For example, when we initially started the program at WorldCom, it was on the heels of the largest bankruptcy in U.S. history. It became clear very quickly that our sales and service leaders were struggling with the questions, concerns and new demands from our clients. Given that they were each working in their respective markets, many didn't realize that they were all facing similar challenges and they were each working independently to gather answers to the same questions. As the primary coach for the sales and service leaders, I brought the concern to the senior vice president of Sales and recommended that the leadership team be given a quick lesson on the rules of bankruptcy. I also suggested that it would be helpful to provide our employees with a forum to supply them with as much information as possible about what was going on: what the changes meant to them as employees and to their clients, and how to respond to inquiries from the clients.

We quickly established a weekly all-hands call, which provided employees (approximately 5,000) the opportunity to receive an update on what was happening, including an explanation of what it meant to them and what they should communicate to our customers. At such a difficult time, when you would think employee engagement would drop, it actually went up. Our employees rallied and really appreciated the open environment where anyone could ask the highest level of their leadership a question and not be embarrassed by the nature of the question or by the asking. I think it's fair to say that this initiative is a big reason that during this difficult time the company retained 100 percent of our key talent and customers.

THE COACHING ADMINISTRATION SYSTEM (CAS)

If your program is progressing and you have multiple coaches, you should consider implementing a coaching administration system or some other way to easily track overall program participation, issues and individual participant utilization. When there were only a couple of coaches at WorldCom and MCI, we used an Excel spreadsheet. When the program expanded, we continued with Excel but on a SharePoint site, and we engaged an analyst to consolidate and analyze the data.

When the program expanded again, and we had hundreds of program participants, we designed our own internal Coaching Administration System (CAS). Now, you don't necessarily need to build your own system; you may find that an existing talent management or learning management system has the capability and is a sufficient tool, or you may have a custom web-based solution. Whatever your approach, you will need to begin with a Statement of Business Requirements (SOBR) in order to determine what type of system will meet your needs.

A statement of business requirements, sometimes referred to as a Statement of Requirements (SOR), is a high-level statement of the objectives and needs of the organization and a description of the opportunities and/or problems that can be realized with the proposed solution. Articulating the goals and being specific in your desired outcomes will increase the probability of implementing a comprehensive solution. Once the SOBR is completed, the program manager can then share it with their business partner in IT, who can help devise a suitable solution. For more information about creating a SOBR and suggestions on what type of information should go into and be captured by your Coaching Administration System (CAS), please go to www.robertsoncoachinstitute.com.

CAS Access

You will also want to consider what levels of access you want to have for your coaching administration system (or process). It will depend on your particular situation, but generally speaking, my suggestion is that the manager be given access to everything in the system, in addition to your system administrator or the individual responsible for inputting the data, pulling information and conducting analyses. As for the coaches, each should have access to their client base and their specific information. This will enforce structure and confidentiality.

The primary importance of having a CAS is to take as much of the administrative, time-consuming and repeatable tasks and automate them. You hired the coaches to coach their clients, facilitate workshops, deliver leadership development programs and more. By having a system that can handle the transactional components of the coaches' work, you free up their time to do more of what you want them to do: coach. Plus, being able to track items like coaching conversation themes, hours allocated and hours utilized for coaching, the system can be beneficial in the planning and budgeting process as well as when it comes to designing learning and development solutions geared toward client concerns or areas for development opportunities.

CAS Benefits

Benefit #1: Allows you to move repetitive administrative tasks and much of the reporting function into the system. Therefore, the system can generate the reports and, depending on what is in your SOBR (Statement of Business Requirements), may provide some of the analysis also. (**Note:** You will need someone to input data, pull reports and analyze data at least part-time, depending on what your needs are and how sophisticated you build your system.)

Benefit #2: Enables you to track your coaches' activity so that you can determine how and where they are spending their time. This will help you ideally allocate their time and efforts to specific groups or types of work (for example, facilitation, consulting, one-on-one coaching).

Benefit #3: Helps you track your program's focus areas/issues/capabilities and how the coach and client are spending their time. This will help you plan more strategically as you can see where the organization is going and what its needs are, enabling you to forecast learning and development programs. In addition, it will help you allocate resources and funding for new programs, additional headcount and, just in case, program justification. Let's face it: people initiatives have a tendency to be first in line when budgets are being cut. Being able to effectively demonstrate how you spend your time, resources and funds, and the impact that the coaching program has on business and talent development, can be critical.

Benefit #4: The system's data output and its analysis can assist the business leaders of the individuals being coached in determining the "brand" of their department and help them to market their department to other groups in the company.

Benefit #5: The analysis that is a result of the data input into the system can help to identify, validate and isolate issues and challenges in a department or organization. By identifying challenges in this way, a solution can be developed and the problem can be solved more quickly than it might otherwise have been.

If you choose to go forward with implementing a system for your internal coaching program, it is important to think through the entire process from beginning to end, as implementing any new system can mean a certain level of effort and resources from your team and from your HR Information Systems (HRIS) or IT counterparts over a period of time. Also, remember that you will need to go through your planning and budgeting process and the HRIS and/or IT planning and budgeting process before reaching approval. Therefore, you must allocate sufficient time in your project plan for these activities. The following checklist is provided to help you with the process.

Checklist for a Coaching Administration System (CAS)

- ❏ Assign a project leader and a team of individuals to gather requirements and determine functionality of the system. (This could be an excellent assignment for a coach with a background in systems and IT or one that supports your IT or HR Information Systems (HRIS) client group.)

- ❏ Have the team prepare the Statement of Business Requirements (SOBR).

- ❏ Get SOBR approval from the internal coaching manager and HRIS manager.

- ❏ Decide if this should be a new system or an added component of an existing Learning Management System (LMS) or Talent Management System (TMS).

- ❏ Once a system decision is made, create employee data feeds to collect participant information in the CAS.

- ❏ Determine costs and timelines associated with creating and/or implementing the system.

- ❏ Submit funding requests and secure project funding.

- ❏ Prepare for and conduct User Acceptance Testing (UAT). Identify all problems (or as many as possible) that could cause delays in your system deployment, then proactively design solutions and workarounds.

- ❏ Identify and assign a systems administrator and determine access levels.

- ❏ Design and deliver systems training for all coaches and administrators.

- ❏ Go live with the system.

- ❏ Provide ongoing support for your coaches, and establish a process to inspect the system's data, its integrity and the timeliness of input.

COACHING & LEADERSHIP INSIGHT:
Use the Playbook to Lay the Foundation for a
Successful Program

It is important to remember that a strong internal coaching program starts with a robust plan, one that will lead to flawless execution and result in returning customers. As the old saying goes, fail to plan or plan to fail—the choice is yours. Therefore, taking the time to build an internal coaching program playbook and clearly communicating your expectations to your coaches will play a key role in the overall success of your program. Similarly, communicating to your clients what the goals of the program are and what a customer can expect will be just as important to your program's success. Remember, based on a client's experience they will either recommend or not recommend your program to others, and what they say about their experience can become the brand of your coaches and the overall coaching program. Therefore, by clearly defining and educating your coaches on their role, the processes and your expectations, of which everything can be defined and placed in your playbook, you leave little room for misinterpretation. This level of clarity, coupled with flawless execution, will result in a positive customer experience and a strong brand for your internal coaching program.

9

The Importance of a Winning Coaching Culture

As we begin to explore what makes for a winning coaching culture, let's look at how the *Merriam-Webster Dictionary* defines the term culture:

a: the integrated pattern of human knowledge, belief, and behavior that depends upon the capacity for learning and transmitting knowledge to succeeding generations

b: the customary beliefs, social forms, and material traits of a racial, religious, or social group; also: the characteristic features of everyday existence (as diversions or a way of life} shared by people in a place or time <popular culture> <southern *culture*>

c: the set of shared attitudes, values, goals, and practices that characterizes an institution or organization <a corporate culture focused on the bottom line>[1]

So when we talk about culture in relation to a company, it's the third definition of the word we're using. Now, an organization has its own unique corporate culture that is composed of the specific values, dynamics and beliefs that are important to, and espoused by, that organization. For example, here is how Google describes its culture:

> It's really the people that make Google the kind of company it is. We hire people who are smart and determined, and we favor ability over experience. Although Googlers share common goals and visions for the company, we hail from all walks of life and speak dozens of languages, reflecting the global audience that we serve. And when not at work, Googlers pursue interests ranging from cycling to beekeeping, from Frisbee to foxtrot.

---

[1] URL: www.meriam-webster.com/dictionary/culture

We strive to maintain the open culture often associated with startups, in which everyone is a hands-on contributor and feels comfortable sharing ideas and opinions. In our weekly all-hands ("TGIF") meetings—not to mention over email or in the cafe—Googlers ask questions directly to Larry, Sergey and other execs about any number of company issues. Our offices and cafes are designed to encourage interactions between Googlers within and across teams, and to spark conversation about work as well as play.[2]

Based on this description, it is clear that Google's culture is largely focused on its people and how they work and engage—which at the end of the day informs its corporate culture. However, Google is also clear about the need for smart, collaborative employees who come from diverse backgrounds and the need for everyone at Google to embrace the differences that individuals bring to the workplace. In addition, Google espouses an open workplace, where hierarchy is absent and where innovation, collaboration, inquisitiveness and a willingness to learn are fostered.

Does Google's culture translate into satisfied customers and success? It's hard to say this definitively I know, but clearly it's not hurting their success. Witness the company's incredible growth over the past ten years, as documented in a recent *Globe and Mail* article:

At 15, Google has reached middle age for a technology company. It remains the biggest success story of the Internet era; so far, no competitor has been able to mount a serious challenge to its dominance in web search, on every platform. This year [2013], it is expected to earn $12.7-billion (U.S.) in profit, and it has already become the third most valuable corporation in the United States behind only Apple Inc. and Exxon Mobil Corp. and surpassing, yes, even Microsoft Corp.[3]

WHAT'S GOOD ENOUGH FOR GOOGLE ... ?

You'll be interested to know, if you didn't already, that Eric Schmidt, former CEO and current executive chairman of Google, works with a business coach. Have a look at what he had to say in the article below (and at http://youtube/kIiwAcnSN1g),[4] which was written by Doris Kovic, business and executive coach of Leading Insight.

---

[2] URL: http://www.google.ca/about/company/facts/culture/
[3] Omar L. Akkad, "What's next for Google, the most successful Internet company in the world?" *The Globe and Mail*, Oct. 27, 2013.
[4] URL: http://ezinearticles.com/?5-Reasons-to-Hire-an-Executive-Coach&id=2691586

5 REASONS TO HIRE AN EXECUTIVE COACH

The best advice Eric Schmidt, Chairman and CEO of Google, ever got was to hire an executive coach.

Initially when board member John Doerr suggested this, Schmidt resisted because as an experienced CEO he didn't think he needed a coach. But now he is a big fan of coaching and states in an interview with *Fortune* magazine that "everyone needs a coach." Why would a successful executive—someone [as] talented as Eric Schmidt benefit from a coach?

Here are the top five reasons why leaders hire executive coaches.

1. **To gain perspective.** At the top of an organization you have a unique perspective, but it is also limited by your position of power. An executive coach is one of the few people [who] is able to tell you what you need to know, but cannot or will not see. Your coach can give you objective and constructive feedback on your blind spots, and provide an outside perspective on the business and your team.

2. **To discuss ideas that are still in the inkling stage and support you in making better decisions.** Ideas and strategy can grow through discussion. We all need a sounding board, but often the only people around us [who] we can talk to are those [who] are impacted by the decision. Coaching is a place to test out ideas and strategy with someone you trust who has no vested interest or competing agenda.

3. **Transitioning into a new bigger role.** "What got you here won't get you there." A good coach can help a leader hit the ground running in a new role. Past success can be a big impediment to moving up the ladder successfully, as we tend to repeat what has worked in the past even though it may not be appropriate in our new role. Executive coaching can accelerate the transition and ensure success.

4. **To have a secure, safe and confidential outlet to vent, when necessary.** Pent-up frustrations, anger and disappointments impair good judgment, and relationships. Everyone needs a safe place and an understanding person to complain to, to vent [to], and to talk things out [with].

5. **To stay ahead of the curve and become a better leader.** To win you need to continually upgrade your skills and think outside the box. Your coach will provide tools, training and insights that support you in playing your best game.

Source: By Doris Kovic, Business and Executive Coach of Leading Insight. San Clemente, CA. Please visit http://www.leadinginsight.com for more leadership articles. Used by permission.

I believe that having a culture which values learning and curiosity, coupled with a coaching component, can be a driving force in a company's competitive advantage in the marketplace—specifically if the culture is one in which employees are encouraged to be innovative and collaborative.

COACHING AND THE CHALLENGE OF INTEGRATING CULTURES

Let's look now at culture from an "across borders" perspective. The world in which many of us work is no longer isolated. Our employees and leaders are now required to have a global mindset. If companies want to achieve large-scale success, they need to understand the buying habits and cultural norms of people from all regions of the world. Internal coaching programs can be instrumental in providing organizations support in this area, and especially for leaders who are transferred or expatriated to other regions, or for companies large and small that have been the target of a merger. Which brings me to the integration of MCI, Inc., an international company with operations throughout Europe, Asia and South America, and Verizon Enterprise Solutions Group (ESG), a US-centric company, which happened in January 2006 and became Verizon Business. Let's turn the spotlight on these two companies and their heritage, and how an internal coaching program aided in the acceleration of the integration of two culturally diverse firms. There are many keys to a successful integration, and the intent of this section is not to discuss all of them, but rather to show how an internal coaching program can be leveraged to positively impact integration, minimize stress in the organization and accelerate the coming together as one company.

Months prior to MCI and Verizon ESG amalgamating, the coaching team at MCI began working with its sales leaders to help them prepare for the change that was coming. We designed a leadership conference entitled "Leading Change," and in an open forum we discussed the forthcoming integration and the realities and challenges that come with being acquired, including the possibility of loss of jobs. We studied the Verizon ESG leaders; the possibilities of who would land where on the organization charts; and their culture. We made certain each leader had a professional biography completed in Verizon's standard format that could be shared with their leaders as needed. In addition, we conducted with each of the vice presidents a personal SWOT analysis to help them determine their strengths, weaknesses, opportunities and threats as they (and their respective organizations) became integrated into the new company. Lastly, we coached them on what questions to anticipate from their new management and how to best position themselves within the new company. This proved to be excellent preparation for the changes to come, as everyone who was a part of the coaching program made it through the integration and, for the most part, all remained in position or were promoted within the initial one to two years following integration.

Now, at the onset of the integration of MCI and Verizon ESG, on the surface all looked like it was going to go smoothly—and for the most part it did. But from a coaching perspective, it was clear that, due to MCI having an entrepreneurial and egalitarian culture and Verizon having a much more hierarchical culture, there was going to be tension somewhere down the line. Remember, we knew there were going to be cultural challenges with integration based on the companies' differing heritages. When it originated, MCI's mission was to bring competition to the telecommunications industry. MCI founders and executives were risk-oriented business people. Their goal was to introduce competition and create better customer service for their customers. The working environment was fast-paced, innovative and collaborative. It had to be—the goal was to out-smart, out-run and out-produce Ma Bell, which was a huge undertaking. Its management were seen as gunslingers and cowboys, only interested in their own organizations and not very compliant with corporate directives (which wasn't too far from the truth, but underlying it all was a fierce dedication to the success of the company, not the individual). MCI's culture was field-based, which meant that decisions were made on the frontline and managers and leaders were empowered to make it happen (within reason, of course). The Verizon culture was steeped in history and regulation. Many employees were from the former Bell Atlantic and Nynex companies, which were spun off after the break-up of the Bell Companies or "Ma Bell." Most of these employees remained in their functional areas and sometimes exact jobs for most of their careers and they were comfortable in the way that they did their work. Coming from a regulated environment, many times they were required to do their work in very specific ways—what I refer to as "inside the box." Adapting to a more collaborative and empowering or "outside the box" approach was not an easy task. Verizon was perceived as stodgy and inflexible. It had a headquarters-based culture, which meant it was about ownership and control, and corporate management held the power. And like most new relationships, trust needed to be established, which is understandable. MCI had just come out of a treacherous ordeal with WorldCom that had led them to bankruptcy. I could see why, despite the due diligence, there would be a strong desire for the corporate Verizon officers to want to maintain control, given that they purchased MCI for $8.5 billion in cash and stock. It was a significant investment that came with great risk, and they wanted to ensure the success of their acquisition. The below model is an excellent depiction of the two companies' distinct cultures. It helps to crystalize the differences and areas where tension existed and opportunities for coaching.

CULTURAL IMPACT OF TWO MANAGEMENT APPROACHES	
Egalitarian Culture	**Hierarchical Culture**
Promotes empowerment	Promotes micro-management
Titles, degrees and age are less important than demonstrated ability	Titles, degrees and age are to be respected
All team members speak up	The senior person speaks up; others listen
Communication across all levels	Communication cascades from peers to subordinates
Servant leader	Paternalistic leader
Collaboration	Top-down information flow

Source: Derived from Global Dynamics Inc., 2011.

The internal coaching team saw the issues that were surfacing and the barriers that were preventing decisions from being made, work being accomplished and responses being provided to customers. We learned about the challenges through the coaching conversations we were having with our clients, and we began to address the issues at a one-to-one level within the confines of the coaching conversation.

As this conversation evolved and expanded into areas of collaboration, communication and leadership, I felt that a more holistic approach to coaching was necessary. We developed broad-based leadership development programs for leaders and managers who held different—even divergent—views of managing their people. The purpose behind these programs was, on the surface, to promote management and leadership development. However, we also knew that they could be used to create awareness for all parties who had different approaches to the business and their work. In addition, it put the coaching team in a position to facilitate the conversations that needed to occur in order to foster collaboration and create a high-performing culture that would benefit all parties.

Through our programs, we created a safe and neutral playing field where everyone had the opportunity to speak, be heard and be acknowledged. Our goal was to foster relationships built on mutual understanding and respect so that partnerships would form and the business could move forward. In addition, in these settings we were able to give the parties a new vocabulary that would contribute to facilitating a new culture at Verizon Business, one in which everyone could make a contribution. For example, in a few of the functional areas, we introduced Gallup's StrengthsFinder assessment and worked with leaders and their organizations on leveraging their strengths. This became a familiar concept to everyone and therefore employees and managers began to have conversations about their strengths, introducing new vernacular and creating one vocabulary everyone could use and relate to.

During this time, while we not only maintained our internal coaching presence in the sales and service organizations, we were asked to expand the program across other functional areas, such as Finance, Legal and IT. We continued to work with leaders and managers in key positions, supporting them as they faced the clashing cultures playing out in their own environments. We offered them support and collaborated with them on how to effectively bring the diverse teams together and achieve success for the client. These were incredible learning opportunities for our leaders that helped them to better handle conflict and manage diversity, leading them to achieve great success.

Let's face it—change is difficult. No matter how much you anticipate it and prepare for it, it is still change. Through our coaching program, we were able to provide a space where leaders and managers could have some strategic thinking time and coaching support to work through the many challenges of a merger and the changes that came with it. Frustrations were worked out privately, and the coaching provided an opportunity for leaders and managers to think through situations and come up with solutions on how to best handle challenging situations. No one sat idle or was stuck, the new entity progressed swiftly into its own.

KEYS TO SUCCESS DURING INTEGRATIONS

When it comes to culture, I believe that leadership is responsible for much of it and that employee engagement and trust are critical components in the employee–management relationship. For without a culture of trust, fear, uncertainty and doubt (FUD) will be present, and when there is FUD, employee engagement will be less than optimum, which will negatively affect the customer experience and therefore business results. Building a culture based on trust, collaboration, learning and coaching fosters a positive work environment. When employees are happy and engaged, good things happen. Simply put, employee engagement drives the customer experience, and the customer experience drives business results.

At Verizon Business we were incredibly fortunate to have a strong senior leadership team. They believed in having elements of learning, development and coaching in a company's culture. They realized the importance of developing leaders and employees—how the professional growth of each was directly connected to the company's results and its overall success, and how the environment in which employees work sets the tone for their productivity.

Think about it: If a company's culture values learning, the key messages that employees will hear from their organization will include the importance of learning and embracing new ideas in a collaborative setting. When employees see that their leadership supports professional development, it sends a strong signal to each of them. They'll understand the importance of investing in their own development, for the sake of their career as well as for the success and growth of the company. Once learning and development are embedded in the culture, then creating a coaching culture is a natural next step.

It is also important to understand the messages that leadership sends to their organizations and the impact of leaders' behavior on members of the organization. So I'd like to share a short personal story about my relationship with two members of the executive leadership team and the impact that they had on my professional development and the internal coaching program. I will always be grateful for their time that they shared with me and the lessons they helped me learn.

During a merger, the chief financial and chief human resources officers typically work closely together to integrate a company and, in our case, emerge with a new entity. I will never forget the day we had our first meeting. It was a Friday afternoon and I was called to the vice president of human resources office, where I met the head of HR and our chief financial officer (CFO). After being introduced, I was offered a cup of coffee and conversation would ensue.

Friday afternoon coffee chats would become an enjoyable routine. Our vice president of Human Resources always kept his door open and welcomed anyone who would enter. I was fortunate to have had the opportunity to partake in several of these Friday afternoon chats, along with whoever else popped in, and we would talk about our business challenges and careers. The VP mentored me in the ways of Verizon and talent management. In his view, your people are an invaluable asset to the company, and supporting them in their professional development is a critical service that Human Resources can provide to the business. He himself shared stories about how he was mentored too. This made me realize the importance of mentoring and I resolved to become a mentor too. In hindsight, these conversations were not only stimulating and thought-provoking, they are some of the most insightful conversations I have experienced.

During that initial meeting, however, little did I know that a test was about to begin. The meeting started off with the usual pleasantries, but very quickly the atmosphere began to change and I found myself on my toes and answering, in rapid fire, questions from our CFO such as, "I hear you are a coach; tell me what that means?" "Are you some kind of shrink?" "Why would a guy like me or someone in my organization need someone like you?"

I remember thinking to myself, "Is this for real?" I decided to let the games begin! I quipped back with, "No, I'm not a shrink; but you're the one sitting on the couch—do you need one?" Later on, I thought to myself, "Wow, I really took a risk saying that—maybe it was the coffee?" But I pride myself on quickly reading situations and people, and at the time it felt comfortable engaging in this way. I also knew that humor has always been one of the best tools in my personal toolkit—we all broke out in laughter and then began a serious conversation about coaching, talent development, and succession planning, and how my team could support his organization. We even discussed the business and I was asked about the legacy MCI sales strategies and product positioning, and even my thoughts on how to structure the new company.

Apparently, I had passed the test. I knew our business well. I understood the industry, our position within the industry, products and services. I also understood our employees, areas for opportunities, and areas of risk. I was able to clearly articulate my perspective and possible solutions. We discussed where there was tension in the system, the differences in the culture, and how to leverage the best of both companies. I demonstrated my open and collaborative style and how my team of coaches and I could bring value to the new company.

It became clear to our CFO that my team and I could be a strategic partner to his organization. Therefore, he invited me to work with him and his talented leadership team within the Finance organization. We would work collegially together in creating succession plans for his top talent; solving talent gaps and challenges; designing career assignments and opportunities to further develop the talent in his organization; and building a pipeline of ready talent for the Finance organization's succession plan. The CFO demonstrated that he is one of the best when it comes to understanding what his employees needed to learn and experience in order for them to move up in a finance capacity.

Passing the test with these gentlemen was a career-defining moment for me and for the internal coaching program at Verizon Business. I had secured the respect and trust of a C-Level Verizon Business executive (who, to boot, was not in my line, Human Resources, or from the legacy MCI side of management). The CFO's endorsement brought immediate visibility and credibility to the importance of talent development and our internal coaching program. Other executives took notice and engaged our services. This was a significant feather in the coaching program's cap.

Always be prepared to discuss what a coaching program can offer and what its value is to your company's overall business. You never know who will want to engage in conversation with you. Be on your game; be the master of your wheelhouse, your coaching program and your business, and understand how it intersects with your business and talent management strategies. If it were not for my ability and preparedness to engage on a deep and meaningful level about our business and how the coaching program could be of great benefit to our human capital, I am not sure I would have received executive endorsement, or the visible endorsement of other executive leaders.

Another example that illustrates the importance of executive support for an internal coaching program dates back to the original program at WorldCom. As I mentioned earlier, the executive sponsor of the program, Steve Young, became my first client. He truly welcomed the support as well as the insights he gleaned from seeing the business through the eyes of his coach. He was an ideal coaching client; he engaged in our coaching conversations and really enjoyed them, pushing me to raise my game as a coach, particularly with respect to how my role contributed to driving sales performance and results with our leaders—every day.

More importantly though, Steve was a great advocate for the program. He knew the challenges that WorldCom's employees, managers and sales executives faced as we fought our way through bankruptcy and struggled to retain our clients and our employees. Investing in our people and their professional development was a key development and retention strategy at a time when it would have been very easy for many to walk out the door.

Steve also knew how important employee retention was to developing a winning culture. The most important message to take away from this chapter is that your company's people and its culture are an extremely critical asset that a company can offer its employees.

And it is the leaders of the company who set the tone for creating and influencing the culture. In a winning culture, everyone wakes up each day and wants to do "good," be productive and make a contribution. We as human beings are naturally curious, and by working in a culture that is based on curiosity and that integrates coaching as a vehicle for success, we are set up to be engaged, productive and fulfilled.

10 Coaching Inside Sales Organizations

After graduating with a bachelor's degree in Political Science from Drew University, I was on a path to study law. I enjoyed studying history, politics and world affairs, but the thought of investing in law school and practicing law did not appeal to me. As much as I wanted to honor my parents' wish for me, my head and my heart were simply not in pursuing law and I made a decision to enter the workforce instead. As you can imagine, my parents were disappointed and could not believe that I was giving up the opportunity to study law and potentially become an attorney. Also of deep concern to them was that I wanted to be a salesperson. I am happy to report that today they are proud of my accomplishments and the career path I ended up choosing.

The first half of my career was spent primarily in sales roles in New Jersey, New York and Pennsylvania. Specifically, I started my career at MCI Telecommunications as a sales representative calling on medium-sized businesses in New Jersey. I started as a commercial sales representative and was the only woman on a team of eight, and it was one of the greatest learning experiences of my life. I was young and incredibly naive, and I knew little about telecommunications, prospecting, the sales process and business in general. My résumé up to that point included selling goods in a Hallmark store, selling a luxury line of women's clothing in an exclusive retail store, clerking in a law firm and working on political campaigns. (I have to say though, that each position served its purpose and provided me with basic sales and business experiences.) Despite my greenness, I was determined to hold my own among a team of competitive and, quite frankly, physically large and impressive former college athletes (I was every bit of 5'5" and maybe a hundred pounds). So I watched, listened and learned, letting them be my teachers.

This was a great time in our careers. The organization and my colleagues were all young, and we worked and played hard as we climbed our career ladders and enjoyed the benefits of success—making good money and winning sales contests and trips to places such as Maui, Lake Tahoe and Banff. We also enjoyed playing softball against other branches and at the annual MCI softball tournament in Towson, Maryland. We took the expression "work hard, play hard" literally. These years were truly a highlight of my life, spent with wonderful colleagues and filled with lots of learning and laughs.

Before the end of my first year at MCI, it all began to click and my career progressed. I found myself on a fast-moving track filled with learning and experiences that would serve me well throughout my career. Over my thirteen years working inside Sales organizations, I received eight promotions and rotational assignments. As a result of my hard work and sales and customer service competencies, I received over fifteen prestigious awards and was recognized nearly one hundred times, either monthly or quarterly, for outstanding performance. Each assignment allowed me to learn about different vertical markets; how local, state and federal government agencies do business; and about selling to a variety of industries, from universities and hospitals to hotels and pharmaceutical and insurance companies. I was also given the opportunity to secure, manage and grow large, complex global accounts such as Becton, Dickinson and Company and AIG. Each recognition and new responsibility I was given increased my confidence and assured me in my career choice.

THE IMPORTANCE OF UNDERSTANDING SALES PROFESSIONALS

So as you can see, I have a fair amount of sales DNA intertwined with my talent management DNA, and as a result I find myself in a unique position when working with my clients. Given my knowledge of telecommunications and IT technologies, sales, customer service, procurement of contracts and account management, coupled with my experiences working with clients in multiple industries, I instinctively begin any type of coaching engagement as I would begin to engage a potential sales client. The starting point is an assessment and analysis of the client's organization, including its achievements, goals and current state, the opportunities and challenges it has, and its strengths and weaknesses.

The key is to learn as much as you can about your clients and their organization so that you can design coaching solutions that will best serve them. This is the first step in any sales process, and by doing so you are actually mirroring what your sales clients do in turn with their clients. Your focused and thoughtful questions will convey your authentic interest in them and their business. It will feel very comfortable to your potential clients and they may actually enjoy not being in the role of the salesperson for once. However, on the flip side, because these are experienced sales professionals they can be your toughest critics if your sales approach, solution or execution is in any way flawed. They may respond to you in a manner similar to how their clients respond to them. For example, sometimes customers have a "vendor mentality." By this I mean that they treat you like someone who merely provides their product or service and is dispensable. In these types of relationships, it is more about the actual transaction and not about the value or actual service that you provide to the customer. On the other hand, there is what is referred to as a "partner mentality," which exists when the client truly values your relationship, experience and services. They see the benefit of having you involved in their business, so they include you in critical meetings and support you in your work with them. This is the ideal relationship and one that any coach or consultant should strive for with their clients. In either case, it is important to know where you stand, and be prepared to engage and execute accordingly—and flawlessly.

> It is imperative that coaches working inside Sales organizations have knowledge and experience working in, or adjacent to, Sales organizations.

CHARACTERISTICS OF THE SALES PROFESSIONAL

Salespeople are a unique breed and very different than the typical employee. After all, they are the primary reason that your company stays in business, since they are responsible for the revenue and growth of the company (as long as your research and development arms provide them with a product, of course). Salespeople are the ones who bring the business in the door. Now, don't get me wrong—all employees are important and each function plays a critical role with respect to the customer and the company. However, I sincerely believe that it takes a certain type of individual to be a salesperson.

When it comes to the differences between sales professionals and other employees, one of the main distinctions is the constant pressure of having to meet monthly quotas and inspect daily sales reports, as well as having your income determined every month by your success or lack thereof. That pressure is responsible for salespeople's sometimes overstressed natures, and yes, sometimes feeds inflated egos. "I know that I am a much more easygoing and likeable person now than when I was carrying a number for thirty years," states Steve Young. And I know the same holds true for me and just about every retired or former sales professional that I know. Although I am more easygoing now, I still behave with the same sense of urgency and focus on results as I did when I was carrying a "bag" or "number" (both of which are sales speak for quota).

As coaches, human resources professionals and business leaders, we need to be aware of the intense stresses on salespeople and acknowledge them in their coaching sessions and in their development plans. For one thing, when coaching sales professionals, coaching sessions should ideally occur outside of prime selling time—before work, at breakfast, during lunch or over a coffee break. This is in order not to compete with their customer or selling time. As a sales coach, I have always offered to coach my sales clients at these times, as well as evenings and weekends. On Saturdays and Sundays especially, salespeople are able to take time to step away from their daily pressures, breathe and clearly focus on themselves and their professional goals.

Another critical point to consider when working with sales professionals is how much of their behavior is driven by the desire for recognition. As human beings, we all have a need for our efforts to be acknowledged and praised, but this need is much stronger in sales professionals. Salespeople typically crave acknowledgment more than money. For them money is simply a way of keeping score and, of course, paying the bills.

I recall when I was working with my first coach, Laura Berman-Fortgang (whom I spoke about in Chapter 1), she asked me to complete a values assignment. At first pass, everything that I valued was extrinsically driven, and it took several repetitions of the exercise for me to reconnect with my core values. It wasn't that I didn't know what my core values were, it was that I had been so conditioned to perform and win (at a cost), and I was driven by the recognition I received from winning sales contests, prizes and making more money. More money meant I could afford to shop in the finest boutiques, and buy luxury suits, shoes and handbags, as well as drive luxury cars such as a BMW,

Audi or Mercedes—further ways I could be recognized for my success. It is easy to lose sight of what is important if we are always focused outside of ourselves and, at the time, these material things were extremely important to me; it was about keeping score and demonstrating my professional achievements.

Now, don't get me wrong, I love luxury goods and driving a nice car, and anyone who knows me is familiar with my affection for the finer things in life—it is part of who I am. I'm not sure if it was always who I am, although I do recall developing an affinity for finer things as I transitioned from childhood into adulthood. Being in sales and constantly aiming to deliver the best customer service placed a brighter light on my desire for quality goods and superior customer service. I still recall the opening of Nordstrom at the Short Hills Mall in New Jersey—I thought I had died and gone to heaven.

But I digress. Moving on, let's look at a common not-so-positive generalization that is applied to sales professionals. Everyone is familiar with stories or has had experiences in which sales professionals behaved unethically or dishonestly, and yes, there are salespeople who fall into this category. There are unethical and dishonest people in all professions, but for some reason sales professionals have this reputation more so than others, which is unfair. I have worked with enough of them over the years to know that for every one salesperson who has questionable morals, there are several honest, stand-up sales professionals who take pride in their work. So my request to coaches or human resources professionals who may have an unfavorable opinion about people in sales is this: Before you pass judgment on these individuals who are trying to make a living just like you are, take some time to get to know them. Understand what is truly important to them in relation to who they are, not what they do. Also, ask yourself, "What would be the state of our business if we did not have a Sales organization?" And then, "How can I be of service to them?" (Quite frankly, the answer to this may be to just get out of their way.)

It's important to realize that sales professionals are always on the firing line. They are responsible for consistently making their quota, and failure to do so puts them at risk of being placed on a performance plan and potentially losing their jobs. How many other positions are you aware of within an organization that are under that degree of pressure? Unlike other functional roles, the salesperson's performance is totally exposed. This can be perceived as a blessing or a curse. It is a blessing to be able to easily determine if sales milestones are being met, so that course-correction can be taken if they are not. The curse is that there is often not a direct line between one's results and one's ability to perform. The challenge can be determining which variables are contributing to or otherwise hindering performance. There can be many variables, including:

- **Economic conditions** – What is happening in the economy? Is the economy rising and therefore all business is growing, or is there a downturn? Even the best of sales professionals struggle in economic downturns and recessions.

- **Industry trends specific to your industry** – Are all companies doing well? Is your industry experiencing a downturn?

- **The deck of accounts or territory and your company's position in each account or territory** – Is your company viewed as the market leader or a new player in the field? The answer to this will determine the level of effort it will take to grow revenue from specific accounts or territories.

- **The sales capabilities of the individual or the team** – Are they seasoned? New to role? New to industry or to the company?

- **The scope of the products and services (i.e., solutions) your company offers** – Are they superior to the competition or subpar? Are there competitive advantages that make it easier to sell through to certain types of clients?

- **The personality and dynamics of doing business with the client** – Is the client difficult to work with? Do they consider companies they do business with partners or vendors? Do they have a complex procurement and contract process, or do they select those they want to do business with and make the procurement process work for them?

- **Any pre-existing or previous issues the client or account may have had with your company its products/services or its customer service** – Do these exist? What level of impact do any pre-existing conditions have on the sales process and the ability to sell services into the account?

Something else that can affect the performance of a sales professional, which is unique to their job, is that their performance is posted publicly for anyone inside the company to see. What are known as "stack rankings" are posted daily, which allow salespeople to see how they are performing *vis-à-vis* their peers. This makes it clear who the top performers are and who the bottom performers are. The rankings can act as an incentive, especially for those who are doing well, but on the flip side, the rankings can be demoralizing for those who aren't performing well, which can perpetuate poor performance.

The message here is that there are lots of opportunities to coach in each of the variable areas that may affect a salesperson's performance. However, it is important to note that, as a coach, you do not want to be in a situation where you are coaching someone who is consistently a poor performer; therefore, it will be important to assess the potential coaching engagement and determine if the individual is a strong candidate for coaching. This is particularly important when it comes to sales professionals, as a sales professional who is consistently underperforming is usually required to achieve their targets or be placed on a performance plan. If they are placed on such a plan, they may have a very short timeframe to make certain goals and therefore need to be 100 percent focused on doing whatever it takes to achieve their goals. In these situations, the salesperson may feel that their employment with the company may be short lived, so they may also be preoccupied with looking for another job. This is why introducing coaching in these situations is not recommended and the coach should expend their time and energy elsewhere.

The bottom line is, as a coach it's important to realize that coaching a salesperson, manager or executive is very different than coaching almost any other type of employee. Given the distinctions, coaches who would like to work in the Sales space should be extremely familiar with Sales and ideally have worked within a Sales organization or an adjacent one, like Marketing, for a fair amount of time. This will ensure sufficient understanding of sales, sales operations, account management and more. Personal experience and knowledge will add to your credibility and increase the likelihood of the sales professional's willingness to engage with you.

THE LIFE OF A SALES PROFESSIONAL

Like many salespeople, I am full of war stories about how and when large accounts were won, the trials and tribulations of complex contract negotiations and, of course, fun times spent with clients playing golf, having dinner and meeting their families. Some of my funniest memories are from early on in my career and involve my first branch director at MCI. One time while playing golf at Fiddler's Elbow in Bedminster, New Jersey, with clients who at the time were from Reckitt & Coleman, the director inadvertently tipped one of the clients from the golf cart as I followed with the other client who happened to be responsible for IT & telecommunications for Reckitt & Coleman. The good news is that no one was hurt. The better news was that we all laughed so hard and the best news is we picked up more business.

My first director and this client in particular were wonderful role models for me early in my career. My director at the time was and remains the ultimate sales professional with a strong natural curiosity, which means he is a constant learner with admirable energy and passion for his work and an inspiration for all. When I think of him, I always smile, as he is not only a bright and funny person, he always does the right thing for the client and ensures that they have the best experience (perhaps this is where I began to learn about making certain my clients always have the best experience possible). My client was very much like my director—he was a kind, warm, funny man and an amazing technologist who also always did the right thing simply because it was the right thing to do. These gentlemen taught me a lot about the telecommunications industry and sales specifically, helping me to lay a strong foundation in business. You could say that they were among my initial career coaches, and for that I am grateful.

Riding the Rails with NJ Transit

The gentlemen responsible for IT & telecommunications at NJ Transit at the time provided me some of the best sales stories and learnings in my career. Our paths crossed in 1990 when NJ Transit was assigned to me. After spending much time learning their business—visiting their control and maintenance centers and learning about their network—my perseverance paid off with winning a new client for MCI, which was one of the largest Tariff 12 accounts in AT&T's home state. Before I go on, let me take a moment to explain the definition of a Tariff 12 and why winning a Tariff 12 customer was such a big deal, as well as give you some background so you'll have a sense of the industry and its mood at the time.

The breakup or divestiture of AT&T Corporation (the telephone company sometimes referred to as Ma Bell) was mandated in January 1982 and placed into effect in January 1984. This meant that, for the first time, the telephone company was now divided into multiple regional phone companies responsible for providing local phone service to their customers. In addition, it would no longer be able to secure equipment from Western Electric, an AT&T

subsidiary. AT&T would be solely a long-distance carrier and would be forced to compete directly against other carriers such as MCI. In order to retain its large customers as well as the federal and local government clients, AT&T designed and began to offer "Tariff 12" contracts for telecommunications services. These contracts included a defined set of services and prices for the specific group or customer. Given this was the first time AT&T was able to compete on price, these contracts required high levels of scrutiny and senior executive approval. AT&T was loath to lose one of these contracts because it would not only represent a significant revenue loss to the company, it would create lots of attention from executives across the company—and I am not talking about the positive kind of recognition that salespeople seek. Therefore, a loss of a Tariff 12 would be a big problem for AT&T and the sales team responsible for maintaining the contract.

Now, back to New Jersey Transit. My potential clients are known for their sense of humor, and it was in keeping with their celebrated sense of humor that they went about telling me I had won their telecommunications business. They were scheduled to make their decision and communicate it to both MCI and AT&T during the week of September 22, 1991, which happened to be two days after my wedding. I left for my honeymoon in Bermuda on September 21 and, as you can imagine, as a new bride one of the last things on my mind was work; however, I could not help but think about the outcome of the RFP (request for proposal), and the strangest thing happened. It was day five of my honeymoon and I received a call from the front desk to let me know a fax had arrived, which seemed odd because only friends and family knew what hotel I was staying at. I immediately went down to the business office and picked up the envelope with the fax and opened it in my room. Inside was the best wedding gift: It was the AT&T symbol crossed out (similar to the Ghostbusters' logo). At first I wasn't sure what it meant, but each day I would receive more faxes, all of the AT&T logo crossed out, until I received the pièce de résistance: the actual Letter of Intent (LOI) from the client indicating that MCI had won the business! This was definitely one of the best jokes that a client has ever played on me.

Now, I make light of the relationship with this story, but I must make clear that these gentlemen had high expectations of me and, through their constant questions and engagement, ensured that I was always at the top of my game and the best sales professional that I could be. They taught me the importance of good customer service—an early and important business lesson.

AIG—The Biggest of the Fish to Catch

Another lesson learned was during my time working to win AIG as a client for MCI. AIG was also an AT&T Tariff 12 customer and spent hundreds of millions of dollars on its telecommunications. At the time, MCI had less than 1 percent of AIG's telecommunications business. It took many sales calls and a significant effort on my end to forge relationships with critical decision makers at AIG. They determined which providers would have what parts and percentages of AIG's telecommunications, equipment and professional services business. After many sales calls that required great perseverance and fortitude, and managing the daily challenges presented by this extremely demanding client, I was able to achieve a position in the account where MCI became AIG's secondary or back-up network to AT&T (and this was only the beginning). Win number one!

This was an incredible win for MCI, even though it only represented a small portion of the business. It meant that MCI was now considered a viable provider, and we would be able to position ourselves to go after the remaining hundreds of millions of dollars of opportunity still held by AT&T. So, putting all of my lessons learned to work, I secured a cube on site and worked from AIG's offices daily. I made myself and the MCI brand visible and ensured that we provided the highest levels of customer service possible. We had to, AT&T was there in full force; we were outmanned and outpriced. But I knew we could beat them with our customer service. Therefore, we turned it on, thanks in large part to my customer service partner. When it came to customer service at MCI, she was one of the best. She and I always made ourselves available and supported AIG to the best of our abilities. So when it came time to bid on their global network, thanks to our proven ability to provide comparable services domestically and to outshine our competition on customer service, we became a viable contender for their international network RFP, which was valued at hundreds of millions of dollars. Our second win!

The RFP process was arduous and competitive. AT&T had heavy artillery in terms of their executive positioning with AIG, their Tariff 12, and a sales and service team that was easily 2:1 (for every MCI employee that was assigned or worked on the AIG account, AT&T had at least two). Therefore, we were always outmanned and had to work twice as hard to be visible and maintain pace with our competitors. However, with MCI's expert business development team, we were able to design a competitive proposal and secure the award. Win number three!

However, being awarded the business was only half the battle. The next stage would be to negotiate a contract, and AIG brought in the big guns to conduct their negotiations—a top-tier firm, LB3, with leading communications lawyers who represented large complex clients. A senior partner at LB3 was brought in to handle the negotiations, and with her we (myself, a representative from the Business Development team and our counsel for MCI—all three women) stayed locked in a room for days negotiating the contract point by point. It was an invaluable lesson for me, proving that it really "ain't over until the ink on the contract is dry!" I am grateful to these ladies for their expertise, leadership and support, and for the grace with which they did their jobs during these very difficult negotiations. After a couple of weeks, we were able to secure a signed contract. Win number four! That experience impressed upon me the true guts and strength that were necessary to succeed in sales and in business.

You may be wondering why I am sharing these stories. Well, it's because I want to make certain that the complex and stressful role of a sales professional is clearly understood by anyone who chooses to work with or support this type of professional. Specifically, that it's understood by those of you who may think that a sales job is only about winning a piece of business. Try to look beyond the actual sale and think about everything that is expected from sales professionals: strong business acumen; critical, analytical and financial skills; personal fortitude; excellent collaboration, communication and presentation skills; and the ability to be (and know when to be) creative and innovative. You need to understand the attributes that contribute to a successful sales professional before you pass judgment on them and certainly before you can be an effective coach for them.

SELLING MY COACHING PROGRAM

Sales organizations are typically composed of people who handle rejection well, enjoy and thrive in a competitive environment, and simply enjoy winning. The atmosphere on a sales floor might remind you of a team locker room where the "players" are full of jokes, pranking each other, talking breezily about challenging contract negotiations and RFPs, and delivering quips and cuts at one another faster than you can blink. I had a lot of great experiences in sales, but one of my best sales experiences did not occur on the sales floor. Let me tell you that story now.

When Verizon acquired MCI, I was so busy working with the leaders and teams in the Sales organization, preparing them for integration, that I had little time to think about my role and what would happen to me or the rest of the coaching team. However, unbeknownst to me, Steve Young and our CEO and president at the time were thinking about us and had my back.

As you might expect in a merger situation, there was a significant amount of due diligence, and it became clear that the internal coaching program could not fly under the radar of such scrutiny, nor should it. They brought the program to the attention of the president of Verizon Business, and directed them to speak with the head of Human Resources. If he bought into the program, it would move to his organization. If he didn't, it was over. When I spoke to Steve about this recently, he shared the following with me:

> I realized that the program had come of age and needed to be expanded to other parts of the company. I also felt confident that with you in charge, you would get the support and the resources needed to continue to grow the program. However, I wasn't going to betray your trust in me by telling you that you had to go with it. The decision would be yours, you would have all of my support, if you wanted to move to Human Resources.

Now, being the salesperson that I am, I wanted to make certain that I closed the deal and our coaching team was viewed as a valuable asset to the newly merged organization. I did not want to see my team moved over and then subsequently be used as headcount for a possible workforce reduction (which is quite common following a merger). So I graciously accepted their support and began to build a strong brand with the new head of Human Resources. I realized, many years later, that Steve and his boss at the time had greased the skids, but at this point I felt that ensuring the program's survival was incumbent upon me, and I wasn't going to jeopardize the fate of my team's positions and my own position of "coach" that I loved. I was going to take responsibility and make certain the head of Human Resources understood the value of what he was about to acquire. To do this, I approached the situation like a salesperson. So what did I do? I designed an account plan and made a proposal!

Thinking in these terms, Verizon was an investment account, one without any prior relationship, an unknown, and one that would require time, relationship building and trust. They would have the same feeling about me and my team. So I thought to myself, Who can help me position myself in this new account? What will I need to do? How can I build trust and do so quickly? I would need to borrow trust to accelerate this relationship. With that thought, a dear friend and colleague came to mind.

She was a human resources director at Verizon and also a member of the ICF's Internal Coaching Committee, of which I was the chairperson. So, I reached out and asked her if she knew the vice president of Human Resources and, if so, if she would feel comfortable making an introduction. She was delighted that I asked her. It turned out that she knew him well, as they were both from GTE and had worked together. So she sent an e-mail introducing him and me to one another, and she provided a glowing endorsement. From there, I knew the rest was up to me.

I sent the vice president of Human Resources a follow-up to the director's introductory e-mail and requested a meeting. In my e-mail I included the press release announcing MCI as the recipient of the ICF's Prism Award, a brief PowerPoint presentation on our internal coaching program and my professional bio (in standard Verizon format). He replied and requested that I meet with him in his office in the next few days. As you can imagine, I was ecstatic and nervous at the same time.

I prepared for the meeting and arrived at the new Verizon campus to meet with the vice president in his office. He was warm and welcoming, and the meeting went well. I could actually see myself working for him and being part of the Human Resources team. In my estimation, he was smart, collegial and had a great sense of humor and collaborative style. We discussed our careers, backgrounds and families. It was clear that our values and work ethic were very similar.

After the meeting, he said he liked what I presented and welcomed me into his organization. There was a place for me as the director of Talent Development. I would report to the new vice president of Learning & Development, and my coaching team would remain intact and continue to report to me. This assignment was new to my new manager as well, as her background was in sales and marketing. She was bright, assertive and a terrific role model for me. Coming from Verizon, she knew its players well and understood how to navigate across Verizon, or what I refer to as the "Big V." We were both high performers and looked at everything we did through the lens of the business.

Needless to say, we made a great team and enjoyed collaborating as we built the learning and development infrastructure and training and coaching programs for the newly formed company, Verizon Business.

My coaching team and I continued to coach within the Sales organization but also expanded our role into the Global Sales and the Customer Service organizations of the company, and subsequently into the other functional areas as well. In addition, my role expanded and I was given additional responsibilities such as succession planning, performance management and employee and leadership development. As the year went on, my areas of responsibility continued to grow and went on to include executive search and placement, implementing a talent management system, compliance and ethics training, as well as diversity and inclusion programs. I was continuously challenged with new responsibilities and thrived with each new project. In doing so, I was able to contribute to an incredible Human Resources organization.

In hindsight, I see that this was a strong move for my MCI sponsors, as it enabled them to have one of their own on the inside of the big Verizon machine and establish credibility with their new boss. By securing a "win" for me, it enabled them to secure a "win" in return. This idea goes back to my experience negotiating the AIG contract—it was all about give and take and determining what you were willing to give in order to get. Yet another business lesson learned.

COACHING AND FACILITATING THE SALES FORCE

There are some key coaching areas to be considered when coaching inside Sales organizations. To begin with, let's look at the "science" side of sales, starting with coaching around the "Go-to-Market" strategy. In this area, topics that can surface during a coaching conversation may relate to channel organization or how the sales force is organized inside the company's Sales organization in order to market or sell to specific customers. For example, will the salespeople sell direct (directly to the client), indirect or through partners (through another entity in order to reach the customer), or has the company established sales centers where internal sales representatives reach a customer audience through telemarketing.

When a company is organizing or reorganizing its sales force as a result of a merger or due to new product or service offerings, these are activities that trigger coaching opportunities. Because the event causes change inside the Sales organization, leaders and managers are required to think through and redesign their organizational structure and account assignments, build new teams and determine how they will "go to market" in light of the change or new goal that is placed upon them. Often the sales manager or leader of the organization can benefit from having a coach to help them think through the change, consider the multiple opportunities that arise from it, and determine how best to align their sales force in order to have success in the marketplace and achieve their goals. In addition, if there is a team involved in the decision-making process, or a combination of the Sales and Marketing organizations, the coach can act as a facilitator of the discussion or be an active participant asking questions or surfacing points that one may not be comfortable raising with the other side.

In addition to aligning with the Go-to-Market strategy, it is important to design sales methodologies to support the type of product/service and sales strategy necessary to properly serve customers. For example, in defining sales methodologies, you need to look at the type of sale by asking the following questions:

- Are you selling a commodity, or utilities?

- Does your product or service call for strategic thinking, or is the product you are selling more of a single transaction that can be sold over the phone?

- How complex is your product or service?

- Are you building a solution? Will it require strategic thinking and multiple interactions with the customer?

- What is the life cycle of the product and how does it live within your client's ecosystem?

- Will strong customer relationships be required or be beneficial in order to make the sale and continue to grow business with specific clients?

These are just some of the questions that sales and marketing leaders need to ask themselves as they're defining their sales methodologies to align with whatever changes are being made to the company or its product offerings. When the leaders are considering these things, it's a great opportunity for a coach to lead a facilitated discussion with the Sales and Marketing teams or talk one-to-one with the sales and marketing leaders who need to design and/or execute the new plan.

One situation where a coach can be particularly useful is when the topic of segmentation is being discussed, as it is a conversation that can cause heated debate. Specifically, how will the territories be organized? Will they be set up by geographic region? Will vertical markets be established? Or will organization be decided by the size of the account or history of the account? Throughout my years in sales, I believe I have experienced every type of design possible, and with each reorganization there is much debate and concern over each and every change. Which is why these are excellent topics for a coach-led discussion. The coach can ensure that the conversation stays on point, that all sides are heard and that a decision is reached in an efficient manner. In addition, the coach can continue to work with each decision maker or leader responsible for the implementation of the decision to ensure that it is executed accordingly in each territory or region.

> From my experiences being involved with several sales reorganizations and restructuring of accounts and territories, one thing I can tell you is that change can be positive and beneficial for some salespeople and not so positive or beneficial for others. Therefore, as with any major change, a clear change management and communications plan is required to minimize the impact on the engagement levels of the employees who are affected by the change. In addition, having coaches assigned to support the managers and key individuals impacted by the change can help them adapt to the new structure or environment more quickly, thus contributing to a strong retention strategy.

Another area that coaches working inside Sales organizations can become involved with, either from a coaching or a facilitation perspective, is the area known as "sales process and tools." This can encompass account planning and management, strategy sessions and opportunity planning, reporting, customer relationship management (CRM), and the necessary sales cadence for each of these activities. These are not only topics that can be focal points in a coaching conversation, they also represent an excellent opportunity for the coach to facilitate the discussion or act as a member of the team during account planning or strategy discussions. The coach is trained to listen and observe and ask questions that may not be on the minds of the typical sales, service and marketing individuals who are sitting around the table. (**Note:** I must caution you, especially if you do not have experience in sales or have not been trained and certified as a sales coach, there will be a low tolerance for naive questions about the sales process and tools mentioned above. Strong sales professionals usually have a lot on their plate and will want the coach and anyone around the table to be able to make an informed contribution to support their clients and their sales success.)

Lastly, the other critical topics that can surface during a sales coaching conversation relate to metrics and rewards. Sales activities and terms that fall under the metrics and rewards category include the following:

- **Sales quota** – the amount of selling or units a salesperson is expected to meet over a given period of time

- **Sales forecast** – the expectation, based on probability, of specific sales and revenue that will be achieved over a specific given period of time

- **Sales pipeline management** – the activity of managing where each sales opportunity lies within the stages of the sales process, including:

  - Lead or prospect – potential consumer of the seller's products or services.

  - Qualified prospect – a potential client who has expressed interest for the products or services of the seller

  - Committed – the customer has confirmed that your products or services have been chosen

  - Closed – the contract or purchase order has been completed

- **Revenue recognition** – accounting principle for when the actual revenue from the sale is recognized by the seller's company

- **Sales reporting** – daily sales, new logos, stack rankings, sales and revenue, sales contests and special recognition awards are some of the reports and topics that sales leaders and sales professionals scrutinize and discuss on a regular basis

- **Sales compensation terms** – such as commissions, bonuses and SPIF (sales performance or promotion incentive fund)

These are all terms and topics that may surface when working with sales leaders, managers and professionals. As the coach, you must make certain that you understand each of them and their importance to sales professionals and organizations.

MCI's Return on an Internal Sales Coaching Program

At MCI, we ran an impact study on our internal sales coaching program that was delivered to the Sales organization, which was responsible for $10 billion in revenue. The organization was composed of accounts and prospects in the enterprise and the federal, state and local government vertical markets. The personnel structure included 6 regional vice presidents, 45 branch directors, 250 sales managers and 3,200 sales and technical professionals. In order to support the sales arm of the company, our internal coaching program focus areas and goals were to:

- retain key customers and employees
- achieve sales and revenue targets
- build and retain top talent
- maintain customers and improve the customer experience
- accelerate leadership development

We felt that it was each manager's responsibility to develop their people and contribute to the talent pipeline. Our belief was that if you invested in your leaders, the results will follow. We also believed strongly in "inspecting what you expect" and to always be thinking about your legacy as well as what, as the managers, we would do to replace ourselves when the time came to be rotated or promoted.

Once the bankruptcy was over, the MCI Internal Coaching Program was redesigned to act as a top-down Sales organization initiative that would ensure alignment, employee engagement and results while supporting the shift to a new sales methodology.

A key element of the program was to recognize the importance of all sales and service managers as drivers of the culture, performance and results. We added coaching to training programs and to operation reviews and account planning. We taught sales and service leaders to coach and to take responsibility for their legacy. We leveraged a "just-in-time" coaching approach to all aspects of the business and implemented a playbook approach to drive alignment, discipline and an underlying cadence to the system. We met each employee/team where they were and designed solutions to close gaps and drive performance. In our program, we had 160 managers and executives in the coaching program. Of the total participants, 69 percent responded to a survey we conducted about their experience with the coaching program. Some results from that survey follow here, and the full report can be found at www.robertsoncoachinstitute.com.

- **98%** experienced improvement in their overall effectiveness.
- **49%** calculated an increase in revenues in the range of $50k–$250k.
- Many indicated that alignment of business priorities and employee satisfaction were strategic to their success.

As it related to sales and the customer experience, respondents indicated that they achieved a:

- **15%** increase in revenues
- **23%** increase in sales opportunities

In the talent management category, the findings were as follows:

- Retained **100%** of key management and employee talent
- **27%** of coaching program participants received a promotion during or immediately following their participation in the coaching program

Now, you may ask yourself, how do I know if my Sales organization could benefit from an internal coaching program? My suggestion would be to use the Environmental Coaching Assessment in Chapter 7 and also ask yourself these questions:

- How would you describe the culture and performance of your Sales organization?
- How engaged are the employees? How are their results?
- On a scale of 1–10 (1 being the lowest), where would you rate the leaders, managers and employees on how prepared they are for the future of the industry?

If your answers to these questions lead you to feel that your Sales organization could benefit from an internal coaching program, think about what areas could use the most support. Following are some other possibilities for how coaching could be delivered to the Sales organization.

Sales executive coaching. This type of engagement involves one-to-one coaching for executive-level sales leaders. The coaching agenda is co-designed by the sales executive and their manager. Common focus areas include leadership style, increasing engagement and results, executive presentations, and enhancing the customer experience.

Sales manager coaching. In my view, this is the most applicable area for coaching within a Sales organization. As we know, front-line managers are critical to employee engagement and performance. They are the connection point between the front-line employee, the customer and the leaders, and are responsible for all day-to-day sales activities and the execution of the sales plan. Therefore, ensuring the development of sales managers is critical to any Sales organization's success. This type of engagement provides one-to-one coaching for sales managers, and the coaching agenda is co-designed between the sales manager and his manager. Potential focus areas may include management, communication and coaching skills; presence and presentation skills; and day-to-day sales operations such as forecasting, funnel management, account planning, building customer relationships and sales force engagement.

Sales effectiveness coaching. This type of coaching is beneficial for sales managers or representatives who may require or would like to secure real-time feedback on their sales effectiveness. A coach observes the participant for a half day or full day, providing in-the-moment coaching and feedback based on pre-established objectives. The engagement is customized for each participant and can be applied to all levels of leadership and individual contributors.

Sales force performance programs. These can be customized in such a way that allows you to work with your sales leaders in order to reinforce the sales methodology of choice. The approach uses one-to-one coaching to drive more comprehensive account plans, improved client relationships, deeper funnels and better results.

On a leadership note, it is just as important to teach leadership capabilities to sales managers and leaders. Therefore, you will want to make certain that you offer foundational leadership development programs for members of the Sales organization, including individual contributors, new supervisors, managers and executives. Also, be sure to provide programs for those who have not had any formal leadership development or who would like a refresher.

COACHING & LEADERSHIP INSIGHT:
Closing the Sales

I find coaching inside a Sales organization to be thrilling and challenging at the same time. It's great to be so close to where the revenue meets the door; however, it can also be hard work engaging clients and building your credibility in their eyes. Therefore, it is imperative, as an internal or external sales coach, to be well versed in sales or have sales experience and be able to think and work quickly on your feet. Sales professionals have a lot on their plate and always have results to deliver. Gaining their respect and support will be the key challenge that you as a coach will face. But I can assure you that once you have gained their trust and respect, it will be one of your most exciting and collaborative coaching relationships.

Part 4:

THE TALENT MANAGEMENT LIFE CYCLE: Integrating Internal Coaching With Your Overall Talent Management Strategy

The Coaching Solution

CHAPTER 13: CAPABILITY (OR COMPETENCY) MODELING

DEVELOPING FUNCTIONAL CAPABILITY MODELS

   THE ROLE AND APPROACH OF THE COACHES

   OWN YOUR CAREER—EMPOWERING EMPLOYEES TO BE RESPONSIBLE
     AND ACCOUNTABLE FOR THEIR DEVELOPMENT

   DEVELOPING LEADERSHIP CAPABILITIES FOR SENIOR LEADERS

ORGANIZATIONAL ASSESSMENTS

COACHING & LEADERSHIP INSIGHT: A Capability Model Is a Powerful Tool

CHAPTER 14: ONBOARDING

DETERMINING WHO TO COACH

COACHING THE NEW HIRE

COACHING & LEADERSHIP INSIGHT: Set Up a Mentoring Program for the New Hire

CHAPTER 15: LAUNCHING TRAINING AND DEVELOPMENT

COACHING THROUGH SALES AND CHANGE MANAGEMENT

THE "MANAGER AS COACH" STRATEGY FOR DEVELOPING YOUR TALENT BASE

   DIVERSITY AND CULTURE—HOW COACHING MEETS CHALLENGES
     IN THESE ARENAS

COACHING & LEADERSHIP INSIGHT: Modeling Reinforces Learning

CHAPTER 16: PERFORMANCE MANAGEMENT

THE ART AND SCIENCE OF PERFORMANCE MANAGEMENT

   HOW TO RESPOND TO A MANAGER'S COACHING REQUEST

   COACHING MANAGERS ON PROVIDING PERFORMANCE FEEDBACK

COACHING & LEADERSHIP INSIGHT: The Leader as Coach

CHAPTER 17: SUCCESSION PLANNING

THE SUCCESSION PLANNING PROCESS

TALENT IDENTIFICATION AND ASSESSMENT

   FINALIZING THE TALENT GRID

   CONDUCTING A BROADER TALENT AND BUSINESS REVIEW

   HAVING THE CAREER-PLANNING CONVERSATION

COACHING & LEADERSHIP INSIGHT: The Most Not-Talked-About Topic of
Succession Planning—To Tell or Not to Tell

Building a Workforce Plan

The Talent Management Life Cycle includes all of the steps and stages from strategic workforce planning and identifying, recruiting and hiring candidates to the development and retention of a company's workforce through succession planning. In this chapter, we will discuss the critical role that coaching can play in the **Workforce Planning** stage of the life cycle.

Figure 11.1: Talent Management Life Cycle

When building your internal coaching program you must make certain that the program is aligned with and supports the company's business, including its key drivers and talent management strategy. In order to do this, it is imperative that you clearly understand your company's workforce plan as it will guide you in designing your objectives for your internal coaching program. Having these objectives clearly defined is like having a road map that illustrates how your program will be integrated into your business and talent management approach. It is also important to note that just because there is a workforce plan, that doesn't mean it is a hard and fast part of your playbook. Organizations are fluid and in constant flux; it is fair to anticipate that change will occur and impact your workforce plan. The key is that, directionally, the plan is aligned with and supports the business drivers. This enables the manager of the coaching program to align and support the drivers of the plan.

Strategic or business objectives are set from the top of the organization and cascade down to each functional area. Each business unit leader will assign goals and tasks specific to their particular organization. As goals and tasks are defined and assigned, the leader of the organization will focus on two key things: how achieving the goals will impact her people and the organization. Does the leader have the right people in the right place at the right time? In other words, does the leader have access to the knowledge, skills and capabilities to meet the goals? If not, how will these be attained? This process is called Workforce Planning and is the initial stage that sets the agenda for much of your talent management and human resources activities. The process for workforce planning typically includes the following:

- **Environmental Scan** – a form of business intelligence that is used to identify the set of facts or circumstances that can surround a workforce situation or event. Information can be from internal and/or external sources, depending on the situation around current trends or futurist studies. The aim is to identify trends, gaps and issues as a basis for future planning.

- **Current Workforce Profile** – a profile of the demand and supply factors, both internally and externally, of an organization's workforce as it stands today.

- **Future Workforce State** – the future view of determining the organization's needs considering the emerging trends and issues identified during the environmental scan.

- **Analysis and Future State** – the product of gap analysis, conducted based on the current and future profiles to determine the requirements.

- **Closing the Gaps** – determining appropriate actions to close the gaps in order to deliver the targeted future.

As the nature of an environmental scan is often misunderstood, let me offer an example here. I recall a time in my career when our talent acquisition team was tasked with hiring very specific technical talent in certain geographic locations, while also tasked with ensuring that they achieved their Diversity Performance Indicator (DPI) objective. Now, the talent acquisition team was exceptional, with very strong recruiters with extensive networks and strength in sourcing candidates. However, the team could not find candidates who met the criteria and achieved the target, and the corporate HR leadership would not accept excuses. Therefore, the team set out to analyze the needs of the organization and benchmark the supply of available talent.

First, an environmental scan was conducted, which involved partnering with our business leaders to identify their workforce requirements, including the number of positions to be filled, specific skills required, technical certifications and business degrees required, and geographic locations that were impacted. Then the team pulled demographic and labor data from several external sources and conducted an analysis. The analysis indicated there was an extremely limited supply of qualified candidates who were diverse and had the specific requirements and were located in the required geographic areas. Leadership appreciated the data and analysis, but the hiring objectives did not change. Therefore, in order to meet the objectives, we needed to adjust hiring in other areas to account for the gap in these areas.

WORKFORCE PLANNING—AN OVERVIEW

As you can imagine, workforce planning for large organizations is no small undertaking and can be a challenging task to complete. There are several variables that can come into play. Organizations are fluid and change can occur daily, especially impacting headcount as revenues and budgets shift. The nature of the business—for example, where the pace of change is very fast—can make it difficult to predict the specific needs of the organization. So it was with the telecommunications industry, which has faced significant opportunities and challenges since the dot-com bubble burst in 2001. In addition, technology is always advancing, competition is fierce and change is continuous, playing out in many ways within companies.

In 2009, I was tasked with a workforce-planning project for an organization newly formed from three different divisions and totaling 17,000 employees and contractors who were located in several countries and who supported over 200,000 customers and were responsible for $22 billion in revenue. As part of this assessment we would need to determine the best geographic locations for our call center and engineering workforce, evaluate the employee skills necessary for current operations and the future state of the business, plus we would need to come up with a solution to consolidate the 198 existing call centers. This would be a collaborative effort between the business leaders, our finance counterparts and the HR team. With some outside help, we would decide which functions and headcount would a) remain in the United States, b) be moved off-shore to our centers or c) be transferred to one of our strategic partners. In addition, we would determine where it was best to consolidate call centers. In Chapter 19, I will walk you through the steps taken to achieve our goal, as the workforce-planning effort was just one component in a massive transformation initiative.

Given this was such a massive undertaking, we knew that we would need outside expertise to assist us. Therefore, we partnered with a very talented team from Accenture to understand the future state of the business and the impact it would have on our client groups, business and talent, as well as where to best strategically consolidate work functions and call centers, and make optimum decisions for our business and clients.

WORKFORCE PLANNING IS NOT HEADCOUNT MANAGEMENT

I remember working with a business partner who had informed me that she had just conducted a workforce plan for her client base and as a result wanted to share the plan with me. I remember being very excited to see this plan as this was prior to my own experiences with workforce planning. She proceeded to share with a slide that showed existing headcount of approximately one hundred employees and a column indicating that given the anticipated business growth that they would require an additional five people (one sales, two support and two technical) to support the new business. I remember thinking to myself, This is a workforce plan? We would compute these calculations on the back of a napkin when we won new business in sales all the time. However, for her client, this is what their needs were and this was their workforce plan. Now, many may refer to this as headcount management—you grow your revenue base and headcount increases to support the new demands. If your revenue base should decrease, in many cases your headcount would decrease also. This brings me to my next point: it is important to understand the distinction between workforce planning and headcount management. In order to do so, let's look at the business and planning life cycle and its impact on headcount.

Annually, budgets are built and forecasts are created based on the goals and expectations that have been set for the company and cascaded into the organization (and sometimes they are rolled up in organizations also). As part of this process, business leaders look at their organizations and assess their current headcount requirements. This is a collaborative effort between the business leaders and their finance counterparts and, one would hope, the Human Resources business partner or organizational development consultant. During this process, business leaders ask their managers to define their headcount requirements for the forthcoming year, based on the needs of the business. Managers must consider the many variables that can come into play such as new products being launched, or winning a new customer or contract that can result in increased demands placed on their employees, or require additional funding for resources such as employees, contractors and so on.

Once all variables are taken into consideration, the departmental manager consolidates the headcount requirements and presents his overall department's requirements to the business leader. The business leader takes this information and works with the finance leader to determine what the company can afford and how to best manage the needs of the business with the allocated budget. It is during this process that there is much debate about what managers "have-to-have" versus "want-to-have." This back and forth dialogue is common practice as budgets are finite and resource requirements and headcount are usually greater than the dollars in the budget. More often than not, the manager is left to manage the needs of their department with either the existing level of resources or a slight increase, but it is possible that budget cuts will result in a decrease in headcount, which leaves the manager challenged to accomplish his goals with fewer resources. Such is the nature of headcount management.

When companies are under financial distress because targets are being missed or costs are impacting profits, they will look for ways to save money. Travel could be restricted, for example, or marketing expenses trimmed. A headcount reduction may occur, also called a reduction in force (RIF). When RIFs occur, depending on their size and which organizations are impacted by the RIF, they can create a shift in the workforce plan.

THE WORKFORCE PLANNING PROCESS

Let's now return to the fundamental building block in your internal coaching program playbook—the development of a workforce plan. This is an excellent opportunity for Human Resources to partner with their clients to conduct a thorough workforce plan assessment and take the time to truly understand the impact of the strategic business plan on the human capital plan. Unfortunately, if this does not happen, areas like talent acquisition and succession planning will be continually impacted.

Preparing a workforce plan can be a challenge for both Human Resources and the Business organization, as business needs and requirements are fluid and can change from moment to moment. Having a strong coach and facilitator can be an asset in guiding and coaching both the HR professionals and the business teams through the process of creating a workforce plan. As discussed in Chapter 8, it is important to make certain you are clear on the company's business goals and to identify where your greatest talent needs are as they relate to these goals. Once the goals are clear, they can be translated into headcount requirements and the actual timing of when shifts in the workforce will occur and how an internal coaching program can best support those changes.

Ideally, the head of Human Resources or Talent Management, or both, are part of the business planning and goal-setting session. Their role is to assess and articulate at a high level the impact of planning on human capital worldwide for the company based on those objectives. At this stage, hopefully, a strategic discussion about the human capital component of the company's business strategy will take place, and members of the C-suite will come away with an understanding and supportive view of the talent management requirements needed to support not only the day-to-day operations of the company but also the long-term strategic plan. From there, the Human Resources and Talent Management leaders will collaborate with the respective business and finance leaders to build the headcount plan. Please understand, if these conversations do not occur or are given short shrift and then handed over to either the business organizations or Human Resources to handle, this can cause a misstep in the budget and planning process, and a golden opportunity to forge a true strategic partnership between Human Resources and/or Talent Management and the business will be missed.

More times than I can mention, I have witnessed organizations struggling to make their goals due to a shortage in necessary talent or a lack of skills and capabilities, or due to an incredibly competitive marketplace. Unfortunately, in those cases the only way to achieve the financial objectives and close the financial performance gap for the company is a workforce reduction. And if a strategic workforce and talent plan is not established, headcount targets can be spread out like peanut butter on a sandwich—everyone gets the same target and talented people are negatively impacted, either being moved into different roles or exited from the company through a reduction in workforce, thereby creating a loss in knowledge, skills and candidates for talent pools. This is where an internal coaching program can play a key role. By involving the coaching team to help develop a company's workforce plan, situations like this can be prevented or, at the very least, minimized.

You may be thinking, *Why is she belaboring this point on workforce planning and business objectives?* Well, these two pieces form a critical part of the Talent Management Life Cycle, as all other talent management requirements will fall into line based on having a clear understanding of the business objectives and having a thorough workforce plan, especially internal coaching programs. Depending on the changes that occur in the workforce plan, the coaching program manager can plan how and when to assign coaches to certain functional areas and individuals. For example, if there is going to be an increase in external hiring, coaches may be designated to work with the new hires to help them assimilate into the company. The workforce planning sessions provide an excellent opportunity for the internal coach to facilitate a discussion between the business and Human Resources. A coaching approach can be helpful to not only demonstrate the value of having an internal coaching team but also to enable both parties to unite as strategic partners and collaborate on issues pertaining to business objectives and human capital. This is an effective way for Human Resources to demonstrate its value and deliver a professional consultative service that benefits all parties and promotes internal coaching.

An Illustration of Not Having a Workforce Plan

It is important to note that, at this time, and as part of my professional development, I was rotated into an HR Business Partner position responsible for a newly formed organization discussed above. This functional area was newly formed and integrated several organizations from multiple companies into one organization, including a labor workforce. It was during this period of massive consolidation and change that Human Resources was hit with a reduction in workforce that impacted my former organization, inclusive of the coaching and organizational development teams. However, the change and workload was not reduced in proportion to the lower headcount. It actually increased, and the newly formed Business Partner team was now responsible for the new organizational development and change management necessary for the transformation.

This Business Partner team was impacted by a 50 percent headcount reduction within the initial two months of the Human Resources integration. Therefore, a newly formed team of six employees who had never met one another (and would not meet for more than six months due to a travel freeze), along with their new-to-role manager, were now faced with managing through a massive organizational change occurring not only in their new client groups but in Human Resources as well. This change came with significant reductions and reorganizations, the disbanding of our self-service model, where employees could call in to a call center to ask for help with day-to-day questions (all of this work was moved to the business partner team), forthcoming labor contract negotiations and, of course, the day-to-day activities that are required in the life of an HR business partner.

Whew! This was some assignment. Unfortunately, at the time there didn't appear to be a workforce plan for Human Resources that could have assessed the state of the business and identified the forthcoming changes in the business plan. If this were available or at least shared with the leaders making decisions for Human Resources, we potentially could have retained the proper number of business partners needed to best support the client as well as the coaches and organizational development consultants. In turn, they could have supported us with our own change as well as with the workforce planning that would need to be completed for the business. The good news is that after approximately eighteen months and the inception of a new HR leader, the gaps were recognized and additional resources provided.

COACHING & LEADERSHIP INSIGHT:
Change Is Inevitable—Put Your People First

The big lesson here is to take the time to plan your business and plan for your employees. Their lives are in your hands, and shareholders are counting on you to make the best decisions for them and their investment in your firm. Take the time to understand the business, its needs, its present and future state, and plan for the inevitable changes, securing the best resources possible to support your company and its employees during a time of transformation.

On another note, remember that when it comes to workforce reductions, these are real people who are responsible for their families and are counting on their jobs for their livelihood. Be responsible, be fair, take the time to listen, and assess and plan accordingly. If a reduction in workforce or a transformation is necessary, do your best to prepare the organization with a strong change-and-communication plan—one that sets out expectations and the training and development necessary for the employees' transformation. (Reflect on the coaching efforts mentioned in Chapter 9, which were used to support employees dealing with change from an integration.) Albeit, this is sometimes not possible or realistic, as technology drives change and as a result reductions in the workforce may happen. Also, it must be recognized that some people can't or won't change and, quite frankly, it is best to identify those employees up front and work with them to prepare an exit strategy. You can't save the world and, let's be clear, I am not telling you to do so. Sometimes, you just have to let people go. It stinks, but it is what it is, and it's a situation that inevitably happens to most managers.

12 Talent Acquisition and Selection

The Talent Management Life Cycle includes all of the steps and stages from strategic workforce planning and identifying, recruiting and hiring candidates to the development and retention of a company's workforce through succession planning. In this chapter, we will discuss the critical role that coaching can play in the **Talent Acquisition and Selection** stage of the life cycle.

Figure 12.1: Talent Management Life Cycle

Once a workforce plan has been established that supports the business objectives, it becomes a key driver for the acquisition and selection of talent. There are many opportunities for the coach to work with the Talent Acquisition and Business Partner teams as well as with hiring managers to identify and acquire the right talent for their needs, at the right time and in the right place.

APPLICATIONS FOR COACHING IN THE TALENT ACQUISITION AND SELECTION STAGE

The talent selection and acquisition components ideal for coaching include:

- Employment brand
- Recruiting

Employment Brand

A company's brand denotes the reputation that a company has as an employer. Similar to a customer brand or value proposition that is used to define a product or a service, an employer has an "employee value proposition" that is used to define an organization's employment offer. The same principles that are associated with branding a product or service are applied to the Human Resources and Talent Management fields with regard to human capital—how to attract, engage and retain talented candidates and employees—using an approach very much like how marketing is used to attract and retain customers.

Figure 12.2 depicts an excellent framework for employer branding and demonstrates how critical the employer's value proposition is to prospective employees as well as customers, market forces and stakeholders. In my view, employee engagement and satisfaction (and, therefore, customer satisfaction) are highest when all of the levers in the Employer/Employee Brand are effectively put to use. The areas that have the most effect on employee engagement levels are career development, compensation, rewards and the work environment. As such, career and leadership development, people management and culture are excellent opportunities for coaching.

Figure 12.2: Employer Value Proposition

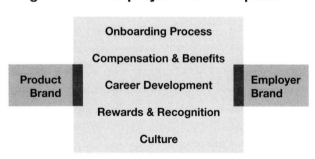

The opportunities for coaches with regard to the employment brand lie not only in coaching managers and leaders in this space with their day-to-day activities and professional development, but also in facilitating the discussion and action planning that need to occur as companies create and modify their employment brand. Given the multiple components that contribute to an employer's brand and everything that is required to develop and build it (brand strategy development, brand testing, message and communication development for both internal purposes and external purposes), not to mention managing and measuring the impact of the brand, multiple individuals or teams are required. These may comprise internal or external consultants and leaders, and managers or individual employees from the business. Their input needs to be obtained, discussed and incorporated into the employment brand plan. The internal coach is an ideal candidate to facilitate these discussions. By using a coach approach, ideas and information can be explored in a positive manner, ensuring that everyone's input is captured and that their contribution is recognized.

Among the questions that need to be considered are: Where and when will hiring and new positions be required? Where will the types of skills, knowledge and experiences be sourced in order to fill these roles? To address these issues talent acquisition, onboarding, and training and development strategies must be developed. In addition, your firm may require new capability models to ensure there is alignment in talent requirements—skills required today and in the future. These models can be used to hire new talent as well as to assess, train and develop the talent that will be needed to support the business changes. Whatever the case, engaging a coach to facilitate discussions around employment branding and to work with the talent acquisition team to design the plan is an excellent coaching opportunity.

Developing an employment brand is no small task, especially for a new company that's not yet well-known in the marketplace. I remember when, shortly after the merger of MCI and Verizon, one of the greatest challenges that our sales leaders overseas were facing was the ability to recruit a qualified sales professional—no one had heard of Verizon Business or understood the value of being a Verizon Business employee. We would hear this in our coaching conversations and it was very frustrating to the managers. Therefore, it was with great focus and collaboration that a team led by the vice president of Talent Management worked with internal and external partners to build an employment brand plan that targeted the potential candidate and explained who Verizon Business was, detailing the value and benefits of working for the company. The team crafted key messaging and worked with agencies to build employment opportunity advertisements and come up with a strategic plan for positioning the ads in order to build employment brand recognition around the world.

I didn't know much about employment branding at this time, but it was extraordinary observing my new manager pull in internal employees and executives from Marketing as well as talent acquisition employees and external consultants in order to develop an employer brand. The end result was a clear brand complete with enticing messaging and an effective process for acquiring external talent that was clearly tied to and aligned with the overall Verizon Business brand and messaging. Fabulous!

Recruiting

A very useful application for coaching in the recruiting process is the facilitation of the discussion between manager and recruiter. Experienced and certified coaches have well-developed listening skills and are able to hear not only what is being said but also what is not being said. In addition, they are trained to ask questions that will surface the truth or needs of the individual or group being coached. A coach's work with a hiring manager can help to establish clear requirements for a position and determine whom the ideal candidate would be. It's a great way to ensure that the job description is accurate and well-defined before the hand off to recruiting. When the needs of the hiring manager are made clear, it saves significant time and energy on the part of the recruiter. It also cuts down on the amount of time the manager needs to spend interviewing, as he or she is already clear on what "good" and "great" looks like, and this alone can eliminate much of the back and forth that can go on between hiring managers and the recruiting team. Driving clarity in this initial step also makes it much easier for the recruiter to be more precise and efficient as they conduct their search. (This also benefits candidates, whose time and energy may be wasted due to a lack of clarity in the initial stage.)

I suggest revisiting the coach selection process described in Chapter 7, as this is a rigorous interview and selection process where a coach can be included. Specifically, the coach can assist with the design of the interview questions and guide and play a role in the actual interview, either as an interviewer or as a member of a panel interview. Remember, coaches who are experienced and certified have expertise in designing and asking questions, and they have unique listening skills that can prove beneficial in the interview process.

COACHING & LEADERSHIP INSIGHT: Leverage Your Coaches' Expertise

So far, we have identified multiple applications for a coach and the use of a coach-like approach. Having a certified coach play an active participant role can add tremendous value to your talent acquisition process. In addition, imagine the impression that it gives candidates when they meet with a coach as part of their interview process. This act, in and of itself, demonstrates the commitment your company makes to its employees—having coaches on staff to support the professional development of employees. The message it sends to the candidate is that it must be a great company with a culture that makes its talented employees a priority. Now, imagine that impact on your employment brand!

13 Capability (or Competency) Modeling

The Talent Management Life Cycle includes all of the steps and stages from strategic workforce planning and identifying, recruiting and hiring candidates to the development and retention of a company's workforce through succession planning. In this chapter, we will discuss the critical role that coaching can play in the **Capability Modeling** stage of the life cycle.

Figure 13.1: Talent Management Life Cycle

Moving along in the Talent Management Life Cycle, we come to the capability and competency modeling stage. (**Note:** I believe the terms competency and capability may be interchangeable, but throughout the book you will see me use the term capability, as that is my preference.) In my view, this is a critical stage as it articulates what "good" looks like for the company's human capital. Specifically, capability modeling:

- articulates the skills, capabilities and behaviors that the company is looking for in its employees

- is directly connected to the business mission and strategy

- drives multiple areas of Human Resources such as employee assessment, professional development, talent recruitment and selection, performance management, succession planning and compensation.

Figure 13.2 again shows the capability model designed in Chapter 6 for selecting and developing professional coaches. As a talent management executive responsible for hiring professional coaches and as a professional coach, I have found these to be the capabilities that my clients desire in their coach. I also have found that the most successful coaches have many of these capabilities and continue to develop them over their careers. I want to share this model with you as, in my view, I believe it ties all of the capabilities together and whether you are a talent management or human resources professional, organizational development specialist, executive coach or business leader, you can benefit from this model.

Figure 13.2: Capabilities of an Internal Coach

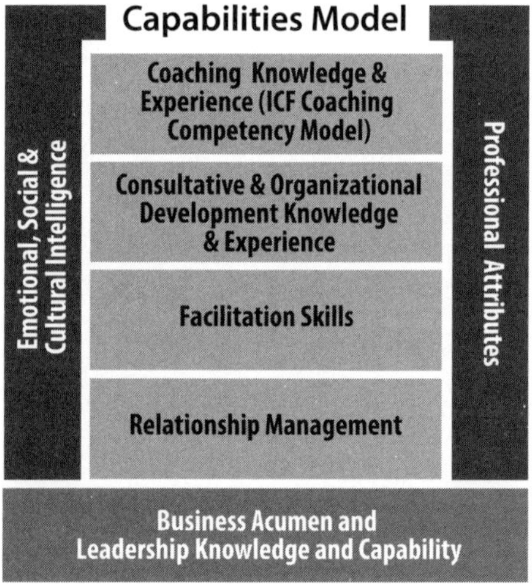

Capabilities Model

Emotional, Social & Cultural Intelligence

Coaching Knowledge & Experience (ICF Coaching Competency Model)

Consultative & Organizational Development Knowledge & Experience

Facilitation Skills

Relationship Management

Professional Attributes

Business Acumen and Leadership Knowledge and Capability

An internal coaching team can provide great value when developing a company's capability models. Specifically, a coach with strong facilitation and/or organizational development training or experience can assist as a lead facilitator to create/validate or develop business values and/or organizational, leadership and functional capabilities. In addition, utilizing the capabilities models in conjunction with one-to-one coaching engagements can prove invaluable to the development of the individual being coached. Specifically, the coach and client can identify specific goals for specific capabilities and work together to design a plan where the client can focus and develop the skills and behaviors of the identified capabilities.

DEVELOPING FUNCTIONAL CAPABILITY MODELS

My internal coaching team at Verizon Business developed the company's general and functional capability models, specifically for sales, customer service and technical functions. In addition, the team created the development capabilities for the employee type (for example, individual contributors, managers or directors). This was the first step for our employees to see and understand what employee development meant to them and to the company. This was an excellent opportunity for the coaches and the business leaders to think through what "good" looks like in terms of their employees and how to coach and develop them.

The internal coaching team designed capability-related models and behaviors for all levels of employees. These capabilities made it very clear to employees and managers what "good" would look like for our employees. In addition, we developed the behaviors to align with each capability for each employee type (individual contributor, manager and director). The capability models were then communicated and employees and managers were trained accordingly, based on what behaviors, skills and knowledge they needed to develop in order to be able to better perform their job responsibilities in their current position, as well as those which they would need in order to perform at the next level.

As for our staff functions (human resources, legal, finance, marketing and information technology), we provided a general capability framework and worked with leadership to make certain they understood the specific training and certifications that were required in their specialty. For example, in order to move up and around in Finance, a CPA (Certified Public Accountant) certification was critical, as was experience in multiple financial areas such as auditing, reporting and analysis.

Once the capability models were established, we mapped the existing training courses (online to the capabilities and then to specific roles). This brought even more clarity as to what education and knowledge employees were required to have in order to progress professionally, and we designed development activities, rotations and experiences that would benefit employees in their professional development. All of these could be found on our intranet site that employees could access 24/7, and our language, images and format matched what was created at the corporate level in order to be consistent and align across the company.

The Role and Approach of the Coaches

Let's explore the coaches' role in this capability modeling project. They were critical in working with each of their client groups to develop the capabilities, their definitions and behaviors; the alignment of the training curriculum as well as the creation of development activities; interpreting and translating how employees would "own their career"; and teaching managers how to support their employees (as well as themselves as they managed their own career). In addition, the coaches were responsible for facilitating the talent assessments and succession planning for their individual client groups, for which the capabilities were to act as a compass and roadmap for progression. (See Chapter 17 for more information on succession planning.)

The coaches began the capability development process by sharing a basic capability model with the senior leaders of their client groups. Each coach was responsible for a specific client group (for example, Sales, Marketing or Customer Service), which meant that this exercise was not only an excellent development exercise for the coaching clients but it also allowed each coach to really get to know their clients. This allowed the coaches to better understand the clients and what "good talent" looked like to them. Based on this knowledge, the coaches were able to provide value-added services in support of their leader clients and managers.

During the process, the coach and the leader of the organization, as well as the person in the next level down (director level), would provide feedback and suggestions on the capability definition and behavior descriptions in order to make certain that it all aligned with the desired knowledge, skills and behaviors that were expected of each role/function and the employee in that role/function.

Once the models were completed, the leaders of each functional area communicated with their organizations about the capability models, the aligned training and development pathways, and how employees were to utilize the models and training and development curriculums. In addition, managers worked with each employee to establish professional development goals, which were then incorporated into the employee's development plan. At this time, we also incorporated training for managers (a learning series we called "Manager as Coach") so that we could teach the managers how to coach their employees on the developmental goals and support them in their success. (More to come on the "Manager as Coach" learning series in Chapter 15.) As a result of this initiative, a clear learning and development plan was established for each employee, and, if followed, the plan would guide the employee in their successful professional development.

Own Your Career—Empowering Employees to Be Responsible and Accountable for Their Development

Our work tied in nicely with a corporate talent management development project that was called "Own Your Career." This was a corporate initiative led by the corporate vice president of Talent Management. As I was the director of Talent Development, responsible for one of the companies, I reported to the corporate vice president in a dotted line and collaborated on many projects with her and her team.

The goal of this initiative was to empower employees to understand what was required for their development and for them to take ownership of their career and career progression. Our focus was to provide the vehicle (system, pathways and programs) for them to easily follow and administer as they took ownership and responsibility for their development. Our capability models were directly linked to an Own Your Career portal, which made it easy for all levels of employees to see where they needed to focus their development and what behaviors were expected of them. It was a terrific project and we were able to provide several online and live resources to support our employees. The feedback from our employees, managers and leaders was fabulous. They were grateful for making it easy to use and understand and, most important, making it clear that every employee was "empowered" to "own their career."

A PERSONAL STORY

The role of director of Talent Development was my first assignment inside of Human Resources and Talent Management. The corporate talent management team who I worked with on the "Own Your Career" initiative, were mentors and incredible resources to me and my team. I remember my first meeting with them and will never forget how gracious and welcoming they were. I knew in a moment that we would have a wonderful and long-lasting partnership. They took me under their wing and made it easy for me to ask questions, offer suggestions and ask for guidance when needed. I consider each of them "the best of the best" when it comes to talent management. They truly are experts in the field, particularly in leadership development, executive education and succession planning.

Developing Leadership Capabilities for Senior Leaders

Another project that my team and I collaborated on with the corporate Talent Management team was the development of leadership capabilities for our senior leaders. The corporate team utilized a similar approach to the one that we used and engaged each of the business units to provide feedback and suggestions as they developed the capability model for our senior leaders. Executive education programs were then developed with the selected partner, Duke University's Fuqua School of Business. The courses were designed for the senior leader level and subsequently these same courses were used with the director level of the company. The initial program was designed around the leadership capability of Financial Acumen with the goal to create a greater understanding of the financial strength of our company, our value proposition, why we made the acquisitions we made and what we needed to do as senior and director-level leaders in order to continue and thrive in our industry. The feedback we received from our senior leaders and directors was very positive, and they indicated that they would be able to better manage their business and make a greater contribution with their new knowledge.

ORGANIZATIONAL ASSESSMENTS

I would like to provide one other example of where coaches can make a contribution and a real difference in the capability modeling area of the Talent Management Life Cycle, and that is organizational assessments. Coaches who already have or would like to develop strength in organizational assessments can conduct them in order to determine where there may be opportunities to develop certain employee capabilities or strengthen a particular organization. For example, the internal coaching team conducted organizational assessments for each functional area. The primary objective was to enable coaches to assess the current state of their client organization, understand their business and talent challenges, and prepare interventions in order to address the areas of concern or gaps in development. The approach that we used for our organizational assessments is as follows. (It is very similar to the workforce planning approach discussed in Chapter 11.)

1. **Current state of the business:** The coach would analyze the performance of their client's business to understand where their client group was performing well and also to identify gaps in performance.
2. **Conduct interviews/needs assessment:** The coach would conduct interviews with the senior leaders and directors in his or her client groups in order to understand what needed to be done to close gaps in performance. Subsequently, they would determine if there was a correlation between the performance gaps and the capabilities required to deliver the results. As a result of their assessments, the coach would work with their partners in the business, members of the training and development team and others to formulate potential solutions.
3. **Make recommendations:** The assigned coach would make recommendations as to how best to close the performance and talent development gaps occurring in the organization. Many times these recommendations aligned with the top organizational development opportunities that connected back to the functional capability model, and were aligned with the training and development curriculum. In addition, in many cases where technical expertise, certifications or advance business degrees were required, the coach would work with the senior leader to leverage the tuition assistance program and leadership development curriculum.

4. **Design solutions and a means to measure success:** Based on the recommendations made to the business, the coach would secure feedback from their client group and determine which recommendations would be most efficacious and that the client would be committed to implementing. In addition, together the coach and senior leader would determine how best to measure the impact of the solutions and establish success criteria and goals.
5. **Deliver solutions:** Once decisions were made on which recommendations to utilize, solutions were designed and implemented.
6. **Measure success:** Following each program that was offered, the coach would conduct a survey/impact study to understand the utilization, engagement and impact of the program against their goals.

COACHING & LEADERSHIP INSIGHT:
A Capability Model Is a Powerful Tool

My final comments on the subject of capability modeling are these: Whether or not you utilize capabilities in your organization, you must make certain that everyone understands the expectations of their position within the company and that they are clear on their goals, responsibilities and what capabilities and behaviors are required to do their job, including what they need to do to prepare for their development and career progression. This ties back to making certain your employees understand what good, or better yet, what great looks like, and from there they can focus on developing the necessary capabilities needed to grow in their role and with the company.

If your company does use a capability-based model, then this presents an incredible opportunity to leverage internal coaches to design and further integrate the capabilities into the company's development planning process, employee and leadership training, and development programs, as well as in your internal coaching programs, which, in turn, will support employee development and help to build bench strength for the organization. From a coach's perspective, using a capability-based model will not only help them to focus in on certain capabilities with their coaching clients, it will also create an opportunity to strengthen the coach's ability to coach in and around each of the capabilities, enabling growth in their professional development.

If your company doesn't use capabilities models, it may be worth exploring or at least be worthy of a discussion with your functional business leaders. By using a coach-like approach, your business leaders may discover the benefits of better defining what "good" and "great" look like for them and their employees.

Onboarding

The Talent Management Life Cycle includes all of the steps and stages from strategic workforce planning and identifying, recruiting and hiring candidates to the development and retention of a company's workforce through succession planning. In this chapter, we will discuss the critical role that coaching can play in the **Onboarding** stage of the life cycle.

Figure 14.1: Talent Management Life Cycle

Onboarding is the process of integrating and orientating new-hire employees within a company. Typically, it includes everything from filling out employment forms to attending orientation and training sessions to completing all of the logistical activities required to integrate an employee into a company.

DETERMINING WHO TO COACH

Regardless of the level of the employee, coaching can be applied in the onboarding stage of the Talent Management Life Cycle; however, it is best targeted at employees who are at a manager or executive level and whose responsibility it is to provide additional support to the new manager/leader being assimilated into the company. As I made clear in Chapter 10, the manager is, in my view, one of the most critical roles in an organization. Managers are the bridge and pipeline to the front-line employees, responsible for executing the tactical activities that support the company's strategic plan while keeping its employees engaged and satisfied. This is not to say a new hire who is an individual contributor cannot participate in your internal coaching program. In my experience, coaching is applicable at all levels as long as most or all of the following criteria is met in the candidate who is being considered for enrollment in the internal coaching program:

1. The individual is top talent (has been identified as someone who can make a greater contribution in the company in the short or long term).

2. The individual is being transitioned to a new role through a promotion or relocation or they have been brought in from the outside, or they are accepting an expatriate assignment; the individual will be required to adapt to a new company, culture, manager or team; or the individual is being promoted or rotated and will be required to adapt to a new position, manager, team or function.

3. The individual's role is complex in nature and requires high levels of intelligence and emotional intelligence.

4. The individual being enrolled in the coaching program is open to coaching and committed to the coaching program. (Ideally, this would have been discussed with the candidate during acquisition and selection.) Their openness to be coached also can be an indicator of the new employee's perspective on and approach to development.

Based on this criteria, you can see that coaching applications for the onboarding stage of the Talent Management Life Cycle can be a good fit for new-hire managers and executives being transitioned into the company. For these situations, I would recommend an onboarding coaching framework that addresses areas such as change management, cultural assimilation, building lasting relationships, and evaluating and/or building your team or organization.

Coaching will result in some early successes and ensure that the new hire and his or her team/organization are aligned to the corporate strategy, have the right goals and are executing and achieving those goals. (Again, this is an ideal application for internal managers and executives who are being rotated, relocated or expatriated for the sake of their professional development or as part of succession planning.)

ONBOARDING & COACHING— A Success Story

A challenge we were faced with at one point was that we did not have the types of employees who were needed in the Global Services organization, which was the company's professional services arm. To address that challenge, growing our professional services business became a strategic imperative.

We needed to acquire some talent from the outside, which meant headhunting individuals at the director level from companies such as IBM and the other leading professional services and system integrator firms. Therefore, we started out by identifying the roles and responsibilities for the positions and the required knowledge, experiences, skills and capabilities. Once each of these components was fleshed out and the job description was written, the compensation team was able to determine the compensation for the position. Given that the position was at the director level and most of the candidates would be coming from outside of the company, we decided to enroll the new-hire directors into a coaching program.

The goal of this initiative was to develop a coaching plan and support the newly hired directors in their transition into the company and its culture. We offered each of them a 90-day coaching engagement. The coaches would work with the newly hired executive to prepare their 90-day plan and provide coaching throughout the initial 90 days. The managers were involved and available to support their new hires in their transition, providing guidance and feedback, which helped them to succeed with the transition.

A special note about this customized version of our coaching program: during the acquisition process of external hires, we discussed the onboarding coaching program with the candidates and how we could customize it to support new hires in their transition. Candidates were very impressed with the development opportunities that would be available to them through our executive education and coaching program, and they saw these programs as an investment in their development and future with the company. So our coaching program proved to be a talent acquisition tactic in addition to helping onboard new hires by easing their assimilation while also accelerating their ability to impact results.

COACHING THE NEW HIRE

Do you remember when it was your first day at your current company or a company you worked for in the past? Recall how you felt. You likely met with an administrative person or your manager who set you up in your cube or office and filled you in on the best foods in the cafeteria and helped you complete any paperwork. Perhaps you were provided with some online training or given some documentation to read. By day two you were probably ready to either continue the online training or maybe shadow a colleague. You may have been offered a live orientation session. It likely wasn't long before you discovered that your new colleagues were overwhelmed with work and, outside of the obligatory introductions or a coffee conversation, the next thing you knew, the honeymoon was over and you were knee-deep in work and learning the culture, systems, processes, protocols and maybe even the business all at once. You were careful not to ask too many questions though, as you could see that your manager and colleagues were swamped, and so you made the decision to struggle quietly and figure it all out yourself—which you did, with some additional stress and anxiety.

Now, imagine this: you are assigned an internal coach and start your first day at your new company getting situated. At some point throughout the day, you have the opportunity to meet with your coach and, during this initial conversation, the coach explains the internal coaching program and the specific type of program you will be a part of as you transition into the company. The coach explains the process and framework and how the two of you will work together. You may even be given the opportunity to start to build a strategic (coaching) plan as to how you will engage with your new manager and your team and/or organization and how you will assimilate into the culture. You then meet with your new manager and your coach, and at that meeting your manager provides you with guidance in terms of specific areas she will need you to target within the first 30, 60 and 90 days. You incorporate this feedback into your plan and begin to work with your coach to think through your approach and your priorities. Going forward, whenever you feel stuck, frustrated or simply confused about something in the new system, culture or organization, you can reach out to your coach for additional support, coaching or guidance. This would make quite a difference, wouldn't it?

The coach can play multiple roles as their client goes through transition, including coach, sounding board and—especially important—interpreter. As many of us who have transitioned into companies or organizations know, there are the published "rules" located in the employee handbook and there are "unspoken rules," the cultural norms, behaviors, ways to work and relationships that exist inside organizations, which are not written down anywhere. The unspoken rules can only be gleaned from being a part of the organization for some time or from having someone (a mentor, coach or engaged manager) to guide you and help you navigate through the new organizational waters. Some examples of "rules" versus "unspoken rules" may look like this:

Rule #1: Work hours are 8:30 A.M. to 5:30 P.M. with one hour for lunch.

Unspoken Rule: Top performers arrive no later than 7 A.M. (this is what the vice president does and she expects to see everyone in the office early). Lunch is eaten at your desk.

Rule #2: As a manager, you are empowered to make most of the decisions at your level.

Unspoken Rule: Your manager is a micromanager and requires you to disclose all activities that require a decision.

Rule #3: Your manager and his manager have a traditional manager–direct report relationship, and they act very formally around one another.

Unspoken Rule: The managers have worked together for over ten years. Their families are friends and they play golf together on the weekends.

COACHING & LEADERSHIP INSIGHT:
Set Up a Mentoring Program for the New Hire

Reflect on the onboarding stages and how much coaching can contribute to the efficient assimilation of a new hire. By providing coaching support to the new hire, he or she can learn about the organization more quickly, including how it works and what the interpersonal dynamics are. Coaching sets up the new hire for success and productivity from day one.

I said in this chapter that coaching is for individuals whose work is complex in nature, and that's certainly true; however, I don't want to neglect the new-hire employees whose roles are more task oriented and repeatable. They also require support as they assimilate into a new company, culture and role. For these individuals, I would strongly encourage that they be assigned a mentor or be enrolled in a mentoring program that provides an individual mentor and is facilitated by leaders (directors and above in the organization). A program such as this, or a mentoring circle, allows employees in similar or different roles to meet on a regular basis and expand their network and their resources (as they build relationships) within the company. If you are going to proceed with a mentoring program, I recommend you do the following:

1. Establish a selection criteria and process for enrolling someone as a mentor. Remember these individuals should be top talent and display the competencies and behaviors that you would like to see in your employees.
2. Develop a process guide and topic agenda for your mentors to follow. Make it as easy as possible for them, as they already have a lot on their plates. This will help you secure mentors and ensure consistency in the program's approach, content and delivery of the materials.
3. If you are able to, prepare the materials for the mentoring forums and train the mentors on how best to facilitate these discussions (another opportunity for your coaches).
4. Check in regularly with your mentors and mentees to see how they are doing. What is going well? Not so well? What goals are suggested for the future? You will probably have some future mentors under your nose and will want to stay connected with them.
5. Be sure to have an end date. If you keep the same employees with the same leaders in place for too long, things can reach a point of diminishing returns, and in some cases the mentor can become a crutch for the mentee who may begin to have a different expectation from the mentor.

15 Launching Training and Development

The Talent Management Life Cycle includes all of the steps and stages from strategic workforce planning and identifying, recruiting and hiring candidates to the development and retention of a company's workforce through succession planning. In this chapter, we will discuss the critical role that coaching can play in the **Training and Development** stage of the life cycle.

Figure 15.1: Talent Management Life Cycle

Training and development is an ideal stage of the Talent Management Life Cycle to incorporate internal coaching programs, especially when it comes to programs for management and leadership—programs that help clients deal with change, the need for a behavior change or the need for an adaptation/

transition to a new way of being and/or doing. Coaching as an add-on to any one of these types of programs is a terrific way to support the employee in making the change and reinforcing the new or desired behavior.

COACHING THROUGH SALES AND CHANGE MANAGEMENT

I would like to share some of my personal experiences using coaching to reinforce a training initiative and sales force transformation. They took place at WorldCom when we were facing the financial crisis. The client decision makers were usually heads of Technology and Information Technology. The focus of our conversations with our customers was mostly about our network, including network management and hardware and bandwidth requirements for applications that traversed the network. Our sales force and its leaders were well versed in the technical components of our network, its operations and the hardware that managed it, as well as our customers' networks, their equipment and their applications.

However, due to the recent events of fraud and bankruptcy within the company, our sales leaders found themselves having very different conversations with a new buyer of our services. Instead of dealing with the telecommunications and technology decision makers, they were having to deal with the chief financial officers and members of the Finance organizations. Of course, the clients were all gravely concerned, and with good reason, about the health and longevity of WorldCom and the potential for a negative impact on their networks and, therefore, their business. In order to quickly prepare our sales force and its leaders for these conversations, our training organization partnered with a firm and designed a training program on how to engage at the CFO level. The program was called "The Language of the Chief Financial Officer." It was the perfect training initiative, delivered at the perfect time, as our sales force had found itself in uncharted territory, having to deal with questions they were uncertain about relating to bankruptcy and its impact on the customer. Everyone in the Sales organization attended training and, with coaching, became much more informed and comfortable with the conversations they needed to have with their customers.

Additionally, our senior vice president of Sales at the time, Steve Young, held all-employee calls each week in order to share with his organization whatever he could about where things currently stood in the fraud and bankruptcy process, what it meant to the organization, and the impact it was having or going to have on our customers. He would open the floor so that anyone on the call could ask questions about the company and its current state. These calls acted as vehicles for providing transparency to employees, helping to support and lead the entire organization.

On the coaching end of things, it was amazing how many calls I received from sales managers and directors asking for coaching support as they prepared to have conversations with their clients about WorldCom's financial situation. They would set up the meeting with the client then review the training materials from "The Language of the Chief Financial Officer" course, requesting coaching support as they thought through their strategies. I would assist with their preparation for their meeting, and we would role-play the conversation in anticipation of the questions the client would ask. This was an excellent application for coaching. The sales leaders knew they had a safe and confidential place where they could think through and prepare for some of the most important and difficult meetings they would ever face in their careers.

We thought this new-found coaching application would work for all types of training programs, and we saw an opportunity to incorporate it into a new training program for sales managers. At the time, our coaching team was quite small: just one coach and myself. As it was just the two of us and the demand for coaching was high, we needed to determine the greatest need in the organization and place as much of our attention in that area. We knew that the most critical link in any organization, especially the Sales organization, was the sales managers, as they were the individuals who would sell, support and execute the move to a new sales methodology (not to mention, they were the face of the company in the eyes of the customer). The endorsement and engagement of the sales managers would be critical to the coaching program's overall success, and our services would be of great help to them during this time. So we decided to offer group coaching to the sales managers in order to reinforce the new methodology, processes, skills and behaviors that they had learned in their training class and would be necessary for achieving the company's goals. Unfortunately though, in this particular application, the vehicle for coaching (small-group coaching) was not the best solution. It was incredibly difficult to find a time when all of the sales managers were available at once. Their meetings with customers were constantly being moved and changed, which made it virtually impossible to have all the managers on one call at the same time.

So we changed our approach and came up with a solution that worked best for these clients, offering one-to-one coaching to the managers, both formally and informally. They were given the option to sign up for one-to-one coaching that would last up to three months after the training, after which time they would have access to us whenever they wanted to work through a particular scenario or application with a coach. Sales managers who were time-challenged but still wanted a regular coaching call were offered ad-hoc coaching on an as-needed basis. This meant that, if they were faced with a specific challenge and wanted to receive coaching, they were able to reach out and schedule a call as needed. We found both of these vehicles for coaching work effectively in Sales organizations, where time is scarce and schedules are always subject to change. We were able to support our clients in a way that was unique to each manager as they began to transition to the new methodologies that required new skills and a shift in their behaviors. I am happy to report that this approach went extremely well and within one year the growth of our coaching program exploded. We recruited a team of coaches to support our expansion, ensuring that all sales and service managers in good standing were able to work with a coach on a regular basis.

THE "MANAGER AS COACH" STRATEGY FOR DEVELOPING YOUR TALENT BASE

Management and leadership development is another area in the training and development stage of the Talent Management Life Cycle that is ideal for coaching. Often the need is to develop certain capabilities of managers and leaders and/or change their behaviors, and coaching can be used in multiple ways to reinforce a behavior change or develop a capability. One such way is a broad approach geared to top talent and bench-strength employees who are given the opportunity to work with a coach in order to focus on specific capabilities that they need to develop.

Coaches are excellent candidates for designing and delivering management and leadership development programs. Think about it: They are accustomed to working with managers and leaders to help them develop their management or leadership style, behavior and presence. They are trained in assessments such as 360-degree emotional intelligence, DiSC, Hogan and/ or the Birkman Method. For these reasons and more, coaches have much to offer as a facilitator of development programs. Additionally, they can provide coaching in the moment in front of the group, allowing them to observe and thereby begin to learn some of the excellent coaching techniques that every manager should master.

On the topic of coaching skills for managers, another excellent coaching opportunity is to offer coaching skills training to your managers and leaders. My team at one point developed a "Manager as Coach" program, which was designed for managers and supervisors who had completed basic manager training. The program could be delivered live to small to medium-size groups or via a WebEx with smaller groups that were, ideally, no bigger than ten people. The purpose of the program was to teach coaching skills and have managers incorporate them into their day-to-day activities in an effort to become better managers, thus increasing the engagement, retention and development of their employees.

In my view, this type of program should be taught after managers and supervisors have had basic manager training, as coaching is considered a higher-level skill, so it is best that managers have established strength in the basics of management first. Ideally, you should introduce the coaching concepts in the basic manager training program and subsequently go deeper into the skills, applications and their use in a smaller and more focused environment. You should also consider including one-to-one coaching for the managers during their coach skills training, as this will enable them to work through some real-time situations with the assistance of an experienced coach.

Diversity and Culture—How Coaching Meets Challenges in These Arenas

In addition to creating a program similar to the "Manager as Coach," there are some other coaching applications that can be used, more specifically, to support the development of managers and leaders from different ethnic backgrounds who may represent a smaller percentage of the employee population or face challenges arising from being in a new culture or geographic region. Such challenges can range from determining the best means to communicate with direct reports, their manager and colleagues, to failing to grasp workplace issues, or struggling to manage and navigate change in a different country or culture. Making coaches available who have experience working in different cultures can be a major source of support for these individuals in their development, and they will develop an affinity with their coach that is likely not to occur with a manager. Another way to support high-potential managers from different ethnic or geographical backgrounds is to provide a mentor to support the manager as he or she grows and their career develops.

I don't want to dive too deeply into the world of diversity; however, I do want to point out that when you are supporting the development of a top-talent individual, it is important to explore their culture so that you can come from a place of understanding. This will allow you to help them see how their behaviors may be interpreted by others in the workplace and, if needed, help them develop alternative behaviors to support them in their success.

When it comes to the workplace, I feel strongly about creating environments that are inclusive in nature. I suspect this comes from my own experiences growing up and feeling excluded at school. I had immigrant grandparents, and I didn't live in a neighborhood with lots of children, nor did I have siblings in the school system with me. Therefore, my connections to my peers at school was limited and I learned very early in life what it felt like to feel isolated and excluded, and the impact it had on one's self-esteem and confidence. Because of this, I have strived my entire career to foster environments built on respect and trust, which result in collaborative relationships based on inclusivity.

My talent development team had an opportunity to build a program to help support inclusion in the workplace. Through our coaching work and our leadership programs we could see that there was a need to build a more inclusive culture throughout the large company, where there were differing cultures, working styles and expectations about the customer experience. So the team of coaches collaborated to find an inclusion program that we could bring to the company and that all employees would be able to benefit from. One of my managers at the time did a fabulous job identifying and incorporating the program we ended up using. It was a program developed by Insight Education Systems titled "MicroInequities: The Power of Small." It suited our needs perfectly, which my manager clearly recognized. Her passion for her work in leadership development and diversity was remarkable. She is one of the brightest and most thoughtful leaders that I have had the pleasure of working with.

Here is how "micro-inequities" is defined by Insight Education Systems:

Listening with your arms folded, losing eye contact with the person you are speaking with, ignoring a female colleague's success while rewarding a male co-worker's same accomplishments, are all examples of small yet powerful biases communicated in the workplace. Also known as MicroInequities, these often subconscious, negative messages and actions can affect company productivity and morale.

MicroInequities are cumulative, subtle messages that occur when these signals are negative or promote a negative bias. MicroInequities are not one-time events. They are cumulative, repeated behaviors that devalue, discourage, and impair performance in the workplace.[1]

The concept of micro-inequities is fascinating, and The Power of Small programs delivers it in such a way that allows individuals to explore their behavior in a non-threatening and fun way. In doing so, managers and leaders become intrigued and begin to take notice of their subtle yet possibly demeaning or, on the flip side, misconstrued behavior, and when they identify it, they want to improve it immediately. So, whom do they call? Why, their coaches, of course! The program was a big hit and got our leaders and employees thinking and taking action. So much so, that we were asked to deliver the program to our colleagues around the world. Additionally, our chief diversity officer at the time held a corporate-wide broadcast for all employees so that they could experience a demonstration and learn about micro-inequities.

Now, you may ask, what does this have to do with coaching? Well, the program was so successful that our leaders were bringing the topic of micro-inequities up in their coaching conversations, asking the coaches to observe them and provide feedback. If they'd caught themselves in a situation in which they felt that a micro-inequity had influenced their behavior, they would bring it to their sessions with their coach to work through how they could respond differently going forward. This was a tremendous breakthrough for not only individuals, but also for the organization. The program placed each of us and our respective cultures, with our similarities and differences, on the same level playing field. We were able to begin to see one another more openly and honestly and speak about the barriers between us, which allowed us to begin taking them down and work toward one culture, one company.

---

[1] URL: http://www.insighteducationsystems.com/faqs.htm

COACHING & LEADERSHIP INSIGHT:
Modeling Reinforces Learning

There are multiple applications for coaching in the training and development space, as this chapter makes clear. If you believe in coaching and your desire is to continue, build upon or create an environment that embraces diversity, inclusion, open communication, collaboration, innovation or all of the above, having a team of internal coaches is an excellent resource to make use of to help you with your goal. Ideally, you want to be able to model "coaching" behavior, teach the skills and, subsequently, reinforce the learning through the actual use of coaching, which again models the behavior and teaches the skills and reinforces the learning—see how this works? Each step builds upon the next step, and so on.

If you are unable to have an internal coach or a team of internal coaches due to budget or headcount limitations, an alternative is to teach coaching skills or have certain top talent managers and individuals become trained and certified in becoming an internal coach. They then could perhaps allocate a small percentage of their time to coaching others, modeling and teaching the skills and behaviors for developing the company's employees and supporting them in their success.

16 Performance Management

The Talent Management Life Cycle includes all of the steps and stages from strategic workforce planning and identifying, recruiting and hiring candidates to the development and retention of a company's workforce through succession planning. In this chapter, we will discuss the roles that coaching should and should not play in the **Performance Management** stage of the life cycle.

Figure 16.1: Talent Management Life Cycle

Performance Management is a hot topic that often creates engaging conversations and debates, especially when it comes to when and how to performance manage employees and the role of coaching in the performance management process. Common performance management topics that arise in coaching conversations can include the following:

- Conducting performance reviews
- Performance conversations
- Counseling and feedback

THE ART AND SCIENCE OF PERFORMANCE MANAGEMENT

In order to help a business better reach its goals, managers have a responsibility to support their employees to succeed—which can be an excellent application for coaching—or otherwise manage them out of their role, department or organization. I'm not going to go into great depth about managing poor performers or offer my views on how to decide whether to release them or give them an opportunity in a different department, role or function. There are many variables that come into play, including the individual's tenure with a company, past performance, business and industry knowledge, and more. I will say, though, that time and time again, we keep non-engaged, underperforming employees in roles for too long. If an employee is not a good fit for a role, then let them go. A square peg does not fit into a round hole, and even if you force the fit, the "peg" will never be truly comfortable and happy, which will negatively affect the employee's performance. This scenario will create a host of issues for you, your team, Human Resources and, potentially, the customer. You will want to kick yourself for spending too much time and energy and too many resources on the situation. Therefore, I don't recommend that coaching be employed for performance management when the goal is to move an employee from a state of "not performing" to "performing."

However, there are legitimate situations in which coaching can be used to help with performance management. For example, a client may approach a coach to discuss employee performance issues, looking to get the coach's perspective on the situation or to brainstorm with the coach potential actions that could be taken to support the situation. I consider this an acceptable request, as the manager is asking for support to address a specific situation and maybe she would like the coach to be a sounding board or to role-play a performance management conversation with her as she prepares to have the conversation. A coach can also be brought in to support an employee, department or organization for the purpose of taking an employee's performance from "performing" to "enhanced performance" or from "good" to "great." It's an acceptable focus area for the coach to engage and support the client.

How to Respond to a Manager's Coaching Request

When a manager requests coaching for an individual employee, the coach should assess the situation and determine (with the manager) at what level the employee is performing and whether they may require counseling more so than coaching. Well-performing employees are better candidates for coaching, whereas poorer-performing employees are typically better suited for counseling conversations. Here are some questions the coach can ask of the manager to help evaluate what kind of support would be most appropriate for the employee:

- How would you describe the employee's performance?

- Describe the employee's behavior and why you believe there are performance issues.

- How long have these issues been occurring?

- What have you done to support the employee and help him/her overcome the challenges? How have you engaged your HR business partner for support?

- Do you believe that a reasonable amount of time and resources have been provided to the employee in order to address these performance challenges?

- What strategies as a manager have you tried? What have you not tried? (Here the coach and client could brainstorm on what other activities, resources or support might be helpful.)

- How does the employee perceive his/her performance? (If the manager and employee see things differently, the coach should ask the manager where the disconnect lies and what needs to happen to close the gaps. Brainstorming may be helpful here also.)

Once the coach feels that the situation has been thoroughly assessed and it's clear what is required for the situation (coaching or counseling), the coach should ask the manager what actions he or she will take within a certain timeframe in order to address the performance issue(s). The manager should be encouraged to sit with the employee as soon as possible to discuss the situation and develop an action plan together. In a negative performance situation, it is important that the manager and the employee document their respective perspectives on the performance issue in addition to the steps that they agree to take in order to try to remedy the situation. This situation needs to be closely monitored by the manager and supported by Human Resources. Unfortunately, sometimes the employee is simply not able to meet the minimum standards or objectives and this can result in termination. If this is the case, it's not a situation in which the coach should be involved. It can create confusion for the employee and make it a difficult termination process for the manager and Human Resources.

Following the manager's conversation with the employee, the coach should ask the manager for feedback on the conversation and ensure that the outcome and action plan are suitable to the needs of the performance situation. At this point, it's a good idea to ask how comfortable a manager is on a scale of 1–10 (1 being the lowest) that the action plan can be taken forward. If the response is less than a 10, the coach should ask what it would take to make it a 10.

COACHING TO RAISE AWARENESS AND ACHIEVE SHIFTS IN BEHAVIOR

This leads to an important point with respect to coaching. Often coaches are brought into a situation in order to help a manager or leader develop more positive behaviors. This can be tricky, especially if the individual does not see the problem with his or her own behavior. What can complicate the situation even more is if the leader's own manager and colleagues are not acknowledging that there is a problem and are tolerating the poor behavior.

If a coach accepts this type of assignment, I advise that he or she employ a 360-degree stakeholder assessment. This type of assessment is based on feedback received from interviews that the coach conducts with the individual's peers, direct reports and the manager. The coach will gather and consolidate the feedback into a written report for the individual, which can then be shared with the individual's manager and possibly also Human Resources, depending on what is decided in the initial coaching agreement.

Based on the findings, the coach and the individual being coached will design a plan taking into account the stakeholder's feedback as well as feedback from the manager and perhaps the HR business partner. The next step is for the individual being coached to present their plan to their manager and the HR business partner (if they have been included in this process). During this meeting, feedback about the plan is provided to the individual being coached and all parties come to agreement on the action plan. At the middle and end of the coaching engagement the individual, manager, coach and HR business partner will have check-point meetings to ensure that the desired change is taking place. Prior to the end of the coaching engagement, the coach will re-interview the stakeholders to secure their feedback on the individual's progress. The feedback is written up and provided to the individual being coached. This is a great way of bringing problematic behavior to the attention of the individual exhibiting the unwanted behavior and dealing with it constructively. Furthermore, it demonstrates the company's commitment for development to the individual and to the stakeholders.

Now, if the manager tells the coach at the outset that the employee is a top performer and that the goal is to enhance his or her performance, or to prepare him or her for a promotion or management role, the conversation between the coach and the manager will have a different focus. Here are some questions the coach could ask of the manager in this kind of situation:

- Tell me what this individual does that makes him or her a top performer.

- If I were to ask your peers and manager for their perspective on this employee, what would they say?

- What do you see this individual doing next in their career? Would this be a promotion? Involve increased responsibility? Be a move into managing people?

- If I were to ask this individual where he or she sees their next career move, what would they say? (Coach: Is this aligned with the manager's response?)

- What has the employee done to "own their career" and prepare for the next assignment?

- As his or her manager, what have you done to prepare the employee for the next move?

- How do you see coaching playing a role in this situation with this individual?

- What would be the desired outcome of this individual working with a coach?

If the answers to these questions confirm that coaching would be suitable for the performance situation, the coach should meet with the employee in person and solicit his or her opinion on working with a coach. If the discussion is positive, the coach can begin to work with the manager and the employee, and perhaps their HR business partner, to design the coaching engagement.

INDIVIDUAL COACHING ENGAGEMENT PROCESS FOR ENHANCED PERFORMANCE

If a coach is going to proceed with a coaching engagement for enhanced performance, I would advise taking the following approach:

Kick-off call/meeting: Have a call or meeting with the manager, employee, HR business partner and coach to establish coaching engagement goals and set expectations.

Objectives/goal-setting meeting: The coach and employee meet to establish specific coaching objectives and outline a plan and activities to achieve the goals discussed in the kick-off meeting.

Ongoing monthly coaching: Define the time parameters of a monthly coaching program (common engagements are a minimum of six consecutive months of coaching and as many as twelve months, with one to two hours of one-to-one coaching per month). **Note:** Length of coaching engagement and number of sessions will be determined by the goals of the engagement.

Mid-point check-in meeting/call: A conversation with the individual who is being coached, the manager, the Human Resources business partner and the coach. The goal of the meeting is to provide the employee with his or her manager's feedback on their progress and identify additional support or resources that may be needed. At this meeting the coach may share any observations.

Ongoing monthly coaching: Monthly one-to-one coaching continues.

Wrap-up meeting/call: A meeting or call in which the employee presents his or her progress to their manager and Human Resources to obtain feedback and answer any questions. In addition, this is an opportunity for the coach to provide final observations and/or recommendations.

Coaching Managers on Providing Performance Feedback

When it comes to providing coaching services in the feedback area of performance management, it is an ideal opportunity for coaches to deliver interactive training. They can work with managers on how to counsel employees, and they can provide training to both managers and employees on how to give and receive feedback. Performance feedback is an area that many managers need to better develop, as they often don't communicate effectively with employees who aren't performing as well as they could be. It's only human to feel reluctant to give negative feedback out of respect for the other party's feelings or because of how uncomfortable it makes us feel. But really, by withholding feedback the manager is doing the employee a disservice, as it's the manager's responsibility to help an employee see when there is a need for professional development—development that will allow the employee to become better qualified and considered for other opportunities, enabling them to continue their growth within the company.

Within corporate cultures that support learning, development and coaching, employees and managers typically do not have as many concerns about giving and receiving feedback. Managers are accustomed to taking a coaching approach with their employees, asking coaching questions, sharing observations and giving fact-based feedback, and the employees know that their manager is there to support them and to coach and develop them. Managers are also comfortable stretching their employee's critical thinking skills and will act as thought-provokers and model the behaviors that they would like their employees to use in the organization.

Supporting Over-Worked Employees

Behavior modeling is a crucial role of a manager, especially when pressures and overwork make it hard for the manager to find time for coaching and development conversations with their employees. Sometimes managers have difficulty handling the pressures of their job and, therefore, may resort to using aggressive language and behavior or bullying tactics as a means of getting employees to work harder and faster. Unfortunately, I hear too many stories about this type of behavior. It's most common in environments where employees are overworked and overwhelmed, making them feel constantly exhausted and stressed.

According to the U.S. Bureau of Labor Statistics,

[the] provisions of sick leave plans have changed significantly since 1992–1993.

The average number of paid sick leave days per year ranged from 10 days with 1 year of service to 17 days with 20 years during the 1992–1993 period. In contrast, the average number of paid sick leave days ranged from 8 days for 1 year of service to 10 days after 20 years of service in 2012. The average number of annual paid holidays declined from 10 days in 1992–1993 to 8 days in 2012. (Holiday provisions are the same for all lengths of service.)[1]

If employers are decreasing paid leave out of fear of abuse of sick time, they are putting employee engagement seriously at risk. People simply cannot mentally process more information and get more done in their 60-70-80-hour workweek. Not only does their work performance suffer, employees may be too emotionally or physically exhausted from their job to be available for their families, friends, communities or any other non-work-related activity, including planning a much-needed vacation.

The January 2014 edition of *HR Magazine* includes the findings from a study conducted by the Society for Human Resource Management (SHRM) in collaboration with and commissioned by the U.S. Travel Association. In an article titled "Unused Vacation Days Take a Toll," it states that within organizations that offer paid vacation plans, 86 percent of full-time employees has sufficient tenure to accrue at least six to twenty vacation days annually, but many fail to take all of their days, which can negatively affect performance and morale. However, only 61 percent of organizations reports that, on average, employees have at least three unused vacation days each year. This same study found that 94 percent of HR professionals thinks that vacation is "extremely" or "very important."

As leaders of the *human* resources of our organizations, HR professionals and internal coaches need to take a stand on employees' behalf and recognize the brutal consequences of decreasing sick time and the impact that not taking vacation time is having on employees' engagement and their work–life balance.

A recent research project was carried out in three hospitals in Ontario, Canada. The project explored the relationship between employee engagement and three key human resources metrics: work stress, injuries and illness from patient handling or contact, and employee retention. The report, published by the Ontario Hospital Association in September 2012 and titled *The Relationship between Employee Engagement and Human Capital Performance*, states that

> 4 in 10 of all respondents [to the survey] experience most days as quite or extremely stressful. However, those employees in the high-engagement group

---

[1] U.S. Bureau of Labor Statistics, *National Compensation Survey–Benefits*, 2013.

are far less likely to experience stress (24%), especially compared with their coworkers who have low engagement. Indeed, more than 6 out of 10 low-engagement employees experience most workdays as quite or extremely stressful.

Other findings from the report show that there are fewer incidences of workplace illness or injury in the high-engagement group, by a margin of 14 percent over the low-engagement group. With respect to retention rates, the high-engagement group was less likely to consider looking for a job change by a margin of 21 percent over the low-engagement group.

In his book *Flat Army: Creating a Connected and Engaged Organization*, Dan Pontefract writes:

> According to Gallup, a global human capital consulting firm, overall employee engagement since 2000 has remained at a paltry 30 percent. More shockingly, levels of active disengagement as well as those simply not engaged in their roles have continued to remain flat at 20 percent and 50 percent respectively.[2] Gallup's most recent report, however, issued in 2011, entitled "State of the Global Workforce," and based on research with over 47,000 employees in 120 countries around the world, tells an even more chilling corporate-engagement tale:
>
> > The overall results indicate that 11% of workers worldwide are engaged. In other words, about one in nine employees worldwide is emotionally connected to their workplace and feels he or she has the resources and support they need to succeed. The majority of workers, 62%, are not engaged—that is, emotionally detached and likely to be doing little more than is necessary to keep their jobs. And 27% are actively disengaged, indicating they view their workplace negatively and are liable to spread that negativity to others.[3]

The outcomes of these findings are clear: If companies fail to properly support their employees, they put employees' health and well-being at risk and significantly decrease their engagement levels, which puts customer relations at risk. It's bad for business. Internal coaches work very closely with and have trusted relationships with their clients, and it is common for a coaching client to discuss work-related stress with their coach. Therefore, the coach is in a very unique position to support their client and advocate for the overall wellness

---

[2] "State of the American Workplace, 2008-2010," Gallup Consulting, 2010. www.gallup.com/strategicconsulting/142724/State-Amercian-Workplace-2008-2010.aspx

[3] "State of the Global Workforce," Gallup Consulting, 2011. www.gallup.com/strategicconsulting/157196/state-global-workplace.aspx

of employees. In addition, it is important to make certain the coach models the behavior that is being requested of the employee. This means that coaches need to make certain that they take the care that is required for themselves in order to be fully engaged for their clients, and this means taking their vacation days also.

COACHING & LEADERSHIP INSIGHT: The Leader as Coach

A goal of one of the coaching programs I was involved with at one point was to teach the company's managers to be more coach-like. This was the reason we created the "Manager as Coach" training program (discussed in Chapter 15), which taught our managers coaching skills through an interactive and experiential learning series. Specifically, we taught our managers how to truly listen and ask thought-provoking questions, how to share observations and deliver feedback, and how to support and hold employees accountable as they work toward their goals. Learning these skills proved helpful not only with coaching conversations but performance management conversations too, where skills such as listening and asking questions were also relevant. In addition, many of our leaders who were enrolled in our one-to-one coaching program began to duplicate the coaching techniques that they experienced with their coach. Sometimes they would practice the coaching conversation they were preparing to have with their employees with their coach.

Everyone who was part of our one-to-one internal coaching program or any of our management and leadership development coaching programs enjoyed the experience and working with a professional coach. It gave them the opportunity for self-development and they appreciated the investment that the company was making in them. Engagement levels rose and, as I noted earlier in the book, we actually had business leaders transferring headcount to our team so we could hire an internal coach to support their organizations! The positive impact that internal coaching was having on our clients' leaders, employees and their business was sensational, and everyone who was involved in one of our programs, or had a coach, took pride in that fact. Because we saw a rise in engagement and productivity, and results, the need for performance management conversations decreased—always a good thing, considering that no one likes to have these conversations in the first place.

17 Succession Planning

The Talent Management Life Cycle includes all of the steps and stages from strategic workforce planning and identifying, recruiting and hiring candidates to the development and retention of a company's workforce through succession planning. In this chapter, we will discuss the critical role that coaching can play in one of the most strategic stages of the life cycle, **Succession Planning**.

Figure 17.1: Talent Management Life Cycle

Succession planning presents an ideal opportunity for internal coaches to play an active role by facilitating the identification process of high-potential talent. Coaches who are either trained on or have been involved with the capability modeling processes for the organization in question can add more value during the talent review process as they are intimately familiar with the functional and leadership capabilities, the on-the-job experiences and the over-all definitions of "what good looks like" for the managers and leaders of that organization. With their coaching and facilitating experience, coaches will be able to design and conduct a talent review session that can drive the identification of high-potentials at all levels of the business.

THE SUCCESSION PLANNING PROCESS

Before the succession planning process is begun, it is imperative that the owners of the succession plans (Human Resources and the business leaders) clearly articulate their goals for the plan. These goals may include the identification of critical positions, and the experiences that individuals need to have in order to move into those positions and progress in their career; establishing a certain number of ready-now and ready-future candidates for such positions; meeting certain goals for the workforce composition; or making a certain amount of development opportunities available to top talent employees each year. Whatever the case, clear goals must be set and, from there, a plan to achieve those goals can be designed. Succession planning should be viewed as a partnership between Human Resources and the business. It is a collaborative effort that is critical to the company's longevity, with both parties sharing that responsibility.

Succession planning typically happens annually, culminating with a presentation to the executive leadership team and board of directors. This presentation requires significant pre-work and preparation on the part of the senior leaders and Talent Management organization. Usually, the succession plan is presented to the board of directors during the beginning or middle of the first quarter. At that time the board will review the plan, direct any questions it has to the president/CEO and the CHRO. Sometimes the board will have specific questions for the individuals in succession for critical positions. If this is the case, the questions are addressed during the presentation or the individual in succession may be asked to join a subsequent meeting. Once the presentation is completed and the questions answered, the succession plan is accepted and it's not long before the talent management team must begin the process again. During the short break, the talent management team will focus on the follow-up items from the meeting and take actions to ensure that the plan's goals are achieved. Simultaneously, internal coaches may be involved in supporting the performance review and compensation planning process that usually occurs in the first quarter, providing training and support to managers.

In addition, based on the output of the succession plan, internal coaches may begin to enroll top talent leaders and managers, who were identified during succession, into the coaching program. There is very little downtime for the internal coach throughout the Talent Management Life Cycle.

One of the challenges many Human Resources organizations have is keeping the succession planning process alive throughout the year. In my view, I believe that succession planning should be an ongoing process including touch points throughout the year, so my recommendation is to include a mid-year step in the planning process to ensure that talent management and business leaders remain engaged and on track to:

- achieve the objectives set out for us the prior year

- make certain we are keeping our fingers on the pulse of our talent

- do everything possible to retain and grow our most senior and talented leaders

- prepare our most critical positions and identify talent for succession

The mid-year talent review session is a high-level meeting with business leaders and their HR counterparts to make certain that the leaders are contributing to the succession plan goals. These discussions may include a review of their top talent and a look at what activities/actions are being taken to develop certain capabilities in their top talent or to prepare them for their next assignments. Taking this approach is an effective way to engage the business leaders and their next level down in the organization to ensure they are doing everything necessary to retain and grow the company's bench strength and achieve the goals of the succession plan.

TALENT IDENTIFICATION AND ASSESSMENT

Many companies have a talent management system (TMS) that houses all of their talent assessments, replacement planning and leader profiles in one place. If you work at a company that does not have such a system, your HRIS or IT team can easily create a simple database to support your needs. If your company is very small, a system may not be necessary, but you may still want to establish a way to capture and store this type of information. (Excel is an easy medium to use, and Word or PowerPoint can be used for executive profiles.)

In whatever manner your company keeps track of its employee information for succession planning, it must have a suitable method of assessing its talent. The assessment method should be based on what is most valued in the organization; what contributes most significantly to the organization's competitive advantage. It may be potential for executive leadership, or it could be skills that are or will be in high demand. Once this is determined, designing a process to find the jewels in your organization may begin. For each company this process can be different, although there is one vehicle that is ideal for assessing your talent in a consistent manner—Lominger's nine-box grid (as shown in Figure 17.2 below). It's the most commonly used assessment tool as it's easy for talent management professionals, coaches and clients to use, and it's an excellent medium for assessing talent. Also, it is quite common in the succession planning and talent assessment space.

Figure 17.2: Talent Assessment Matrix

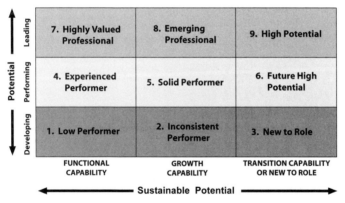

Once a manager has assessed his or her high-potential candidates, the coach should meet with the leader (the manager's manager) for a conversation about the employees to find out where he feels they fit on the talent grid. Sometimes what the leader of the organization believes is top talent and what a manager believes is top talent may not be the same and, therefore, a calibration may be necessary. This can take place in the broader talent review discussion. In preparation for this discussion, the coach, Human Resources business partner or talent manager (whoever it is in your organization) should prepare a preliminary talent grid with the names of the high-potential employees posted on the talent grid, unless a TMS is in place and a grid can automatically be generated. Having a visual aid with the employees' names placed in the relevant boxes—and juxtaposed to one another's—is an excellent tool to facilitate the discussion. It will help to trigger questions and thoughts about the placement of the individuals.

Finalizing the Talent Grid

When looking at the preliminary talent grid together, the coach can begin by asking the leader to voice any observations that come to mind about his or her team. Then, beginning with the employee who is currently in the top talent box, the coach should ask the leader to what extent he or she feels the person is top talent, and continue with these questions: What are his/her strengths? Opportunities for development? Blind spots? How ready is he/she to be promoted to the next level? How does he/she demonstrate the expected leadership capabilities? Are there any areas that the employee is particularly strong in or requires development in? Are there any assignments or experiences that he/she needs to have or would be beneficial to have prior to being promoted? What positions would you consider this employee for now and in the future?

Note: A designated note-taker should be capturing the manager's responses to each of these questions and repositioning the employees on the grid accordingly. The coach should also be taking note of who the top talent/high-potential employees are, as they more than likely are candidates for the coaching program.

The coach should repeat the above questions for each employee, working around the grid from top talent/high-potential to emerging talent, then to core performers, new-to-role and low performers. During this process the coach, who is trained in the art of questioning, will compare and contrast the employees by asking thought-provoking questions of the leader in order to challenge their assessment and make certain everyone is evaluated in a fair and consistent manner. A bonus of this exercise is that it allows the coach to glean some terrific insight on the manager's perception of her employees and the talent in her organization.

Ensuring that an organization's employees are accurately placed on the talent grid is crucial to a successful succession plan. But it can be challenging to achieve this, as it can be difficult for some managers to speak in terms of an individual's true capabilities and potential. If their comments are along the lines of "He is a great guy" or "She is a workhorse," and that is the extent of how the manager articulates their employees' performance and potential, it can result in an individual being incorrectly placed on the grid, leading to false expectations being set and a strike against the designers of the plan. (It could also signal that the manager is not familiar with or does not understand the purpose of the capabilities and how to develop his people using capabilities.) Again, this is strong justification for having the coach, as a neutral third party, act as the facilitator of the talent review. Remember, the coach is skilled at asking thought-provoking questions, in-depth listening and getting to the truth.

Another challenge that can hinder the success of the development of a succession plan is the company's ability to develop talent through movement within the organization. Perhaps opportunities to rotate individuals in order for them to gain the experiences that they need to progress their career are simply not available. If this is the case, then it is a strike against the succession plan designers and business leaders. In my view, I see the responsibility of talent development falling to the leaders of the organization, with Human Resources acting as the facilitator of the process. It's the organization's leaders who should know their top talent and which employees need to have what type of experience. By creating one open position for someone to move out of the organization or around the company, several other positions can become available, creating a domino effect and enabling movement for several top talent ready-now succession candidates. The coach can facilitate and brainstorm with the leaders of the organization to help identify target areas for rotations and promotions in order to provide their top talent excellent development opportunities. Remember, all it takes is one good move to be the catalyst for multiple moves and, subsequently, multiple coaching engagements.

Before moving on, I'd like to shine some light on a few performance types who typically aren't considered when it comes to succession planning. The first is the *new-to-role performer.* Sometimes new-to-role employees get neglected in the succession planning process because there is no immediate expectation of them to be moved or change positions too soon. But from a coaching perspective, I believe that each individual should be considered in the discussion, even if only briefly. Depending on the level and the role, new-to-role employees can be ideal candidates for the internal coaching program, especially if they are a new manager or executive, or they find themselves in a new functional area or in an expat assignment, or they have been relocated or newly hired to the firm.

The other type of employee often not included in the succession planning discussion is the *low performer.* This is typically because these employees are usually on their way out of the organization. However, if someone was a high performer or top talent in the past, and currently has been identified as a low performer, I recommend a conversation be conducted about the employee either during the performance management or succession planning process. The key is to make certain that the employee's situation is being managed accordingly. Specifically, questions the coach can ask the manager should include: How did this employee go from being top talent, high performer, to now being considered a low performer? What may have changed in their role and responsibilities when their performance started to fail? What actions have been taken to support this individual or what actions have not been taken? What about their manager? How is their track record in developing employees? I am always curious when I see someone who was once a consistent top talent subsequently fall from grace and be identified as someone who should be managed out of the company.

BEWARE OF BLIND SPOTS WHEN ASSESSING TALENT

Let's view this issue first with regard to high performers. These individuals consistently exceed their objectives and, as a result, they stand out in organizations and management identifies them for challenging assignments or projects because of their reputation to get things done. High performers are excellent in their role and take pride in their accomplishments, but they may not have the potential (or desire) to move to a higher level, learn a more complex role or accept a more challenging assignment.

Throughout my professional career, I have witnessed countless high-performing sales representatives being promoted into management roles. But just because someone can deliver results day in and day out does not necessarily mean that they will be a good manager of people. High performance can create a blind spot for the manager who is looking to promote someone, as it can mask the attributes and behaviors that are critical in a good manager, such as change management, mentoring, coaching and overall general people management skills.

With regard to low performers, I have seen employees classified as such on the talent grid because they are either new-to-role and not fully up to speed, or they are struggling to perform and the manager to whom they report has not looked past their performance and has assumed there is a lack of potential. This is critical to recognize because, while there is an element of performance in the talent assessment process, the main objective of succession planning is to identify individuals with potential who may move up and around the organization to fill critical positions. Sometimes it is difficult for a manager to spot potential when, for any number of reasons, an employee is underperforming, or it may just be the case that the manager does not have the capability to identify potential. This is why I suggest having at least the next level above the manager (ideally an executive) also review and approve the talent assessments. In addition, having the coach facilitate the talent review discussion is beneficial, as they have had insight into the larger picture and can provide guidance around where and why individuals are placed in certain boxes.

Another blind spot that can occur and be problematic for the manager looking to promote someone into a managerial or critical role is if the company has not clearly articulated the capabilities and behaviors that it values in their employees, or perhaps it has but the linkage between the words on paper and the actual behaviors is absent. I'm sure we can all think of a time when we have read a company's values or mission statement and then observed behaviors in the organization that are at the opposite end of the spectrum. Such companies fail to walk the talk, which leads to confusion and anxiety for the employees and their managers within the organization and it can also make it challenging to identify candidates for succession, or justify why certain candidates are in succession.

In my view, high potentials who have demonstrated aptitude for their initial technical abilities and who show signs of having future potential are more likely to make a greater contribution to the organization. Something to always keep in mind is that if you have an individual who is assessed as a high potential but is consistently performing below expectations, that individual may not be in the right role or may not be a good fit for the organization's culture. Some form of action is required. This is again why I believe that everyone on the talent grid deserves to be included in the talent review discussion. Remember, these employees are assets of your company. To lose them or have them in a role that does not play to their strengths can be a waste of your firm's investment in them. Therefore, having a coach leading these discussions can make certain that you have a rigorous talent discussion and uncover all blind spots.

Once the coach and the leader have worked their way around the talent grid and situated the employees among one another appropriately, the coach should ask the leader the following questions:

- What do you see?

- How do you feel about the changes we've made?

- How comfortable do you feel in presenting the members on your team and where they are placed on the talent grid to the leadership team?

- What questions will your manager or your peers ask you about your employees in relation to where they're placed on the grid?

- Who is likely to challenge you on where certain employees are positioned? (This is an especially important question for the coach to ask, as the manager may need to be prepared to justify an employee's location on the grid, especially if it's known that others have a different perspective of that employee.)

The leader should take one last look at the talent grid and ensure that each employee is in the right position in relation to the other employees. If the leader feels confident that he or she can explain and, if necessary, defend the positioning of each of their employees on the grid, then the meeting can be closed and the next step begun. If there is any uncertainty, the coach should pinpoint the areas of concern and walk through the grid with the leader again. This can be time consuming and many leaders may feel that this step is not necessary; however, I can tell you that it most certainly is worthwhile. The leader will be much better off when it comes time to present their employees in the broader talent review conversations. In addition, it forces the leader to truly know his or her employees' strengths, their potential and the areas for growth and opportunity. It also helps leaders view their organization at a higher level and identify the strengths and the opportunities for development, allowing them to provide direction on training and development initiatives for their organization.

Executive-Level Discussions

Ideally, an internal coach would be assigned to a specific organization and subsequently facilitate the talent review discussion with each of that organization's leaders. So, for example, depending on the size of the organization and how far down within the organization the talent is going to be assessed, the coach could start these meetings at the director level. Following the completion of the director conversations, the coach could then prepare a preliminary grid for the more senior executives and review it with them before a talent review discussion with the director and his director-level direct reports.

Now, this brings up a common and interesting issue. Typically, executives (director/vice president and higher levels) are involved in succession planning, and depending on how many levels deep you conduct your talent assessments, you may have high-potential employees who report to a manager who reports to a director who, in turn, reports to a vice president. When the vice president looks at his overall talent grid and conducts a talent discussion, it raises the question "Who should be in the room?" Would the manager take part in the succession planning discussion, or would she be excluded because of her level? In these situations, the director should be capable of discussing his employees.

A similar question that can come up is, if the employee reporting to the vice president is an individual contributor or at the manager level, should that individual be included in the succession planning discussion? The way I see it, if the person is a high-potential and a high performer who is competent enough to work for an executive and has a comparable level of responsibility as the other direct reports of the vice president, then I suspect that that individual is capable of contributing to a talent review and keeping the discussion confidential. However, if the employee does not have a comparable level of responsibility (for example, he or she is an administrative assistant), then being asked to the table may not be appropriate.

I must stress that it is imperative that these discussions be kept confidential, as employees should not know an executive's perception of them or their performance, especially if the perception is negative. This could cause significant damage to the employee and manager's relationship, or that of the employee and peer manager or executive, and may even cause the employee to mistrust his manager or others in the organization and possibly re-think his purpose at the company. Conversely, sharing with an employee too much positive feedback may create a false impression of her relationship with her manager, her peer manager or another executive. This false sense of security may lead the employee to change her level of performance as a result of feeling too comfortable in her position.

Conducting a Broader Talent and Business Review

As leadership changes occur in organizations, employees who are aligned with certain executives may be rotated out of succession, despite their knowledge, expertise and leadership capabilities. This is unfortunate but a reality. At the end of the day, organizations are systems, and within systems there are political currents and personal agendas at play. When a new leader assumes a role, that leader will naturally want "her people" in the support roles and will, if necessary, try to use her influence to place them there. I can understand why a leader would want individuals whom they know and trust close to them. However, if the leader is left entirely to her own devices to choose her entire team, it can limit diversity of thought which, in turn, could impact innovation and growth.

This is a situation where having an experienced coach who is assigned to a specific organization, and therefore truly familiar with the talent in that organization, can be an invaluable asset to the organization. He will have a deep understanding of the current and future business state, including the challenges and the opportunities. The coach will be able to look holistically at the organization and the business and provide very "charge-neutral" feedback and guidance on the talent review discussion. In addition, having an internal coach facilitate this discussion frees up the Human Resources business partner to play a more active role. Commonly the business partner prepares and conducts the preliminary meeting and the broader talent review discussion, but with a coach available to look after these things, the business partner is free to be an active participant and valuable contributor to the discussion.

Now, in preparation for the next stage of the succession planning process—a broader talent review with the leaders from across an organization—the coach, talent management consultant or whoever is leading the succession planning project for that organization must consolidate the individual leader's talent grids, creating new ones based on the employees' position levels. So, for example, one grid would be for vice president level, another grid for director level, and so on. These grids are presented in the talent review, at which time the organization's leaders' peers appraise and discuss each of the employees and calibrate their placement on the grids, as they compare and contrast the leaders' perspectives on their employees.

During this review or calibration meeting, the coach would act as facilitator and moderator of the discussion, ensuring that a) each employee receives ample discussion time, b) employee positions on the grid are challenged and adjusted accordingly, and c) the amount of time devoted to the session is properly managed. If you have ever been in one of these sessions, you know exactly what I mean by this last one. It is very easy to stray off course or spend too much time on one individual compared to the others, and it requires a very skilled facilitator to keep the meeting on track. Additionally, a skilled coach will ensure that the right questions are asked and that employees are fairly placed on their talent grid.

Once all of the employees are vetted and a grid for each level of employee is finalized, the coach will make recommendations regarding the trends observed during the review. For example, a certain competency or knowledge gap may have surfaced several times, in which case the coach should collaborate with his colleagues on the talent development team or the learning team and come up with recommendations to help the leader develop specific competencies or increase knowledge and close skills gaps. Doing this will also create an excellent opportunity for the coach to meet with the leader again and provide in-depth observations and recommendations for her organization.

Talent Assessment and Leadership

This reminds me of a time when I was the director of Talent Development and we were preparing for our annual talent assessments and reviews. One of our objectives was to create a means to easily identify internal ready-now talent and promote or rotate them into open positions. By doing so, it would enable us to proactively present opportunities to our employees and develop our bench strength while also reducing external hiring costs. The process we designed was simple. Once a requisition was opened, we would provide a short list of candidates for the position to the talent acquisition managers for their review (candidates were pulled from our talent management system and based on the information gathered during the talent assessment). After reviewing this list, the manager seeking to hire would speak with the manager of whichever employee she was interested in, and if there seemed to be a fit for the open position, the individual would be pre-screened and included with the other candidates under consideration. This process worked fairly well and, as you can imagine, employees were thrilled to receive calls about potential job opportunities. And managers were pleased to know that they would be supplied with a list of qualified candidates to replace their employee if that employee was selected for the open position.

In addition to this project with the talent acquisition team, we were preparing for a large-scale business transformation project that would require the company's leaders and managers to truly know their employees—their talents, their strengths and their areas for development. In order to ensure that the leaders were prepared for what was coming, we decided that we would conduct a talent assessment on all of the employees (approximately 50,000 of them!). The data gathered would be used to help us determine the capabilities of certain organizations and where we had talent with certain strengths or who would be a candidate for a future opportunity (for example, a relocation or an expatriate assignment). As you would expect, this was a complex and demanding project, but it was made a little easier with the help of our skilled internal coaches, which enabled us to duplicate the succession planning process that we had been carrying out with our senior leaders and bring it down to the manager level.

The initial step was for all directors to complete talent assessments in our talent management system. Once these were completed, we asked each of the directors to vet the positioning of the managers on their teams. We then asked the managers to complete talent assessments on their employees (this is where the bulk of the employees were, at the individual contributor level). After these assessments were completed, we asked the directors to review the placement of the individual contributors. During the vetting process, the coach would be involved, conducting a session with the director to validate and calibrate the employees' positions on the talent grid. When the talent grids were final, the information was updated in the talent management system. Then we began the process again, this time with the vice president and their directors, conducting a review session to calibrate all of the manager or manager-level employees in their organizations. We had visual documentation to support talent development programs (for example, executive education and executive coaching), which also demonstrated the respective levels of engagement in those programs and how engagement in one particular organization stacked up against engagement levels in the overall organization. We followed the same process as we did with the senior leader/director calibration meetings. The coach would act as the facilitator, questioning and challenging, calibrating the talent based on the discussion and ensuring that each employee was represented and fairly discussed during the session. Once these discussions were completed, the TMS would be updated accordingly.

The final phase of this undertaking involved the coach conducting a review of individual contributor level talent with the vice president, director and managers present. For larger organizations, these kinds of discussions can be several hours long; however, because our leaders were committed to knowing all of the employees in their organizations, their strengths and their areas for development, this part of the process went quickly. In total, the coaching team, comprised of ten coaches, completed over 200 live talent review sessions with a result of nearly 50,000 talent assessments loaded in the company's TMS— a remarkable achievement.

Figure 17.3: Talent Assessment Results

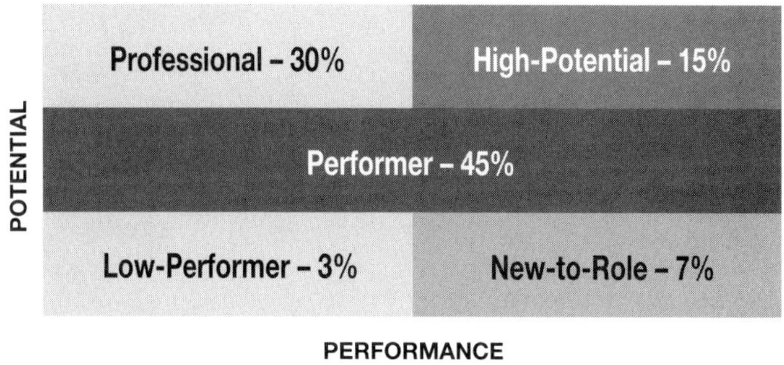

PERFORMANCE

Note: Nine boxes, as described in graph 17.2, have been consolidated into five boxes in the above graph (i.e., High Potential and Future High Potential = High Potential; Solid and Experienced Performer = Performer; High Valued Professional + Emerging Professional = Professional and Low and Inconsistent Performer = Low Performer).

After the talent assessments and review sessions were completed, it was the perfect time to speak to our leaders about their organization's development. Because we had visual documentation of their talent it was easy to discuss development programs with them (for example, executive education and executive coaching), as well as the respective levels of engagement in those programs and how engagement in their organization stacked up against the overall organization. In addition, we showed the leaders the competencies that their managers who were enrolled in the coaching program were identifying as areas where support was needed. This information enabled us to design targeted workshops and training. Moreover, these conversations would lead to greater support from leadership and greater participation in training and development programs.

Having the Career-Planning Conversation

Another common coaching conversation in the succession planning stage arises when a manager wants to prepare for a career-planning conversation with an employee. The coach may meet with the manager and the employee separately or together but, in either case, the onus is on the employee to take responsibility for his career and the conversation with his manager. The coach can help prepare the employee for that conversation by asking the following questions:

1. Tell me what you like and dislike in your current position.

2. In this position, what do you think you do well? Not so well?

3. What would you like to do more of, and less of, at work?

4. Where do you see yourself in one year? Three years? Five years? Ten years?

5. At what age would you like to retire?

6. What do you think you need to learn and what work experiences will you need to have in order to achieve the optimum position you would like to hold before retirement?

The goal is for the coach and employee to determine what critical assignments, projects and experiences would be beneficial in helping the employee achieve their ultimate position. Once all of this information is gathered, the employee, with the help of his manager and coach, can build a plan to support the employee's goal. As a coach, it is important to stress to the employee that assignments and experiences may not always be of a vertical nature or be in the employee's functional area. The employee may need to navigate a career lattice across functions in order to secure the necessary experiences needed in order to reach his desired position. It should also be pointed out that even the best-laid plans may fail due to unforeseen and unanticipated environmental variables.

Note: The coach can work with the manager to help build a career map that may look like a ladder or lattice for the employee. In addition, the coach can support the manager in helping them with how to "coach" this type of employee on their career.

Career planning conversations are an excellent opportunity for an internal coach to provide support during the succession planning stage of the Talent Management Life Cycle. Most coaches have had at least some training and experience in career planning and, if not, their coach training and the process of coaching itself can prove incredibly beneficial to the executive as she and the coach work together to plan her career and/or retirement plan, as well as her exit strategy. (**Note:** There are career coach management certification programs available to those who would like to learn more and work with employees in transition.)

Coaches must, as a matter of course, reflect on the service that they provide to executives with regard to managing their career and preparing for retirement. Many companies invest in the selection, onboarding and training of their employees but, when it comes to the end of the employee's time at the company, they choose to outsource the handling of what was once a great asset to an external company. Now, don't get me wrong, I completely agree with providing outplacement services to employees who are transitioning or who have been affected by a workforce reduction of some type. However, consider what it would be like if you could provide some type of support to these individuals as they prepare to make a transition or to retire. Think of the positive impact it would have on the employment brand. We say we have respect for our employees, but do we really when we give them notice?

I remember hearing stories from friends of mine in the pharmaceutical industry who were told that there was a reduction in force coming and they were to be in their offices on Friday at 11 A.M. If they were being affected by the reduction, they would receive a phone call. If they didn't receive a phone call, they were safe. Can you imagine? How respectful is that? Another story that a friend of mine told me was about how several employees at her company were called into a conference room and told their fate. Some were safe and others were told they no longer had jobs. Again, how is that being respectful of your employees?

I'm not saying that employees being affected by reductions should be coached, but imagine the experience if, first of all, the employee was told they were being let go in private, by their manager, and given time to collect their things or remain in the office to inform colleagues and friends and share their personal contact information. Then imagine if they were given the opportunity to speak with a coach to discuss next steps and their exit strategy and a farewell message, and begin to formulate the beginnings of a plan for what they'll do next career-wise. The employee would have time to prepare for outplacement and know what to expect. Reflect on how you would feel being treated in such a respectful way. A difficult situation can be turned into a somewhat positive situation by offering support and respect for the employee.

In the case of an employee who is retiring, companies typically provide financial planning services. These financial firms help retirees plan for the next phase of their life. Can you imagine how appreciative you would feel, as a retiree, if you were also provided with coaching support as you transitioned? You might be inclined to become a recruiter for the company and a representative of the brand, explaining to candidates why they should choose your former company rather than the competition. Perhaps you would become involved in your community and share your career experiences with others who indirectly will support your employment brand.

Unfortunately, today, we are all moving at the speed of light, and many are struggling to find work. However, there is a tremendous asset leaving the workforce that could be mentoring and providing stewardship to thousands on how to prepare for their future in certain industries or specific functions. Through these conversations, students and other professionals could be preparing for their future by getting the right training, experiences and support. By creating a positive experience for retiring employees, we can be creating opportunities for them to continue to make a contribution while helping to build the future for generations to come.

COACHING & LEADERSHIP INSIGHT: The Most Not-Talked-About Topic of Succession Planning—To Tell or Not To Tell

Now the million-dollar question: Do you tell your employees where they are placed in succession? Well, every company has a different perspective. If that sounds like a canned answer, that's because it is! I have heard this topic discussed and debated time and time again. The discussion is circular and there are advantages and disadvantages to both sides of the debate; however, at the end of the day, you need to do what is best for the company and the individual.

If you have decided that you will disclose this information to an employee, you should be prepared to clearly explain your decision when asked later: What was the purpose of telling the individual? How did you tell them? What was the context? What action will be taken as a result of telling them their position in succession? This situation is an excellent opportunity for a coaching conversation, as a coach can help the manager prepare for the disclosing of succession information to an employee. It's important for both the manager and the employee to remember that, when someone is told where he or she is in succession, it is a moment in time, a snapshot if you will, and there are many variables that can change or cause one's position in succession to change. Also, remember that all employees are assets to a company, despite where they may fall in succession, and it's important to tell them that they are valued (unless you are speaking with an underperforming employee). In any case, when an employee asks where he or she stands within the company's succession plan, you can turn it into a coaching conversation and ask them where they think they stand. What did they do to be placed in that position, or what do they need to do in order to progress in succession? From there the employee can come up with an action plan and leave the conversation empowered, "owning" their career and their position in succession.

Part 5:

HOW TO MEASURE THE IMPACT OF AN INTERNAL COACHING PROGRAM

The Coaching Solution

CHAPTER 20: TOP TEN REASONS A COMPANY SHOULD HAVE INTERNAL COACHES AND BUILD A COACHING CULTURE

18 | What Does Success Look Like?

One of my favorite questions to ask clients is, "What does 'good' look like for you?" I like to start any project or coaching engagement with this question because once we all know what "good" will look like, we can define success and thereby identify the goals, timeframes, and type of support and resources that will be needed to achieve success. The same goes for internal coaching programs. Knowing what "good" looks like helps to determine the resources that will be necessary, the programs that will need to be developed and who the participants will be in those programs. "Good" and "great" can come in many shapes and sizes; it can vary depending on the size of the organization, the focus areas of the program and the timeframes and resources available. For example, the purpose of your pilot internal coaching program may be to gauge the level of interest among the employees in being coached, and whether your culture is open to having coaching programs developed. Therefore, your measure of success might be what percentage of eligible employees signed up for the program as well as how much did they utilize their coach.

METHODS OF MEASUREMENT

So, how will you measure your internal coaching program's overall success? There are many ways to measure success and they include the following:

- Utilization and Net Promoter Score (NPS)
- Return on Investment (ROI)
- Return on Engagement (ROE)
- Impact Study (a hybrid model including all of the above)

Utilization and Net Promoter Score

The first way to measure success is simple: utilization and feedback. At the end of the day, do your customers use your services? If so, that alone is a pretty good indication that the program is considered valuable. The metric of utilization is relatively simple: determine how many hours you would like to allocate to coaching per participant per month and set that number as your target. Measure how much time is actually utilized against that allocation to calculate an individual participant's utilization score. Then, take the average for all of your participants' time spent in coaching and measure this against the targeted allocation to calculate the percentage of utilization. This is a quick and basic method to assess program participation, which is a driving factor of the program's success. The thinking is, why would your employees participate in a program if they were not seeing value?

You may also wish to track the utilization of your coaches' time and the amount of time that clients are spending with their coaches. This is helpful to you as the program manager because it can help you manage workflow. For example, if you find that there are some months where coaching is utilized more than others, how might you be able to integrate this information into your overall learning and talent development schedule? This is a simple way to monitor activity—a first gut-check, if you will, which will ensure that you are planning your coaches' workloads accordingly. With regard to how much time the participant is spending with the coach, if it is under or over the amount of time that is allocated, this is something to explore with both the coach and the client separately. If underutilization is occurring, it could mean that the participant is not engaged, is not interested in coaching or doesn't have time for it, or the chemistry between the client and the coach might not be right. If utilization is much higher than expected, the participant may be over relying on the coach or there could be something significant occurring for the participant and he requires additional support for a short period of time. If there is a trend with overutilization, the program manager should explore this with the coach, the participant and perhaps also the participant's manager.

The following chart illustrates how you can depict participation within your internal coaching program.

Figure 18.1: Participation Chart

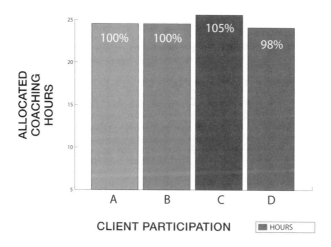

After the clients use the coaching services, what do they say about the coaching experience? The answer to this question is the basis for the Net Promoter Score (NPS), which lies at the core of the Net Promoter System developed by Fred Reichheld, introduced in his 2003 *Harvard Business Review* article "One Number You Need to Grow." The NPS is a measurement of customer loyalty, how loyal or committed a customer is—or, in this case, how committed a coaching program participant is—to the internal coaching program. So, when it comes to using the NPS model to assess your internal coaching program, you need to ask your program participants one simple question: "Would you refer the internal coaching program to a colleague?"

If the feedback from your customers is positive and they wish to continue to use the program, then continuing to monitor interest and engagement levels may be an adequate way to measure your program's success. If the response is, "No, I wouldn't refer the program to a colleague," then I would encourage you to have a conversation with program participants to understand why that is. Find out what their issues and concerns are, and explore opportunities to improve the experience for them and, in essence, the program overall.

ROI and ROE

Let's begin this section by defining the two key terms that surround measurement when it comes to the learning and development of people:

Return on investment (ROI) is the concept of an investment of some resource yielding a benefit to the investor. A high ROI means that the investment gains compare favorably to the investment cost.

Return on engagement (ROE) is used to describe the concept of measuring the positive impact or results of engaging with people. This concept originally began in terms of measuring people's response to social media; however, now it has expanded to include many types of people engagement programs.

Identifying and measuring the business impact of learning and development programs has traditionally been the subject of robust discussion and debate. The same is true when it comes to measuring the benefits of an internal coaching program, particularly the program's ROI or ROE for an organization. When the coaching profession was less mature, there was a greater demand for ROI information to help inform those who were uncertain about the viability and impact of coaching. As the coaching profession evolved, so did the understanding that coaching is effective and valuable. Consequently, there is no longer as strong demand to quantifiably demonstrate the impact and effectiveness of coaching. However, the discussion still occurs and I would be remiss if I neglected to discuss the much sought-after quest for the ROI holy grail.

Collecting return on investment data and calculating the actual ROI requires enormous commitment on behalf of the sponsoring organization. Creating a structure that would allow for the collection of ROI data for a coaching program takes a great deal of time, effort and resources (that could otherwise be applied to the coaching initiative). This can be challenging for even the largest of organizations.

The other option that many organizations adopt, especially government and non-profit organizations, is return on engagement. Return on engagement is measurable, and research on ROE has produced consistent outcomes:

- A highly engaged organization has the potential to reduce staff turnover by 87 percent and it can provide a corresponding increase in performance by 20 percent.[1]

---

[1] "Driving Performance and Retention through Employee Engagement," Corporate Leadership Council, 2004. www.mckpeople.com.au/SiteMedia/w3svc161/Uploads/Documents/760af459-93b3-43c7-b52a-2a74e984c1a0.pdf

- Companies with an engaged workforce improve operating income by 19 percent, while companies with low engagement results see operating income decline by 32 percent.[2]

- An engaged employee has a willingness to do more than expected (39 percent), produce a higher level of activity (27 percent), have better working relationships (13 percent) and have more satisfied customers (10 percent).[3]

Measuring ROE is more practical than measuring ROI for those organizations whose budgets have a tendency to be restricted. It's also particularly useful in the federal government space, where one must contend with confidentiality matters and levels of clearances, and it is simply not possible to disclose, discuss or measure the investment.

Now, the problem with using ROI to assess a coaching program's value is that, despite its intense rigor, ROI doesn't capture the impact and costs to the organization of not doing coaching. As many of us know, coaching can mitigate poor behavior and mistakes made in an organization, and it has facilitated conflict resolution in a timely and effective manner. These outcomes can contribute to the effectiveness, performance and the ability of a company to deliver results, whether it be on behalf of the individuals being coached or as a result of the impact they have on their team, their peers and other employees or the overall organization.

Years ago there was much anxiety about the idea of calculating ROI for coaching programs (internal or external). It's a commonly accepted fact now that coaching adds value to organizations and to the leaders and employees who participate in the programs, but for the longest time the coaching profession felt the need to justify or provide ROI on the value and expense of their coaching initiatives. One measure that would have relieved the anxiety would have been to evaluate the impact of the coaching program on its participants and their organizations at the end of each coaching program cycle. So, for example, if program participants were enrolled in the coaching program in January and completed their coaching engagement the following January, if an impact study were conducted at that time it would effectively measure

[2] "The ISR Employee Engagement Report," Towers-Perrin-ISR, 2006.

[3] Sean Bakker, "A Study of Employee Engagement in the Canadian Workplace: Control, Opportunity & Leadership, Psychometrics," 2010. www.psychometrics.com/en-us/articles/engagement-study.htm

the impact of the coaching on the participants and business results. (I discuss using impact studies as a measurement tool in more detail later in this chapter.)

I am not suggesting that it's unnecessary to measure the impact of your coaching program or that you should implement such a program on a whim without proving its effectiveness. However, I do think it needs to be remembered that implementing a coaching program is not like buying a piece of equipment that can be treated as an asset and depreciates over time. The program facilitates behavioral change at an individual and an organizational level, and it can be difficult to capture the precise moment of the change and, therefore, measure the impact of the change over time. With that said, and based on your company's culture and philosophy, you will need to determine which level of measurement is best for your program and company.

The Five Levels of Learning & Calculating ROI

The most common measurement utilized in learning organizations is called "Four Levels of Learning" and it was developed by Donald Kirkpatrick, who was professor emeritus at the University of Wisconsin and past president of the American Society for Training and Development. The "Four Levels of Learning" is a progressive metric with these four levels:

Level 1 – Reaction: Measures participants' reaction to the training.

Level 2 – Learning: Assesses the increase of knowledge and skills during training.

Level 3 – Behavior: Assesses post-training the transfer of knowledge and skills from the training in the workplace.

Level 4 – Results: The impact of the training on the business.

Jack Phillips is the founder of the ROI Institute and a thought leader in measurement, accountability and evaluation. He took the "Four Levels of Learning" one step further and incorporated a Level 5: Return on Investment. Many learning organizations and programs use either the four-level or the five-level approach. The combination of Kirkpatrick and Phillips' work is depicted in the following chart:

Level	Measurement Focus
Level 1: Reaction, Satisfaction & Planned Action	What are participants' reactions to the program and what do they plan to do with the material?
Level 2: Learning	What skills, knowledge or attitudes have changed and by how much?
Level 3: Job Application and Implementation	Was there behavior change and did the participants apply what they learned on the job?
Level 4: Business Impact	Did the on-the-job application produce measurable results?
Level 5: Return on Investment (ROI)	Did the monetary value of the results exceed the cost for the program?

Phillips believes that when a learning program is implemented, it should create a chain of impact at several levels, resulting in ROI. A chain of impact needs to occur as skills and knowledge (Level 2) are learned and applied on the job (Level 3) to produce business impact (Level 4). At each level, measurements need to be taken to determine whether the business impact was actually generated by the program. If there is a negative ROI, it should be easy to identify which link in the chain was the cause. For example, did the participants not assimilate the learning (Level 2) or were they not able to successfully apply the new learning on the job (Level 3)?

Calculating ROI is not an easy process. Figure 18.2 is a visual depiction of Phillips' ROI Methodology.

Figure 18.2: Phillips' ROI

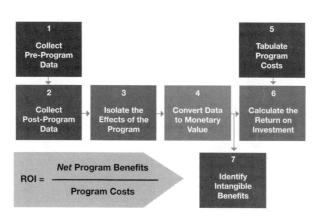

As I said earlier in this chapter, ROI evaluation is extremely complex and time-consuming. Phillips advises that organizations should consider measuring learning and implementing ROI impact studies very selectively, on only 5 percent to 10 percent of their training programs. As noted at dashe.com:

> [Phillips] recommends that training measurement and evaluation focus on an individual program or a few tightly integrated courses. For organizations implementing the ROI concept for the first time, he suggests that only one course be selected for an ROI calculation as part of the ROI learning curve. In the final analysis, the selection of programs for ROI calculations should yield a level of sampling where top management is comfortable in its assessment of the training and development functions.[4]

Impact Study

A coaching measurement model that I have a great appreciation for (and have used in the past) is one that is based upon Merrill Anderson's model. It is a means of assessment called an Impact Study, and is used specifically for measuring the impact of coaching and coaching programs.

Anderson cites an impact study in his book *Coaching that Counts* in which he and his team worked with a client who launched a leadership development initiative that targeted middle managers from different business units and functional areas within a company. The leadership development activities included group mentoring, individual assessments, development planning, a leadership workshop and work on strategic business projects. Anderson's team utilized coaching as the key enabler of achieving results because the coaching program participants could work privately and individually with each coach. Participants spoke highly of the program and an assessment of the program's success was conducted using the following questions:

1. How did coaching add value to the business, and what was the return on investment?

2. How could coaching be best leveraged in the future, especially if coaching was to be expanded to other business regions?

The process that was used to collect the data involved a two-part questionnaire. Part one was completed by the participants via e-mail. The purpose was to gather information on their initial reaction to coaching, what they learned

---

[4] URL: http://www.dashe.com/blog/evaluation-2/more-on-re-evaluating-evaluation-jack-phillips-and-roi/

and how they applied what they learned. In essence, it assessed the coaching program's business impact. The second part of the questionnaire was conducted over the telephone with each respondent, and it probed more deeply into business impact and the financial return on investment.

Impact Study Results

In both of my internal coaching programs, we conducted impact studies to further validate the positive feedback we were receiving from our clients. The goal was to determine if the coaching program was of great value in terms of the individual participants' professional development, productivity and results. (The setup and findings from the study conducted in the MCI Sales organization may be found in Chapter 10.)

As you now know, once MCI was acquired by Verizon and became Verizon Business, we were asked to take our successful program and expand it across all functional areas. By 2008, we had a fully operational coaching team deployed globally, supporting the company's different regions and functions. When it came time to determine the impact of the coaching program, we had learned many lessons about calculating ROI and the level of effort (LOE) required to conduct such a study, and so we felt that our time, energy and budget would be much better spent working with our clients than trying to calculate ROI. Plus, the company had adopted the Net Promoter Score (NPS) methodology in order to measure their customer experience, so it made sense for us to align with the NPS concept and utilize that approach in measuring the coaching impact. We invited program participants actively enrolled in the annual program (approximately 300) to complete the survey. Approximately 70% completed the survey and the following are the key results.

Net Promoter Score Questions:

"I would recommend the coaching program."
- 98% agreed/strongly agreed (and over 70% strongly agreed)

"I would recommend my coach."
- 99% agreed/strongly agreed (and over 80% strongly agreed)

In July 2014, the Human Capital Institute (HCI) produced the *Building a Coaching Culture* study (underwritten by the International Coach Federation). A survey was given to 545 HR and business managers, and four subject-matter experts were interviewed in-depth. The conclusions drawn from this study support the business case for having a strong coaching culture, including the following:

- "Organizations with a strong coaching culture have higher employee engagement (65% of employees rated as highly engaged compared to 50% of rest of the organization)."

- "They also reported stronger financial performance; among organizations with a strong coaching culture, 60% report being above their industry peer group in 2013 revenue compared to 41% of all others."

- "More organizations are realizing the importance of coaching, thus increasing the scope and offerings—especially for managers/leaders using coaching skills. 80% report they are expanding the use of managers/leaders using coaching skills within the next five years."

Research continues to support not only the use of coaching inside organizations, but how much coaching inside organizations has grown and will continue to grow in the future. To download or purchase the study, please go to http://coachfederation.org/coachingculture. For additional internal coaching resources, please see www.robertsoncoachinstitute.com.

COACHING & LEADERSHIP INSIGHT: What Does "Good" Look Like? The Answer Is with Your Clients

Over my years of building and implementing internal coaching programs, it is clear to me that internal coaches provide value to the organization in many ways. I have seen coaching positively impact financial results in sales force performance and revenue growth, as well as in the customer experience and in expense reductions. In addition, I have seen coaching positively impact the attraction of new talent to organizations, and the retention and development of all types of talent—new hires, managers, leaders and entire organizations. If programs are designed properly and you have strong coaches with actively engaged participants, the results will follow.

But even though I know internal coaching programs positively impact engagement, productivity and business results, I am still an executive who wants to see results in black and white. And I know many executives feel the same, especially when it involves making a significant investment in time and money. Conducting surveys to assess the success of your program requires a significant level of effort and, therefore, I encourage you to keep the surveys simple yet quantitative and trust the feedback of the program participants. If they are engaged in the program and are consistently working with their coaches, change will occur. Also, the managers of your program participants will have a view both on the participants' and program's success. They will tell you if the program and results are not meeting their expectations. It is an excellent idea to check in with them along the way and ask them if they are seeing the changes in behaviors or the results that they expect to see. If so, excellent; if not, this is an opportunity to course correct and adjust whatever is happening or not happening in your coaching program in order for you, your coaches and the coaching participants to drive the change in behavior and results that are desired.

Companies spend hundreds of thousands, if not millions, of dollars on training and development programs annually, and not every single program is measured in terms of ROI. I think what is most important is that you ask yourself these questions: Every time our company implements an initiative or a change, do we measure it? If so, to what degree? Depending on your company and its culture, the responses to these questions will signal to you the degree of measurement necessary. The key is to demonstrate "what 'good' looks like" and have your program participants become strong advocates for coaching. Once that happens, I suspect the idea of measuring ROI or ROE, or even using impact studies, will fall by the wayside.

19 The Trilogy of Change Management

Change. It's constant. It impacts us in many ways. The choice we do have is how we respond to change. Can we stay calm and focused in the face of change? Or do we let it control us, which is going to lead to chaos and calamity.

Back at MCI, we would refer rather ruefully to our company's acronym as "Many Changes Imminent" in light of the inevitable annual or bi-annual organizational change, which in those days felt as though it happened much more frequently. These days, changes in organizations occur at a much faster pace and do not wait for a new year, the year-end or a new quarter, sometimes with devastating effects on the people impacted and those left behind to pick up the pieces.

Change can also impact our psyche and our ego. Over my career, I adopted an approach to dealing with change that has its origins in the ancient Japanese martial art of *Aikido*. Aikido is often translated as "the way of unifying with life energy" or as "the way of the harmonious spirit." Its creator, Ueshiba (1883–1969), had a goal to create an art that practitioners could use to defend themselves while also protecting their attacker from injury. Therefore, Aikido is performed by not opposing the attack with direct force but by redirecting the force of the attack. This requires very little physical strength, as the Aikido practitioner "leads" with the attacker's momentum and uses precise movements to go with the energy and achieve success without harm or injury to oneself.

What, you might ask, does this have to do with our psyche or ego? Our psyche or ego can suffer if change results in demotion or a lateral and unwanted move. Perhaps long-term colleagues are let go or leave voluntarily if the change doesn't align with their expectations or values, or it simply takes them out of what is familiar to them—out of their comfort zone. This sudden shift can impact one's psyche, spirits or personal morale. When this type of change occurs consistently and is relentless, it can cascade through the organization until the organization becomes an organism in stress.

By using Aikido and going with the energy force, not opposing or resisting it, you are least likely to cause harm to yourself or the organization. It is to the mutual benefit of the individual and organization as we experience change to keep this thought before us, and also with clients who are going through change. On this note, I will now offer some stories, concepts and an approach that I found extremely helpful when I was leading change initiatives or being affected by change initiatives.

THE "THREE A" APPROACH TO CHANGE

From a personal perspective (and this works organizationally as well), I like to deal with change by using the "Three A" approach: **Anticipate, Adapt** and **Adjust Accordingly**.

When I know that change is inevitable and I need to prepare my team, I always advise my employees and clients to "think globally and act locally." I ask these questions: What is your company's vision? Its purpose? How is its performance? How is your department performing? How are *you* performing?

Based on their responses, I ask them to come up with multiple scenarios and flesh out each of the outcomes in the context of WIIFM (What's in it for me?), WIIFMD and/or WIIFMO (What's in it for my department and/or organization?). Together we assess the possible outcomes and determine the best way to *anticipate* change. This completes step one in the process.

At step two, the *adapt* part of the approach, we identify the top three possible outcomes and design multiple responses to each of the possible changes. This may result in a change in organizational structure or, if I am working with a sales and service leader, it could include redesigning account assignments and designing new ways to "go-to-market" and support existing customers. If we are preparing for a reduction in force (RIF), we'll discuss how the work will get accomplished and by whom (for example, who stays in positions, moves to different positions, can be placed in other roles and, unfortunately, who would be impacted by the reduction in force).

At step three, we consider what will need to happen to *adjust* and/or course correct during the onset of the actual change and how individuals may be likely to respond to those potential adjustments. Of the possible solutions decided in step two, we work with the one that applies to whichever change is occurring and discuss what needs to happen and by when; for example, how will the manager and team members react, who is most at risk or to be upset by the change and how will those situations be addressed. We begin to draft a plan inclusive of all actions/items and determine who will be responsible for what and by when.

The second part of the adjust step is focused on the execution of the change, in accordance to (or *accordingly* with) the expectations that have been set by leadership or the leader of the change initiative. Therefore, it is important to keep an eye toward the future while continuing to steer the business and accelerate through the change. During this stage, it is important to make certain you are taking into consideration the a) degree of communciation, b) management or leadership engagement and c) support, as well as _____ (fill in the blank with whatever else you believe will be needed to not only accelerate the change but to maintain employee focus and engagement and result in minimal downtime and impact to efficiencies).

A change strategy brings clarity and confidence to the equation. It's sort of like preparing for takeoff and going through the safety procedures, where in the event of loss of cabin pressure you are instructed to put on your oxygen mask first and then help others. It's not about saving yourself but, rather, it's about making a shift (internally) that is aligned to the overarching goal of working with change in a way that is the most calm, efficient and least disruptive to your employees and the organization. Also, quite frankly, it's about getting your head around what is happening so that you can be the best individual contributor, manager, leader and change agent your company needs you to be. From that state you will be able to offer assistance to others, helping them to put on their own oxygen masks and prepare for the drop in cabin pressure—the change.

I have worked on several business transformation projects over my career and have listened to colleagues discuss change theories, create change architectures, complete RACI (Responsible, Accountable, Consulted, Informed) charts and more. But at the end of the day the goal is to make the change as smoothly as possible and mitigate impact to the business. This sounds easier than it usually is, especially when it comes to transformational change. Without getting too technical, the larger the change or level of transformation that needs to occur, the greater probability of disruption to your people and your business.

TRANSFORMATIONAL CHANGE

Transformational change initiatives typically share these dynamics:

1. They are long-term initiatives—ones that that may extend over several years, expand across several functional areas and impact succession plans once considered inviolate. Complex change does not occur overnight, nor should it. It takes strategic and tactical planning and the orchestration and coordination of many organizations, their people, systems and processes.

   To achieve a change project or a transformational initiative, many complex initiatives and projects may be integrated into the overall plan. This includes projects that may address the changes that need to occur in business strategy as it relates to things such as:

   - markets served
   - products and services distributed
   - sales and customer service strategies

   and supporting requirements such as:

   - organizational structure
   - required skill sets and other talent capabilities
   - technology
   - process

   These complex changes may require multiple support levers to be pulled and projects to be launched. However, the first lever, if you will, that needs to be pulled is with respect to the alignment of leadership across and down into the organization. This is critical to accomplish and can be one of the most difficult challenges a leader of change will face, which goes back to my earlier point about how our natural tendency is to resist the force of change. Resistance is much more keenly felt in a culture that is risk-averse or has been stagnant for a long time. Therefore, I strongly encourage any leader undertaking a large transformational change to conduct a thorough analysis of their future state of the areas that will be impacted by the change, inclusive of systems, processes and, most importantly, people.

As Geoff Colvin writes in his best-selling book *Talent is Overrated: What Really Separates World-Class Performers from Everybody Else*, ". . . the best organizations assign people to jobs in much the same way that sports coaches or music teachers choose exercises for their students—to push them just beyond their current capabilities and build the skills that are most important. . . . Organizations tend to assign people based on what they're already good at, not what they need to work on. The merciless competitive pressure on every company makes it difficult to pull accomplished employees out of jobs they do extremely well and put them into positions where they may struggle. That's a tension every organization must deal with in order to become more successful."[1]

For those individuals who are not willing to adapt or even capable of doing so, it is best for them and the organization that they move on. For organizations and individuals who find themselves in the "tension" that is mentioned above, it is most important to remember that the decision to place an individual in a "stretch assignment" was intentional and they must be patient as the individual adapts and grows through the experience. Often, I see these decisions made and the expectation to have impact is immediate; patience begins to wear thin, creating additional tensions for the individual and the organization involved.

2. Collaboration and cooperation from multiple leaders, departments and business units across geographic areas will be required. Large transformational change by its nature impacts an organization on a wide scale, be it quickly or over a longer time horizon, depending on the complexity and breadth of the transformation. Many times, those involved in the change or asked to be change agents also have a full-time job in addition to the role they are playing in the change or transformation project. Therefore, an individual, manager or leader, who already has a very full plate, can now be easily overwhelmed. Especially at your manager level (recall my views on managers from Chapter 15), you will find critical connectors in your organization to align, motivate and engage your

---

[1] Geoff Colvin, *Talent Is Overrated: What Really Separates World-Class Performers from Everybody Else* (New York: Portfolio, 2008, 2010), 128.

employees and impact the customer, as well as interface with leadership. Do not underestimate their ability to be a change agent or change resister or to become burnt out or suffer from what I refer to as "change fatigue."

3. Education, communication, monitoring progress and recognizing success are critical elements of executing a successful change or transformational plan. Anyone impacted by the change needs to understand why the change is occurring; how it will affect them, their team, their work and their livelihood; how it may alter the vision for the company; and why the company will be in a better place as a result of the change. (For example, the company will become more agile, flexible and adaptable to change while developing its change capability.) Therefore, monitoring progress—"inspecting what you expect"—and communicating these expectations and progress are critical to all those involved with or impacted by the change.

The Application of Transformational Change Initiatives for Internal Coaching Programs

The process and discipline of transformational change management is a hands-on collaborative endeavor involving key executives from across organizations and, in many cases, an external partner who can provide an essential outside perspective and help put plans into action. Typically, there are multiple areas in which a coach who is experienced with change management can play an instrumental role. Some possibilities include being assigned to individuals leading change initiatives at an organization or department level, as well as coaching groups or teams who are impacted by the change or involved in the change management. For example, the coach and the change leader may partner and support the leader as they work through their strategies and approach, as well as support the leader as challenges arise by creating a safe and trusted place where the leader can think and work though the issues.

In terms of the groups that are impacted, the coach can provide group coaching to work with the team in order to help them assess the change and, therefore, prepare for the change. In addition, as it relates to the change team, the coach can provide group coaching and facilitation support or be the quiet observer on the sidelines, stepping in when the team gets stuck or fails to see a challenge or an opportunity. The coach can surface thoughtful questions or ideas for consideration. All of the above contribute to establishing a high-performing team and can accelerate the change and impact of the change on the organization.

Readying for and Managing Through Change— A Four-Step Process

Let me walk you through a transformational project and show how coaching and consulting was applied throughout it. Please note that this approach is derived from Accenture's Journey Map approach, which some leaders I have worked with have used in their business transformation journeys. It is very similar to a "coach" approach, in the sense that it is about coming from a place of inquiry and learning. I believe that this approach, when deployed by internal coaches across an organization, can drive alignment and accelerate through most organizational changes.

Step 1: Assess the Current State

At this stage, the executive leadership team comes together in a workshop type of forum to access the "state-of-the-state" of the business while identifying the drivers for the change. It is important during this step that the forum not be about judging or blaming, and that leaders are comfortable opening their organization's kimonos and indicating what works well and not so well, and truly be open about their own capabilities and limitations. During this step, an internal coach may act as a facilitator and guide the group through the discussions, asking the uncomfortable questions with the intention of getting the facts and the truth out on the table. In addition, the coach may need to manage the egos in the room by providing a space for the leaders to share their perspectives in such a way that it does not cannibalize the floor or meeting purpose while providing equal "airtime" for all participants. This is a fundamental exercise in determining a baseline and to be able to measure your progress against your starting point. During this step it is crucial that the leadership team identifies the drivers for the change, airs contrasting points of view and, most importantly, works to achieve alignment across the leadership team as well as articulate responsibility for shared leadership of the business's transformation and the challenges the team is facing.

Note: This type of session is important to be conducted not only at the executive level, but at each level in the organization where and when needed. These sessions help to not only surface the details of the good, bad and ugly, they can also begin to build momentum, alignment and support for the change. During these sessions, change agents and resisters may surface, making it easier to address problem areas as well as to leverage strengths accordingly. If alignment does not exist at the sponsor level, and the sponsor does not have the political support, then the change/transformation is doomed. To ensure growth or change, there are times when leadership needs to remove those unaligned for the greater good.

QUALIFICATIONS AND CHARACTERISTICS OF CHANGE AGENTS		
respected	trusted	proactive
approachable	open to change	a good communicator
influential and has gravitas	motivated	a formal or informal leader

Some leaders may show up and participate in these meetings and appear to have the qualifications and characteristics of a change agent and be supportive of the change; however, once they leave the room, their behavior betrays that they are anything but supportive of change. In these situations, it is imperative that the behavior is eliminated or the individual is removed. Otherwise, their nonsupportive thinking and behavior will carry forward and impact the design as well as the achievement of the future state.

Step 2(a): Setting Up for the Future State

At this stage, defining a vision for the company in its new form is critical. Management needs to know what the common objectives are and how best to communicate this vision to their organizations and be able to demonstrate tangible and measureable benefits as to why this change is important to the company. This step is conducted again with the next level of the leadership team. Subsequently it can be shared with the next level down, as senior executives must have time to interpret how the change will impact their organization and what needs to be done to onboard their people and adapt processes and systems accordingly. Again, a coach can facilitate the discussion and work with the leaders individually to think through and design their change plans. This is an important step, as this is where the WIIFM (what's in it for me?) begins to take shape and messaging can be developed. Each employee impacted by the change will be looking for the WIIFM and, therefore, ensuring messaging is geared toward them can be an accelerant to the change.

Step 2(b): Assessing the Current State

As a corollary to step 2(a), leaders of the organization must conduct an assessment of their current state (people, process and systems) and determine what areas will be impacted by the change or require a direct change. Tools that can be used include custom-designed assessments, interviews with key stakeholders and members of organizations, and perhaps surveys of those to be impacted by the change. The goal is to establish a benchmark in terms of capability as well as identify where support or in fact resistance to change resides, as well as to understand the scope, scale and level of effort required to execute the change. Subsequently, the internal coach and the leaders of the department can bring together members from different parts of the organization who can realistically analyze the gap between their department's current state—inclusive of systems, processes and people—and the desired state, and collaborate to design the solutions required to prepare and execute the change. As part of this process, existing training programs, leadership development and culture initiatives as well as leaders, directors, managers and employees will need to be assessed to determine their effectiveness to lead and support the change in their organization, as well as their own competency/capability to make the change themselves. The following is an example of a change assessment summary slide.

Figure 19.1: Change Assessment Summary

Business Function	Rating	Key Impacts
HR		• Processes have significant manual activities • Lack of process standardization, scalability and internal controls • Job role changes as a result of eliminating manual processes
IT		• Processes are executed and updated manually • Job role changes as a result of elimination of manual processes • Current policies are mixed between global and local as a result of lack of corporate governance
FINANCE		• Process require manual activities • Job role changes as a result of elimination of manual processes • Function is decentralized

Degree of Impact	Low	Medium	High

Step 3: Change Architecture Design

Once all of the assessments, interviews and processes described in steps 1 and 2 are completed, the internal coach can lead the change team to design a change architecture plan. The plan defines all activities required to achieve the desired future state. It will also prioritize the activities (training, executive communications, use of social media platforms, and so on) and include a communications plan that will keep the entire organization aligned to the goals and on track to monitor and communicate its progress. The ability to deliver the plan and the capability of the business and the people to absorb the work and the plan will be critical. Doing too much, too soon, is not a good idea. However, not doing enough is not good either. Finding the balance can be a challenge, however, it is possible.

Step 4: Monitor the Progress

Communication is critical in any change initiative, and progress must be monitored and communicated. It is imperative to define specific goals, objectives and critical milestones. If course correction is required, it must be communicated. Typically, the change lead or program manager is responsible for monitoring progress with respective team members, department and/or organizational leaders involved with and affected by the change. A common approach is to use a dashboard prepopulated with goals and milestones. Many times these reports are color-coded red/yellow/green in order to easily depict the status. When a project or work stream is depicted yellow or red, this creates an opportunity to understand where there is an issue or a milestone may be missed and its impact on other projects and milestones.

I know this sounds like simple project management, but in many change initiatives, change occurs at intersecting points or hand-offs between organizations. It is at these intersecting points where progress can be slowed and the change delayed. Having a dashboard, monitoring progress and open communication can prevent projects getting stuck or delays from occurring. For example, once a circuit in a network is provisioned, it no longer resides with provisioning; the responsibility moves to the installers and from the installers to maintenance to customer service. Can you see all of the intersecting points? When a change impacts one point, more than likely change will impact the hand-off point. It is within the intersection that both sides must be clear on the change and willing to implement and manage the change for their respective areas. And this change then flows through the entire service delivery life cycle. An error here can negatively impact the customer and their experience. The execution of change at intersecting points, especially when those points affect the customer, is critical.

INTERNAL COACHING AND CHANGE INITIATIVES

Internal coaching programs, when incorporated into your change initiative, can truly make the difference between "good and great." First of all, through coaching you are proactively caring for the execution of the change by proactively caring for your employees who are leading and/or impacted by the change. Engaging coaches at the leadership and especially management levels where change will occur creates a forum for the manager to proactively work through and design a change plan for themselves as managers. A coach can cover specific topics with a leader/manager who is being impacted by change and support the manager or leader to manage and accelerate through the change. Following are some questions that the coach can ask the managers and leaders leading or being impacted by change:

1. How will you, as the manager, need to change?

2. What will you need to do? Do differently? What behaviors will you need to change? What new behaviors will you need to adopt?

3. What work habits will you need to adopt? Change? Stop doing?

4. What will you communicate as it relates to the change? How and when will this communication occur?

5. What impact may you expect from the change? De-motivated employees? Over-worked or over-stressed employees? What can you do to anticipate, prepare and minimize or eliminate these situations?

Engaging a coach can help leaders or key individuals in organizations affected by change to adapt and align or help them see that they need to be removed from the situation. Having a coach provides these individuals with a unique opportunity to think through, process and adapt to the change. By doing so, they are able to better manage themselves during the change and, therefore, they are better equipped to manage their departments or organizations. In addition, coaching creates the space for confidential and thoughtful thinking and planning, which in many times is neglected, especially in the midst of rapid and/or constant change.

Case Study: A New Entity Is Launched

At this point, I would like to walk you through a large change initiative that I was part of. I was responsible for one of the work streams that impacted the people-part of the change in addition to other accountabilities. I will use the approach described above to walk you through the transformation and how we achieved our desired outcomes.

A newly formed entity, one of the largest and most complex organizations, emerged from the integration of three different organizations within the company. The new organization housed approximately 15,000 employees, approximately 2,000 contractors, multiple vendors and strategic partners. Over time, the three separate organizations grew and grew to support the needs of their customers, and work was duplicated in many areas across multiple functions in several countries. The goal of the new organization was to evaluate and streamline operations, reduce costs and, ideally, maintain and enhance the customer experience. The task of evaluating and integrating these massive organizations was tremendous. One organization was composed of provisioning, maintenance and repair, and operations, while the organization from the other side of the company was composed of customer service and service delivery. Given the size and complexity of these organizations and their different cultures, this would be a tremendous undertaking, and the change component would be even greater. As a result, the new entity would be faced with significant change and disruptions that would directly impact its employees, systems and processes at many levels. These changes would occur over a two- to three-year period and would be constant. As well, the organization would remain in flux and continue to experience change for the following three to five years.

As part of this complex transformation, which included over forty work streams and subchange initiatives, at the client's request I took the lead on one of the work streams, "talent transformation." There were three subprojects within this project:

1. Workforce Optimization & Call Center Consolidation

2. Skills & Capabilities Assessment & Development

3. Alignment of Titles and Compensation

Each of these components was integral to the overall workforce plan for this new organization, as mentioned in Chapter 11 on workforce planning. To illustrate an aspect of the change initiative, I will focus on the subproject Skills & Capabilities Assessment & Development, and the execution of a plan to achieve the talent transformation's project goals.

Step 1: Assess the current state – After the leadership team partnered with Accenture, established its vision and determined "what good would look like in the future," I met with the next level of leadership for each of the functional areas to see how the vision would impact their organization. In these conversations, we identified the areas or employee types that would be impacted by the change and began discussions on next steps.

Coach Approach: I acted as a coach to my client in these meetings. I prepared by studying their organization charts and understanding what their various departments were responsible for, and designed questions to facilitate the discussion. Gathering this information enabled me to understand the current state for the client and the organization as a whole.

Step 2: Setting Up for the Future – We worked with the leaders to define what "good" would look like for the future state—what skills, capabilities and behaviors would be required, thus allowing us to establish a plan for how to achieve the future state. Based on the feedback from the leaders, and help from our partner, we designed an assessment that managers could complete on their employees. The goal was to help us identify existing skill and capability gaps on each employee at the department level, and look for trends across the organization. In addition, we wanted to be able to design training, technical certification and development programs to support the employees as they developed themselves for the future. We learned that many of our employees had the requisite skills for the immediate period and were optimally located; however, we also learned that in order to best compete in the marketplace, we would need to upgrade their knowledge and capabilities in some very specific areas. Based on our findings, we were able to design training curriculums and certification programs that, over a two-year period, would allow us to up-skill a significant percentage of the workforce. An added benefit was that since all employees would be going through this process, it would automatically create a common bond and language for the new organization—a culture accelerator.

Coach Approach: In my role, it was important to not only ask well-designed and thoughtful questions, but to support the leaders and managers as they began to realize that change was upon them. I would meet with the managers most impacted by the change and offer support, helping them to anticipate where the challenges would arise with the forthcoming changes. Together we would come up with a plan to be prepared to address the concern—whether it be for an individual, a group, or a system utilized by their department, and if additional training would be required to make the change happen. It was paramount that the managers communicated with their employees and teams, and motivated them during the change.

Step 3: Change Architecture – A critical step in our transformation initiative was to identify the key actions and milestones necessary to achieve our transformation. Right from the beginning of our work, through the assessment and gap analysis stage and through the training and certification stages, we would need to have a thoughtful communications plan. The plan would need to be broad as well as go deep into the organization and be specific and targeted in some areas. Therefore, we made absolutely certain our communications partner was engaged from Day 1, and together we designed a comprehensive, consistent plan using multiple means and media to deliver the key messages and points that were fleshed out in the communications planning process.

Coach Approach: When designing the change architecture, coaches can play an active role as the facilitator of the plan. They can bring together the appropriate contacts to form a team in order to collaborate and design the key messages, communication and training plans. In addition, they can be a coach to each of the team members as they work through the change individually for themselves as well as when issues arise in their area. The key is to not let anyone get stuck, not for a minute, or a day, when it comes to these change initiatives. If a group gets stuck and falls behind for a week or even a day, it has a downstream impact on other teams and the overall project. Therefore, getting stuck is not an option, and neither is not having a coach.

Step 4: Monitor Progress and Recognize Success – As important as it is to communicate, it is even more important to measure your progress (as the saying goes "inspect what you expect"). Therefore, it will be important to determine up front what "good" looks like in terms of measurement, and setting up a red/yellow/green report dashboard will make it easy to see what is going well and not so well or your areas that may be "stuck." Remember, red or "stuck" may be an excellent opportunity to deploy a coach to help understand why a stuck point exists and what needs to happen to get things moving. In addition, a progress report, assessed regularly and communicated accordingly to the appropriate employees, will enable you to achieve success. This is particularly important and can make or break a change. Also, when you are in the midst of a long-term change initiative, it is very easy for employees and managers and even leaders to lose their focus and stamina. Therefore, keeping everyone focused and on track is critical.

Recognizing individuals and teams for their success is also critical. Even when small goals are achieved and obstacles overcome, recognize the challenge and the win with a reward or acknowledgment relative to that goal or challenge. The same goes for major milestones—communicate and celebrate the employee's success. Success breeds success and builds momentum, and when employees see progress and forward movement, momentum will build, focus will remain and energy to complete the project will increase.

Coach Approach: *During this phase of the transformation journey, the coach can be an active participant—reviewing the dashboards, asking thoughtful and appropriately placed questions, and surfacing opportunities for acknowledgment and recognition. It is important for a coach, who is trained to listen deeply and to come from a place of inquiry, to be aware of who, how and when their questions are offered. For example, in a group setting, a coach may come from a place of learning and curiosity and ask a question about a certain project or a challenge and what actions can be taken to move the project forward. This question may be on many people's minds, but sometimes surfacing questions or challenges carries risk. The internal coach always needs to be aware of this dynamic and their role on the team. Ideally, the coach's role on a team should be addressed up front. Everyone needs to be aware that the coach is working with them in a supportive role and that in that role, they may ask uncomfortable questions. These questions are not to put anyone on the spot; they are to surface the truth and, as we all know, sometimes the truth is difficult to hear. Remember, the coach's role is to help uncover challenges and obstacles, and to move the group along and achieve their objectives.*

COACHING & LEADERSHIP INSIGHT:
The Leadership and Change Trilogy

Many years ago, I adopted a personal philosophy around leadership and, over time, it grew into my approach to leadership development. It is based on a three-prong approach or what I refer to as the "trilogy of leadership and change," if you will.

I believe, as many do, that development is an ongoing process and it begins with oneself. I call this "personal leadership" or how one leads oneself. It includes many pillars, including one's values, vision and personal mission for their life and career. This process begins with an introspective view that becomes one's foundation and personal compass or guiding principles for their life and their career. It includes components of building strong and healthy relationships, clear and direct communications, and a developed or developing sense of emotional intelligence. I believe that once an individual has a strong personal foundation in these areas, as demonstrated in their own "personal leadership"—as these behaviors have been integrated into who they are and how they work—it is at that time that the individual is ready to pursue the second aspect of the "trilogy," and that is the ability to lead others.

Management of others includes the multiple facets of management development such as:

- higher level of emotional intelligence;

- a developed interpersonal communications style;

- the emergence of a leadership style or better yet, multiple styles, supporting the ability to manage conflict and change and use influence to create win–win situations;

- proficiency in the capability to provide feedback and coach and counsel team members; and

- the ability to be the role model that others would like to emulate.

Once a manager has been able to develop these areas and become highly proficient in them, she will be ready to approach the third aspect of the "trilogy," which is the ability to lead organizations. Organizational leadership incorporates a strong foundation in all of the above as well as mastery in organizational savviness and navigation; the ability to flawlessly execute initiatives; to motivate, engage and align their employees toward a vision and mission and subsequently execute the mission; and, most importantly, to *manage and lead through change*. In my view, it is also extremely important to recognize that one's "performance" and ability to deliver results and achieve targets is imperative to their personal brand and success.

A strong personal brand drives a strong company brand in the eyes of the industry and the company's clients and shareholders. To do so consistently and over time requires the ability to change and adapt, and it is through the development of self-change, coupled with all of the above that creates leadership mastery and a consistency and trust for all the key-stakeholders involved from employees to customers to shareholders. I consider this a sustainable leader. We are constantly growing and changing as individuals and so are the companies that we work within; therefore, our own development of our "trilogies" is fluid and constant. It is with a watchful and ceaseless eye that we must care for our development as individuals, managers and leaders.

Top Ten Reasons a Company Should Have Internal Coaches and Build a Coaching Culture

When I set out on the journey of writing this book, I wasn't sure where the path would lead me. One of the joys of the experience has been reflecting back on the numerous coaching conversations I have had over my career with employees, colleagues and business leaders. These individuals all had a resolute desire to make a bigger contribution to the greater good, and they recognized how working with a coach could help them achieve their goals. That I have been able, as a coach, to guide people to a breakthrough, to make a positive shift in thinking or behavior and to take actions that benefited their career, their business and their life—this has been the greatest gift of all. That is what coaching does; it makes a difference.

As I write this final chapter, I am flying back from Austria, listening to Vivaldi's "Four Seasons," feeling energized and inspired. While in Vienna I participated in a two-day workshop with a strategic business partner. During the workshop we discussed business opportunities around change management and corporate development, and in each of the discussions, there was someone who played the role of coach. Again, I was reminded of how invaluable coaching skills are in facilitating productive dialogue and improving group performance.

I am fortunate to have an alliance with Doujak Corporate Development, a company founded by Alexander Doujak about a decade ago. Doujak's business-savvy consultants are smart, well-educated and richly experienced. They have written extensively and delivered keynotes all around the world, sharing their talents and knowledge with others who have the desire of making a greater contribution; they support their clients to be the agents of change, on a personal and a professional level. My colleagues at Doujak inspired me to write this final chapter offering my readers the top ten reasons for taking action now and either 1) become trained to be an internal coach and/or have masterful coaching skills, 2) design and deliver a coaching program in your organization and/or company, or 3) begin to build a culture of coaching in your company. No matter what action or path you choose, now is the time to set goals and take action. Be confident in achieving what you set out to do. The evidence to support creating internal coaching programs is clear.

REASON #1: INTERNAL COACHING PROGRAMS CAN ACCELERATE AND FACILITATE CHANGE

I have personally experienced this time and time again. During the fall of WorldCom, I saw the impact that the internal coaching program had on employee retention and the rapid shift required in the sales force and its management team during that incredibly challenging and dark time. I also personally experienced the positive impact that the program had on performance at MCI; during the integration of MCI and Verizon ESG; and when it was a powerful resource in a comprehensive leadership development program.

REASON #2: COACHING IS A MODEL FOR EMPOWERMENT

Anyone who has ever been coached well knows the feeling of empowerment that comes along with the experience—it is a direct result of the coaching process. When managers and employees feel empowered, great things happen. For example, employee satisfaction rises, causing customers to enjoy a more positive experience and, therefore, enjoy doing business with your company. When customers enjoy the service they receive they are more apt to be repeat customers. When customers buy more of your services, your company's performance rises. When performance rises, so will profits and shareholder value. It's a win–win for everyone.

REASON #3: INTERNAL COACHING PROGRAMS CAN BE A CULTURE AND PERFORMANCE GAME CHANGER

When companies are being integrated, acquired or looking to make a culture change, or they have taken steps to build a coaching culture, success can hinge on deploying internal coaches. They can teach coaching skills or support critical leaders and contributors to culture, helping them to think through their culture change strategies and design supporting actions, behaviors and messaging. The more quickly leaders embrace and adapt to the change around them, the more quickly their employees will do the same. The sooner the change is embraced, the more quickly results can be achieved.

REASON #4: INTERNAL COACHING IS ESPECIALLY EFFECTIVE IN SALES ORGANIZATIONS

Sales leaders are unique from other professionals. They are always thinking about making their numbers, and no one puts more pressure on a high-achieving sales professional than the sales professional him- or herself. Given their constant need to be in motion, it can be challenging to find the time to think through the development of their sales forces, let alone their own professional development. Their quota never goes away, and relief is rare. There is only a split second between the close of one month or quarter and the beginning of the next when the vicious quota renews and repeats itself. Being able to coach sales leaders and teach them how to coach their teams is a strategic capability and resource that can make the difference between "good" and "great" sales managers and their sales forces. Recall the findings I told you about earlier in the book, based on feedback from the 160 sales leaders who were surveyed after participating in internal coaching:

- 15% reported an increase in revenues

- 23% experienced an increase in sales opportunities

- 49% calculated an increase in revenues in the range of $50k–$250k

The question to ask is this: If having your sales professionals or managers coached would accelerate performance and results, what is preventing your company from doing it?

REASON #5: COACHING DRIVES BUSINESS RESULTS

The world is changing and how we do business is constantly evolving. As the business world becomes more of a global marketplace with our talent constantly in motion, traveling the globe and changing assignments, employees and their companies need to maintain a competitive advantage. If a coaching program or engagement is designed and delivered well, utilizing a well-trained coach who is familiar with your business environment and needs, then the return on investment will be substantial.

REASON #6: THE PROCESS OF BEING COACHED DEVELOPS NEW WAYS OF THINKING AND BEHAVIORS

As coaches, we wish for our clients to achieve more effective ways of engaging both with their work and in their lives. There is significant scientific evidence that the brain demonstrates neuroplasticity. Canadian psychiatrist and award-winning science writer, Dr. Norman Doidge, has noted, "The human brain is as malleable as a lump of wet clay not only in infancy, as scientists have long known, but well into hoary old age."[1] Dr. Abigail Zuger's article, "The Brain: Malleable, Capable, Vulnerable,"[2] points out examples of how the brain can be rewired. Given that coaching is a process, it is through the process of being coached that one can not only learn and perfect their coaching skills, they can begin to develop new thinking patterns and change their behavior. Through the coaching process, one can also further develop their ability to think critically and strategically and to problem solve. I have witnessed this in the individuals whom I have coached and I have experienced this for myself. Critical thinking and problem-solving skills will be required more and more in the workplace as time goes on. Now is the time to develop those skills and invest in our talent, our companies and our world.

REASON #7: COACHING IS AN EXCELLENT TALENT AND LEADERSHIP DEVELOPMENT TOOL

Coaching can be used in many talent development scenarios; for example, to support a manager in learning a new skill, to reinforce training, to change leadership styles and behaviors, and to improve the performance of a group. In HCI's *Building a Coaching Culture* study, participants were asked: "Why offer coaching?" The top five reasons were ranked in the following order:

1. Leadership Development
2. Improve Communication Skills
3. Improve Teamwork
4. Improve Decision-Making
5. Increase Productivity

---

[1] Norman Doidge, M.D., *The Brain that Changes Itself* (New York: Penguin Books, 2007).

[2] Abigail Zuger, M.D., "The Brain: Malleable, Capable, Vulnerable," *New York Times*, May 29, 2007.

The motivations for offering coaching remain the same despite the use of different types of coaching modalities (internal/external coach or managers/leaders using coaching skills). Coaching is used in organizations as a leadership development strategy, to increase employee engagement, to improve communication and teamwork skills, and to increase productivity.

Coaching is a proven technique that can be easily integrated into your learning and talent development programs. Employees, managers and leaders recognize its value and embrace it, and research confirms it.

REASON #8: COACHING IS GOOD FOR EMPLOYEE RETENTION

As human beings we like to do well at whatever we are doing; we are natural learners and like to achieve. We like to feel good about our contributions. Having the encouragement of a coach allows us to breathe as we think, take action and change. Being coached is a thoughtful and considerate approach to professional development, which leads to higher engagement and retention rates. Recall the results of the internal coaching participant survey that my colleagues and I conducted and the findings from HCI's *Building A Coaching Culture* study, which I shared with you in Chapter 18:

"I would recommend the coaching program."

- 98% agreed/strongly agreed (and over 70% strongly agreed)

"Organizations with a strong coaching culture have higher employee engagement."

- 65% of employees rated as highly engaged compared to 50% of the rest of the organization.

Net/net, if we have good employees why wouldn't we want to make certain they are engaged and retain them and make them great employees?

REASON #9: INTERNAL COACHING IS EASILY INTEGRATED INTO ANY TALENT MANAGEMENT STRATEGY

Whether a company chooses to integrate internal coaches into its overall infrastructure or teach its Human Resources business partners and Organizational Development consultants coaching skills, its employees, clients and business leaders will all reap the benefits. Mastering the basics of coaching fosters improved thinking, innovation, collaboration and problem solving. What employee or company couldn't benefit from having an empowered, engaged, innovative and collaborative leadership team and workforce? We have seen that coaching drives changes in employee behavior that, in turn, drives company performance and results. In today's competitive marketplace everyone is looking for a competitive edge, and coaching can be that solution.

REASON #10: IT'S GOOD FOR A COMPANY'S EMPLOYEES, ITS CUSTOMERS AND ITS BUSINESS

I can't say this enough: people who are coached develop faster professionally and become better problem-solvers, managers and critical thinkers. They are a reflection of your company's brand in the marketplace, so the better equipped your employees are to do their jobs, the better your customer experience and, therefore, the better your company's reputation and its results.

It should be abundantly clear to you now that possessing masterful coaching skills is invaluable in the work world, especially for anyone working inside an organization responsible for people development. Being able to take a coach approach and utilize coaching skills is a talent that successful leaders and business and organizational development consultants as well as human resources professionals should have in their repertoire. Having the ability to facilitate a coaching conversation demonstrates a leader's emotional intelligence and their confidence in their employees. It shows a willingness to empower others as well as an ability to bring great people and minds together to collaborate, to be innovative and to solve business challenges, or create new products and solutions. Coaching acts as a stimulus for all of this and more, which begs the question, Why wouldn't a company want their employees to be coached?

I hope that you found what you were looking for in this book and more. Thank you for taking time to read about my journey to coaching and about the incredible impact it has had on me, the employees who have been in my coaching programs and the impact of coaching on organizations and business results. I invite you to e-mail me with questions at renee@trilogydevelopment.com or post a comment on my blog at www.trilogydevelopment.com. I look forward to hearing from you and wish you the best of success in your coaching endeavors.

ACKNOWLEDGMENTS

Each individual whom I recognize below has, in his or her own unique way, helped me develop as a professional, executive and coach. I am immensely grateful that our paths have crossed and for the opportunity to work together. Thank you.

Kelly Adams
Nataliya Adelson
Madelin Adkins
Teresa Ahmad
Mani Allu
Keith Altman
Shawne Angelle
Shelly Ashwill-Powers
Denise Austin
Brian Bailey
Kerry Bailey
Chuck Balch
Nick Balletta
Kevin Bandy
Alan Barnes
Claire Barnes
Bryan Barretto
Mary Basel
Paul Bates
Brenda Belleville
Bill Berkowitz
Laura Berman Fortgang
Mike Bickel
Jane Biggerstaff
Rich Bisagnano
Rich Black
Laura Brody Heltebran
Mike Brown
Darlene Bruno
Martin Burvill
Steve Cafiero
Kathi Caldwell
Larry Califano
Becky Carr
Tara Carroll Briggs
Lorenzo Cavallaro
Ed Chanod
Kate Chesney
Jack Chidester

Cliff Cibelli
Cindy Clark
Jane Clements
Pam Cohen
Alex Coleman
James Condo
Sean Connoly
Brady Connor
Regina Corales
Susan Corbett-Klein
Vince Corica
Jon Craver
Jane Cresswell
Troy Cromwell
Blair Crump
Jim Davy
Mike Dawson
Terry Dean
Peggy DeCarlo-Dufill
Brenda Dewey
Karen Diebel-Sessions
Jeannie Diefenderfer
Kori Diehl
Ian Dix
Ben Doherty
Linda Dolceamore
Terry Donohue
Alexander Doujak
Jay Dowling
Michael Duke
Jim Duncan
Scott Eason
John Edmunds
Rick Ellenberger
Denise Farinaro
John Faugno
Aldo Figueroa
Tracey Fitzgerald
Michael Flanaghan

Pat Flynn
Bill Foster
Judy Frank
Brian French
Jeanne Frizzel
Chad Gagnon
Dom Gaillard
Rick Gallagher
Dave Gann
Kathy Gardner
Helen Gaskill
Jim Gauthier
Jim Geary
Laura Giadone
Lisa Giambattista
David Gill
Nancy Gofus
Mary Gorman
David Gray
Anthony Gruber
Bob Guccene
Maggie Hallbach
Kyle Hardy
Cynthia Hart
Shary Hauer
Claudia Healy
Chris Heffernan
Linda Heimer
Steve Heller
Charles Hellings
Mike Henderson
Holly Hess
Paul Higuchi
Michael Holland
John Hudson
Karen Huff
Wayne Huyard
Deborah Hyman
Michelle Ifill

Becky Incorvia
Nori Insler
Maria Jimenez
Jared Kearney
Mark Kearns
Dana Keefer
Mike Keil
Kate Kelly
Kevin Keyser
James Kilmer
Chris Kimm
Lisa Kleitz
James Knego
Charles Koman
Peter Kunk
Jane Lamperski
Adolfo Lantigua
Richard Lenahan
Chris Lichko
Edwardt Lictenauer
Janice Losen
Bonita Mackey
Dan Macmillian
Mike Mahoney
Peppy Margolis
Elena Martinesque
Don Maruska
Phil Masci
Bob Maute
Susan McCandless
Caryn McGarry
Tamara McMillen
Maggie Mcphail
Chris Meinelt
Wes Merritt
Randy Milch
Sarah Miller
Tim Miller
Anna Miranda
Rich Molina
James Montgomery
Richard Montgomery
Suzanne Moore
Meryl Moritz
Siobhan Murphy
Brian Myre

Tom Napoli
Kyle Natchioni
Dottie Neuf
Dave Nichols
Dan Nicita
Dwayne Norton
John Nunziata
Bob O'Connell
Jill Oletsky
Bruce O'Neel
Rachel Ong-Villa
Steve Orlando
Joe Owen
Bill Owings
Kelly Oyola
Mike Palmer
Vince Pastorello
Michelle Perrella
Jay Perry
Nancy Philabaum
Scott Pierce
Rob Pilgrim
Karen Pinks
Max Portey
Susan Powderly
Tammie Quinn
Pava Radocovich
Sandra Ray
Tony Recine
Jay Redmond
Wendy Ribbons
Peter Ritchie
Maximo Rocha
Bob Rodgers
Keith Rodgers
Bruce Rosen
Mark Ruhl
Michel Ruhnke
Brian Ruschevics
Joe Russo
Mike Russo
Andy Rutcofsky
Mark Ruth
Traci Sanders
Ron Sauder
Vernon Saunders

Marc Schaub
Bill Schiemann
Valeria Schiemann
Robin Schlee
Johan (JC) Schoeman
Chester Scott
Margaret Sears
Fran Shammo
Claire Shields
Linda Shinimoto
Craig Silliman
Jonathan Singel
Julie Slattery
Dan Smith
David Smith
Kimberly Smith
Mike Smith
Shaun Snow
Ron Spadaro
Odessa Stapleton
Michelle Starks
Dan Stewart
Jerry Strigari
Jim Stupak
Michael Sunderman
Trish Taylor
Charlie Tito
Robert Toohey
Frank Traditi
Harnet Tsehaye
Ben Urzendowski
John Vasina
Paul Vincent
Barbara Voigt
Victoria Vojonovich
Meg Walters
Judy Moyers
Mark Wiley
Cindy Williams
David Wilshire
Michael Windeler
Ann Woonton
Steve Young
Tom Zahay
Susan Zeleniak

INDEX

Page numbers in **boldface** indicate a Coaching & Leadership Insight

N

Net Promoter Score (NPS):
    and design of coaching program, 103, 108–109, 227–29, 235–36
    methodology of, 229, 235–36
new hires:
    coaching of, 185–86
    determining whom to coach, 183–84
    mentoring of, **187**
NJ Transit, 143–44

O

obstacle chart(s), 55–56
onboarding:
    as stage of Talent Management Life Cycle, 182–86
organizational assessments and issues:
    coach's role in, 179–80
    identifying issues, 118
outsourcing:
    and succession planning, 221
overworked employees:
    supporting, 201–204
Own Your Career initiative, 177–78

P

partnerships:
    lobbying for, **49**
passions:
    pursuing, **19**
PEF. *See* Position Evaluation Form
people:
    and principles, **32**
    putting people first, **167**
performance feedback, 201–204
performance management:
    and capacity modeling, 174
    coach's role in, 198–204
    and coaching program, 46–47
    process and objectives of, 39, 100–106, 112, 201–204
    and remediation, 113
    in Talent Management Life Cycle, 196–204
performers:
    low (and succession planning), 211–12
Personal Certified Coach (PCC) designation, 75
Phillips, Jack, 232–34

S

sales:
- activities and terminology, 152–53
- as "home" for coaching, 41–42, 44–45
- initiatives, 92–94, 98–99, 102
- involvement of in coaching process, 28–29, 189–91
- methodologies, 150
- need for understanding of, **156**
- performance programs and types of coaching, 155–56
- sales forecast, pipeline management and quota, 152
- sales force (coaching of), 137–46, 149–55, 258
- as stakeholder, 56

Schmidt, Eric, 125, 126

selection. *See* interview; recruitment

social media:
- as source of recruitment, 94, 95

Society for Human Resources Management (SHRM):
- and unused vacation days, 203
- capability model, 78
- Relationship Management, 86–87

sponsor:
- defined, 28
- lobbying for, **49**

Stakeholder Positioning Matrix, 51

stakeholders:
- approaching and identifying key, 50–54, 56–68
- assessments of, 74, 199
- identifying key, 51–54, 56–58
- relationships with, 87

statement of business requirements, 119–120

stress and illness:
- responding to, 203–204

success:
- measurement of, 227–36

succession planning:
- and capability modeling, 176
- and disclosure to employees, **223**
- process of, 61, 207–208
- role of executives in, 214–15
- as stage of Talent Management Life Cycle, 206–22

T

talent acquisition and selection:
- as stage of Talent Management Life Cycle, 168–72

talent assessment:
- blind spots in, 212–13

ABOUT THE AUTHOR

Renée Robertson is the founder and CEO of Trilogy Development, a boutique learning and consulting firm with a proven track record in designing and implementing internal coaching programs; sales force performance initiatives; and talent development solutions. A veteran Fortune 500 executive, she has served as a trusted advisor and coach to many top business leaders.

Robertson is one of only nineteen recipients of the International Coach Federation's prestigious Prism Award, a recognition bestowed upon her twice for her groundbreaking work on designing and implementing an internal coaching program during the fall of WorldCom and resurgence of MCI Telecommunications Inc. and her innovative and comprehensive coaching program at Verizon. At Verizon, the program engaged more than 600 leaders from all functional areas over a four-year period. It reinforced key training and change initiatives and was a critical component to succession planning. It was combined with key leadership development programs and professional development initiatives for female and ethnically diverse executives, managers and top employees too.

In addition to her success in the coaching industry, Robertson has designed and implemented talent transformation and system initiatives, including:

- A 10,000-person global organization talent transformation initiative which included the evaluation and alignment of job titles and functions as well as the design of future state job titles and descriptions and the use of customized training and certification programs to support the transformation.

- An initiative to design career paths for 34,000 employees globally by building competency models, assessments, training curricula and development activities.

- The scoping, design, and implementation of performance management, talent management and internal coaching systems.

Robertson holds an MBA from Fairleigh Dickinson University and a BA from Drew University where she also completed studies at the University of London and the United Nations. In addition, she has taken postgraduate studies through Duke University's Executive Education Program. She is proficient in French and enjoys being active, doing yoga and spending time with her family.

TRILOGY DEVELOPMENT

Trilogy Development, founded in 2012, has proven results in utilizing coaching and people development programs to expand and sharpen executive leadership and management capabilities; drive sales force performance and accelerate business integration and change initiatives. Trilogy's clients benefit from higher levels of engagement, increased positive customer experience, higher retention rates, sustained training impact, and an improved bottom line.

Trilogy's guiding principle is the belief that investment in human potential leads to achievable and measurable business results. We guide and assist our clients in the growth of stronger, more profitable and fully engaged organizations through the development of their human capital. Our strength is our capacity to build robust and sustainable programs integrating coaching as a primary methodology.

The success of Trilogy Development led to an even more ambitious initiative—the launch of the Robertson Coach Institute (RCI). RCI is a leading source for HR, Talent and Organizational Development professionals and coaches to learn and become trained on how to design and deliver internal coaching programs. RCI offers webinars, hosted learning sessions and live training events on internal coaching. In addition, coaches, HR and OD professionals are trained and mentored on how to coach inside organizations.

To learn more about Trilogy Development and its offerings, please contact us at www.trilogydevelopment.com or email us at info@trilogy development.com.

For information about our internal coach learning programs, visit us at: www.robertsoncoachinstitute.com.

Renée Robertson has in-depth experience in the many aspects of talent management and enjoys speaking on various topics such as Internal Coaching Programs, Leadership, Sales Force Performance and Change. For more information or to schedule a speaking engagement, please contact us at info@trilogydevelopment.com.